Mountain Top to Table Top

A Mountain Community Cooks with Love

HANDS OF FAITH

I saw no giant hands in the east
strain to push upward
a golden ball of fire,
or twirl the earth beneath me
to meet a dawn
hidden during my spinning flight
through dark of night.

I saw no gentle fingers
peel back sepals of a rose
and take brush in hand
to tint delicate petals
only a season ago awakened
from frozen earth by hidden hands
of warmth and beauty.

I saw no hands grasp bellows
to give breath to make a baby cry,
signaling new life
claiming its place
on Time's unmeasured string
played out with plan and order
by hands of an unseen Power.

If I can believe in dawn
and bloom and baby's cry
and see no giving hands,
can I but put faith
in God's waiting arms
to welcome me from eternal emptiness,
all that faithless earthbound eyes
can see at the end of the string?

William L. Davenport

Mountain Top to Table Top

Big Canoe Chapel

The Heartbeat of the Community

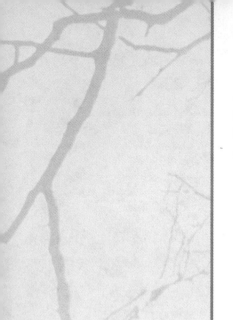

ISBN: 978-0-9816057-0-8

Copies of MOUNTAIN TOP TO TABLE TOP may be obtained by sending $25.00 plus $5.00 shipping and handling to the following address:

Mountain Top to Table Top
Big Canoe Chapel Women's Guild
10455 Big Canoe
Big Canoe, Georgia 30143

Cover Art: Bell Tower
Big Canoe Chapel
Photographer: Lassie Dye

WIMMER
COOKBOOKS

A CONSOLIDATED GRAPHICS COMPANY

800.548.2537 wimmerco.com

Guild Presidents

Devon Collins   Fran Saling

Cookbook Committee

Susie Brogdon   Ann Burton
Devon Collins   Liz Davis
Thelma Davis   Peggy Dickey
Alice Eachus   Millann Funk
Cynthia Junger   Judy Lacey
Charlotte McCloskey   Louise Prescott
Fran Saling   Emily Thurman

Marketing

Valerie Doll   Alice Eachus

Photography

Lassie Dye

Historian

Charlene Terrell

Proofreaders

Ann Burton   Pat Girdler
Louise Chumbley   Betty Hickman
Devon Collins   Marilyn Klask
Thelma Davis   Charlotte McCloskey
Peggy Dickey   Louise Morgan
Alice Eachus   Fran Saling
Millann Funk   Emily Thurman
Gayle Giles   John Thurman

*Proceeds from the sale of **Mountain Top to Table Top**
will be used to the glory of God to benefit those in need in
the Georgia counties of Dawson and Pickens.*

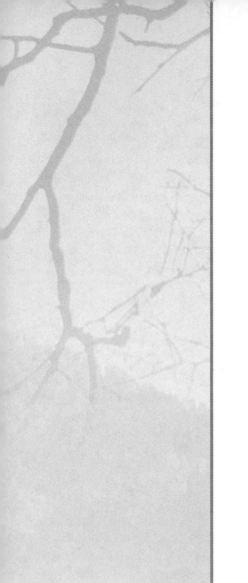

Big Canoe Chapel Women's Guild Purpose Statement

*The purpose of the Women's Guild is to
bring together all women of the Big Canoe community:*

To encourage Christian fellowship

*To understand God's will for
our lives through Bible study*

*To promote activities that benefit the
Chapel and our surrounding areas.*

Big Canoe Chapel Women's Guild

MOUNTAIN TOP TO TABLE TOP

By the Chapel Women's Guild

The Big Canoe Chapel Women's Guild has a dramatic history. Like the Chapel, it started small and the Guild's original goal was a weekly home prayer time for women. At the organizational meeting on January 21, 1988, seven women met and decided they wanted to expand their goal to include Bible study. From this small beginning, the numbers grew until Guild membership became too large for meetings in private homes and they moved to the Broyles Center.

In 1989, Guild members decided to have a fundraiser to purchase furnishings and equipment for the Broyles Community Center, which was under construction. The first Tour of Homes was held on Saturday, May 27, from 10:00 a.m. to 4:00 p.m. The event attracted about 200 and it was co-chaired by Rebecca McDaniel and Dorothy deAlbuquerque. Nancy Moseman chaired the bake sale. Big Canoe was much smaller in 1989 but the tour was so successful that Guild members voted to make it an annual event.

The year 1995 was an important one in the Guild's history. That year, the "Guild Boutique" was added (now known as the Gift Shop) and the fundraiser became even more successful.

Also in 1995, the Guild published a cookbook called a "Culinary Tour of Homes." The cookbook was very successful and its success inspired a second cookbook in 2001 called "Served with a View." All 1,500 copies of the second cookbook sold in record time. Since 2001, many people have expressed a strong interest in the publication of another Guild cookbook — and here it is! Mountain Top to Table Top is another gem compiled and published by the Guild and it promises to more than satisfy the yearning for another treasure trove of great recipes.

Cookbooks are fitting accomplishments by the Women's Guild because hospitality has been a big part of the Guild from the beginning. In fact, the very first Bible study at the first regular meeting back in February 1988 was called: "Open up Your Life: A Woman's Workshop in Hospitality."

Hospitality means caring and as the old saying goes, "Nothin' says lovin' like something from the oven." And for the Chapel Women's Guild, showing love to others is what it's all about — from the Tour of Homes that benefits those in need in Pickens and Dawson Counties to this wonderful cookbook. It's all about love and nurturing.

Charlene Terrell

The Women's Guild Cookbook Committee would like to express our deep appreciation for the enthusiastic response and support from the Big Canoe community in sharing so many wonderful recipes. We regret that due to constraints of space and similarity of recipes we were unable to publish them all. However, we did endeavor to use at least one recipe from each contributor. It is our sincere wish that you will enjoy them all.

The Big Canoe Chapel Women's Guild
Cookbook Committee

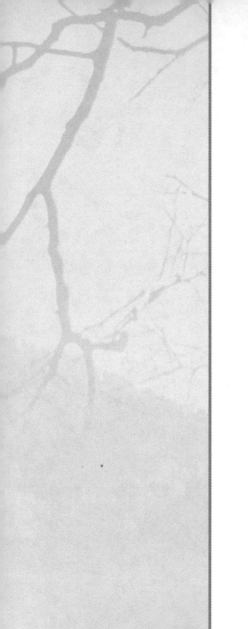

Winter Contentment

From inside my cozy house,

Smelling of warm bread,

I gaze with wonder

At the mountain blanketed

With new fallen snow.

JOYCE REID RALEY
2001

TABLE OF CONTENTS

Appetizers

WINDING ROADS

Winding roads, twisting, turning, canopied by trees,
rays of sunlight shifting through billowing clouds,
yellow stripes that stretch beyond,
on that winding road
that takes you to a special place
and then back home again.

Rolling hills and fields of grassy meadows,
pastures with horses and cows,
gates that spread their open arms to homesteads,
on that winding road
that takes you to a special place
and then back home again.

Queen Anne's lace, wild berries,
brown-eyed Susans,
quail, wild turkey, deer,
hawks that glide overhead,
on that winding road
that takes you to a special place
and then back home again.

Far distant mountains, ascending, descending,
cliffs, rocks, steep declines,
suddenly you are there,
on that winding road
that takes you to a special place
and then back home again.

Jayne Beske
Big Canoe

ANTIPASTO

1 (14-ounce) can artichoke
hearts, drained and
quartered

1 cup cherry tomatoes, halved

½ cup pitted ripe olives

½ cup pimiento-stuffed olives

1 (10-ounce) jar pepperoncini
salad peppers, drained

1 (4-ounce) jar button
mushrooms, drained

1 (8-ounce) bottle zesty Italian
dressing

1 (8-ounce) package block
mozzarella cheese

1 (6-ounce) package thinly sliced
ham

Leaf lettuce

- Combine artichoke hearts, tomatoes, olives, pimiento olives, peppers and mushrooms in a heavy-duty zip-top plastic bag.
- Pour dressing over vegetables. Seal bag.
- Refrigerate 8 hours, turning bag occasionally.
- Cut mozzarella cheese into sticks. Roll ham into logs and secure with a wooden pick.
- Drain vegetables, reserving marinade.
- Arrange vegetables, mozzarella cheese and ham on a lettuce lined serving tray. Drizzle reserved marinade over top.

May lighten appetizer by using reduced-fat Italian dressing.

Yield: 6-8 servings

MARILYN KLASK

ARTICHOKE BALLS

2 garlic cloves, crushed

2 tablespoons olive oil

2 eggs, slightly beaten

2 (14-ounce) cans artichoke
hearts, drained and mashed

¾ cup Parmesan cheese,
divided

¾ cup Italian bread crumbs,
divided

- Sauté garlic in oil about 2 minutes. Add eggs and artichokes. Cook over low heat 5 minutes.
- Remove from heat. Add ½ cup Parmesan cheese and ½ cup bread crumbs.
- Shape mixture into balls. Roll in remaining Parmesan cheese and bread crumbs.

Yield: 6-8 servings

LINDA SCHNEIDER

*Breathe on me
breath of God*

Fill me with life anew,

*That I may love what
thou dost love*

*And do what thou
wouldst do.*

Edwin Hatch

NOTES

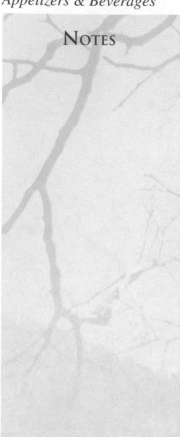

HOT RYES

1 cup shredded sharp Swiss cheese

¼ cup crisply cooked and crumbled bacon

½-⅔ cup chopped ripe olives, drained

¼ cup finely sliced green onions

1 teaspoon Worcestershire sauce

¼ teaspoon salt

¼ cup mayonnaise

1 loaf party rye or pumpernickel bread

- Preheat oven to 350 degrees.
- Combine Swiss cheese, bacon, olives, green onions, Worcestershire sauce, salt and mayonnaise.
- Mix thoroughly.
- Spread a slightly rounded teaspoon of mixture over each bread slice. Place on a baking sheet.
- Bake 10-15 minutes or until cheese melts and is slightly browned.
- Serve immediately or keep warm.

May spread mixture on bread, cover and refrigerate for several hours or overnight.

Unbaked appetizers may also be frozen for several weeks. Increase bake time 3-5 minutes if frozen.

Yield: 18 servings

ALMA TONEY

THE MAN *who says it cannot be done, should not interrupt the man who is doing it. ~Chinese proverb*

CHEEZY BURRITOS

1 (16-ounce) container sour
    cream
1 (8-ounce) package cream
    cheese, softened
1 (4-ounce) can mild chopped
    green chilies
1½ tablespoons fresh lemon
    juice

Dash of Tabasco sauce
Dash of garlic salt
2 (10-ounce) packages small
    flour tortillas
Picante sauce

*This recipe is from
a friend in San Antonio.*

- Combine sour cream, cream cheese, chilies, lemon juice, Tabasco and garlic salt. Mix well.
- Spread mixture over tortillas. Roll up tortillas.
- Refrigerate for several hours.
- Slice tortilla into 1-inch pieces and secure with toothpicks.
- Serve with picante sauce.

Yield: 25 servings
CAROLYN OMUNDSON

Delicious '09 HOT SWISS SHELLS

2 cups freshly grated Swiss
    cheese
1 (8-ounce) package cream
    cheese, softened
¼ cup mayonnaise
¼ cup finely chopped onions
    (yellow, white or green)

Tabasco sauce to taste
2 (2-ounce) package mini phyllo
    shells
Cooked and crumbled bacon
Chopped sweet red or bell
    peppers
Paprika to taste

*This makes an
easy-to-serve and
enjoyable finger food.*

- Preheat oven to 350 degrees.
- Cream Swiss cheese, cream cheese, mayonnaise, onions and Tabasco.
- Spoon a small amount cheese mixture into phyllo shells.
- Top with choice of bacon and/or peppers. Sprinkle with paprika.
- Bake 8-10 minutes or until slightly browned.

Yield: 15 servings
CHERYL GREGORY

HOT PEPPER CHEESE TORTA

1 (8-ounce) package cream
   cheese, softened
1 (9-ounce) jar hot pepper jelly,
   divided

1¼ cups grated sharp Cheddar
   cheese
2 garlic cloves, minced
1 egg
Assorted crackers

- Preheat oven to 350 degrees.
- Blend cream cheese, half pepper jelly, Cheddar cheese, garlic and egg.
- Spread mixture into a greased 6-inch springform pan.
- Bake 30-35 minutes.
- Cool completely. Remove from pan.
- Spread remaining jelly over top.
- Serve with assorted crackers or hearty bread.

Yield: 6-8 servings
BETTY ROBINSON

MANDARIN ORANGE CHEESE BALL

6 (8-ounce) packages cream
   cheese, softened
1 stick butter, softened
1 teaspoon almond flavoring
1 teaspoon ground ginger

1 (15-ounce) can Mandarin
   oranges, drained and juice
   squeezed out
2 tablespoons packed brown
   sugar
2 cups toasted almonds, divided
Gingersnaps

- Combine cream cheese, butter, almond flavoring, ginger, oranges, brown sugar and 1 cup almonds.
- Shape mixture into a log or ball. Roll in remaining cup of almonds.
- Refrigerate 6-8 hours. Do not freeze.
- Serve with gingersnaps.

Yield: 40 servings
MARGARET MORRIS

MISS MAGGIE'S POPPY CHEESE STICKS

1(16-ounce) loaf thinly sliced bread
1 cup grated Italian Parmesan cheese

2 tablespoons poppy seeds
1 teaspoon celery salt
1 teaspoon paprika
4 sticks corn oil butter, melted

- Preheat oven to 325 degrees.
- Trim crust from bread and cut into thirds.
- Combine Parmesan cheese, poppy seeds, celery salt and paprika.
- Brush bread strips with butter. Roll bread in cheese mixture. Place on a greased baking sheet.
- Bake 15-20 minutes or until crisp and browned.
- Cool on paper towel.

Yield: 30-35 servings
JANE WYETH

HONEY'S CHEESE STRAWS

1½ sticks butter, softened
2 (8-ounce) packages shredded sharp Cheddar cheese

2 cups all-purpose flour
½ teaspoon salt
½ teaspoon cayenne pepper

- Preheat oven to 325 degrees.
- Cream butter and Cheddar cheese.
- Gradually add flour, salt and cayenne.
- Using a cookie press with star attachment, make straws at length of choice.
- Bake 20 minutes. Freezes well.

Yield: 12 dozen
JERRY JUSTICE

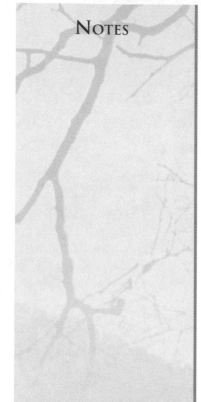

AVOCADO DIP

2 cups sour cream
2 tablespoons mayonnaise
1 envelope dry Good Seasons
   Italian Salad Dressing mix
3 ripe California avocados,
   diced

3 small to medium ripe
   tomatoes, seeded and diced
Salt, pepper and Tabasco sauce
   to taste
Tortilla scoops

- Blend sour cream, mayonnaise, dressing mix, avocados, tomatoes, salt, pepper and Tabasco.
- Mix well.
- Refrigerate for several hours. Serve with tortilla scoops.

Yield: 6-8 servings
SUE BACIGALUPO

ARTICHOKE DIP

1 (14-ounce) can artichoke
   hearts, not marinated
1 (8-ounce) package cream
   cheese, softened

1 (8-ounce) container sour
   cream
½ teaspoon dried dill
1 (8-ounce) package shredded
   Parmesan cheese

- Preheat oven to 375 degrees.
- Cream artichokes, cream cheese, sour cream and dill. Spread mixture into a 9-inch pie pan.
- Sprinkle Parmesan cheese over top.
- Bake 45 minutes.

Yield: 15 servings
JULIE BARNARD

CREATE-A-HOT-DIP

1 (8-ounce) package cream
   cheese
½ cup mayonnaise

2 green onions, sliced
1 tablespoon dried parsley

- Microwave cream cheese in a glass bowl on roast for 2 minutes until softened.
- Stir in mayonnaise, green onions and parsley.

Yield: 2 cups

HOT CRAB DIP

1 (6-ounce) can crabmeat,
   drained and flaked
½ cup slivered almonds
2 tablespoons dry white wine

1 tablespoon horseradish
¼ teaspoon Worcestershire
   sauce

- Add crabmeat, almonds, wine, horseradish and Worcestershire sauce to cream cheese mixture.
- Microwave 4-5 minutes on roast or until hot.

HOT SPINACH DIP

1 (10-ounce) package frozen
   chopped spinach, thawed and
   well drained

6 slices bacon, cooked crisp and
   crumbled
⅓ cup grated Parmesan cheese
2 teaspoons lemon juice

- Add spinach, bacon, Parmesan cheese and lemon juice to cream cheese mixture.
- Microwave 3-4 minutes on roast or until hot.

BARBARA (DOLLY) BLAKE

*The ocean's wide,
my boat is small,*

*But God who
watches over all,*

*Will bless me with a
gentle breeze*

*And guide me safely
through the seas.*

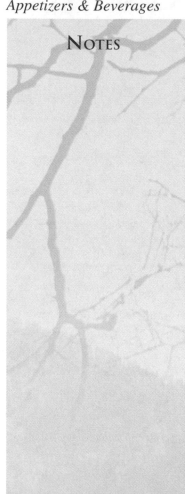

BUFFALO CHICKEN DIP

3 boneless, skinless chicken breast halves, cooked and shredded
½ bottle Frank's hot sauce
1 (8-ounce) package cream cheese, softened

½ bottle blue cheese dressing
1 (8-ounce) package shredded Cheddar cheese
Pita chips

- Preheat oven to 350 degrees.
- Toss chicken with hot sauce in colander and drain.
- Place chicken in bottom of a greased serving dish.
- Combine cream cheese and dressing. Spread over chicken.
- Bake 20 minutes.
- Remove from oven. Top with Cheddar cheese.
- Return to oven. Bake until cheese melts and is bubbly.
- Serve with pita chips.

May substitute ranch dressing for blue cheese.

Yield: 20 servings
DEVON COLLINS

FRESH AND CHUNKY GUACAMOLE

3 ripe avocados
3 tablespoons lemon juice
½ cup diced onions
1 medium tomato, seeded and chopped

½ teaspoon salt
2 tablespoons minced cilantro
Tortilla chips

- Cut avocados in half and remove the seeds.
- Scoop out pulp and place in a bowl.
- Drizzle with lemon juice. Mash avocado until chunky.
- Add onions, tomatoes, salt and cilantro. Mix well.
- Serve with tortilla chips.

Also good spread on a sandwich.

Yield: 6-8 servings
BETH HAMPEL

PUMPKIN DIP

1 (29-ounce) can pumpkin pie
    filling
2 (8-ounce) packages cream
    cheese, softened
4 cups sifted powdered sugar

1 teaspoon ground ginger
1 teaspoon cinnamon
Gingersnaps and apple slices

- Blend pie filling, cream cheese, powdered sugar, ginger and cinnamon until smooth.
- Serve with gingersnaps or apple slices.

Serve in a small clean pumpkin. This makes a large quantity but freezes well. Also great as a gift.

Yield:
GLENDA MOLTON

LAYERED SHRIMP DIP

2 (8-ounce) packages cream
    cheese, softened
1 (12-ounce) bottle cocktail
    sauce
2 (4½-ounce) cans salad shrimp,
    drained

1 cup shredded mozzarella
    cheese
2 cups chopped tomatoes,
    drained
1 bunch green onions, chopped
Assorted crackers

- Spread cream cheese on a serving dish with a rim.
- Layer cocktail sauce, shrimp, mozzarella cheese, tomatoes and green onions.
- Serve with assorted crackers.

Yield: 6-8 servings
LEWISE NEELY

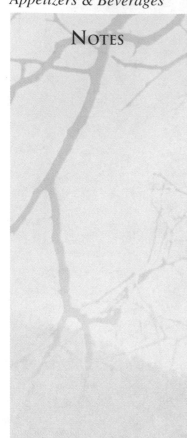

GREG'S HOT BEAN DIP

1 (8-ounce) package cream cheese, softened

1 (15-ounce) can refried beans

1 (8-ounce) package shredded jalapeño pepper cheese

Tortilla chips

- Spread cream cheese on the bottom of a microwave dish. Layer beans over cream cheese.
- Top with pepper cheese. Cover with plastic wrap.
- Microwave 5 minutes or until cheese melts.
- Serve with tortilla chips.

Yield: 6-8 servings
GREG MOORE

MUSHROOM ESCARGOT

12 medium escargots

12 medium mushroom caps

1 stick butter, melted

1 tablespoon fresh minced parsley

1 teaspoon minced garlic

Salt and pepper to taste

2 tablespoons fine dry bread crumbs

- Preheat oven to 350 degrees.
- Combine escargot, mushrooms, butter, parsley, garlic, salt and pepper.
- Set aside 15 minutes.
- Transfer mushroom caps to a baking dish. Sprinkle bread crumbs into each cup.
- Spoon escargot mixture into each cup. Cover with garlic butter mixture.
- Bake 10-15 minutes.

Yield: 6-8 servings
PEGGY DICKEY

TIPSY FRANKS

2 cups ketchup
¾ cup packed light brown sugar
1¼ cups bourbon
1 garlic clove, minced
¼ cup chopped onions

⅛ teaspoon dried oregano
¾ teaspoon dried rosemary, crushed
2 pounds franks, cut into 1-inch pieces or cocktail franks

- Preheat oven to 350 degrees.
- Combine ketchup, brown sugar, bourbon, garlic, onions, oregano and rosemary.
- Stir in franks. Pour mixture into a baking dish.
- Bake 45 minutes. Transfer to a crockpot. Serve warm.

Yield: 10-12 servings
BLOSSOM HOLYOAK

CHAFING DISH MEAT BALLS

2 pounds lean ground beef
1 egg, slightly beaten
1 large onion, grated
Salt to taste

1 (12-ounce) bottle chili sauce
1 (10-ounce) grape jelly
Juice of 1 lemon (3 tablespoons)

- Combine beef, egg, onions and salt. Shape mixture into small balls.
- Combine chili sauce, jelly and lemon juice. Add meat balls.
- Simmer in a skillet until browned.
- Transfer meat balls to a chafing dish. Serve warm.

Yield: 12 servings
EVIE DILLIPLANE

This recipe was used in one of our gourmet dinner club menus 40 years ago, when we lived in Lancaster County, PA.

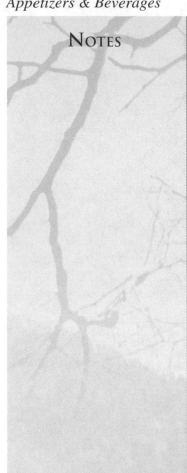

MUSHROOM LOGS

2 (8-ounce) cans refrigerated crescent rolls
1 (8-ounce) package cream cheese, softened
1 (4-ounce) can mushroom stems and pieces, drained and chopped

1 teaspoon seasoned salt
1 egg, beaten
1-2 tablespoons poppy seeds

- Preheat oven to 350 degrees.
- Separate crescent dough into 8 rectangles, sealing perforations.
- Combine cream cheese, mushrooms and salt. Mix well.
- Spread mixture evenly over each rectangle.
- Start at long end and roll up each rectangle jelly roll fashion.
- Pinch seams to seal.
- Slice each log into 6 (1-inch) pieces. Place seam side down on a baking sheet.
- Brush each log with egg and sprinkle with poppy seeds.
- Bake 10-12 minutes.

Yield: 4 dozen
KAAREN ARTHURS

OLIVE CHEESE NUGGETS

1 cup shredded sharp Cheddar cheese
¾ cup all-purpose flour
4 tablespoons butter, softened

½ teaspoon paprika
⅛ teaspoon salt
Stuffed green olives

- Preheat oven to 400 degrees.
- Combine Cheddar cheese, flour, butter, paprika and salt. Mix to form dough.
- Shape 1 teaspoon dough around each stuffed olive.
- Bake 12-15 minutes. Watch carefully.

May prepare 2 days in advance and freeze. Bring to room temperature before baking.

Yield: 10-12 servings
JOYCE DMETRUK

OYSTER ROLL

1 (8-ounce) package cream cheese, softened
2 tablespoons mayonnaise
½ teaspoon garlic powder
½ teaspoon salt
½ teaspoon pepper

½-¾ cup pecans, chopped and lightly toasted
1 (3¾-ounce) can smoked oysters, chopped
Paprika to taste
Wheat crackers

- Combine cream cheese, mayonnaise, garlic powder, salt and pepper.
- Refrigerate until firm.
- Roll out mixture on wax paper to a rectangle shape.
- Refrigerate until quite firm.
- Spread pecans and oysters on top. Gently roll up into a log. Sprinkle with paprika
- Serve with wheat crackers.

Yield: 6-8 servings
CHERYL BAILEY

The dictionary is the only place that success comes before work.

Anonymous

CHEESE PÂTÉ

6 ounces cream cheese, softened
1 cup shredded Cheddar cheese
3 tablespoons dry sherry
¾ teaspoon curry powder

¼ cup mango chutney
¼ cup chopped green onions
Assorted crackers

- Combine cream cheese, Cheddar cheese, sherry and curry powder.
- Spread mixture on a serving plate in a circle to ½-inch thick. Refrigerate until ready to serve.
- Before serving, spread chutney on top. Sprinkle with green onions.
- Serve with crackers.

Yield: 6 servings
PATRICIA MACARI

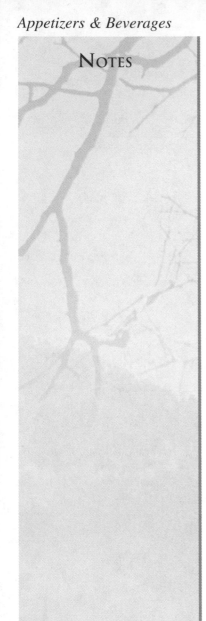

CRAB PÂTÉ

1 (10¾-ounce) can cream of
   mushroom soup, undiluted
1 (¼-ounce) envelope unflavored
   gelatin
3 tablespoons cold water
¾ cup mayonnaise

1 (8-ounce) package cream
   cheese, softened
1 (6½-ounce) can crabmeat
1 onion, chopped
1 cup chopped celery
Garnish: Parsley
Assorted crackers

- Heat soup. Dissolve gelatin in water. Add to soup.
- Stir in mayonnaise, cream cheese, crabmeat, onions and celery.
- Spoon mixture into a greased mold. Refrigerate until firm.
- Invert mold onto a serving plate. Top with parsley.
- Serve with crackers.

Yield: 8-10 servings
PATRICIA APPEL

HOT CRAB SPREAD

1 (8-ounce) package cream
   cheese, softened
6½-ounces crabmeat, fresh,
   frozen or canned
2 tablespoons finely chopped
   onions

¼ teaspoon salt
Pepper to taste
½ teaspoon creamed horseradish
⅓ cup slivered almonds
Assorted crackers or carrot or
   celery sticks

- Preheat oven to 350 degrees.
- Combine cream cheese, crabmeat, onions, salt, pepper and horseradish.
- Spoon mixture into a small baking dish. Sprinkle with almonds.
- Bake 15 minutes.
- Serve with crackers or carrots or celery.

Yield: 8-10 servings
PATRICIA APPEL

PINWHEEL APPETIZERS

SPREAD

2 (8-ounce) packages cream cheese, softened

8 small green onions, finely chopped

½ bell pepper, finely chopped

½ cup finely chopped pecans

½ teaspoon garlic powder

Dash of seasoned salt

Milk

PINWHEELS

6 (10-inch) flour tortillas

1 pound thinly sliced deli ham

1 (10-ounce) package fresh spinach

SPREAD

- Blend cream cheese, green onions, peppers, pecans, garlic powder and salt.
- Add enough milk to reach spreading consistency.
- Refrigerate. May make the day in advance to allow flavors to blend.

PINWHEELS

- Spread cream cheese mixture over tortillas.
- Place ham and spinach to cover two-thirds of tortilla.
- Roll up tightly, starting with spinach and ham side.
- Cut into 1-inch slices. Refrigerate until ready to serve.

Yield: 50 pinwheels

ANNELISE GREEN

ALTHOUGH *the world is full of suffering, it is also full of the overcoming of it.* ~Helen Keller

JOY'S BBQ

1 bottle favorite barbecue sauce   **Hamburger buns**
2 pounds pork tenderloin   **Dill pickle chips**

- Generously rub sauce over tenderloins. Place meat in a crockpot.
- Pour half the sauce over meat.
- Cook on high heat 5 hours.
- Pull apart meat with two forks until completely shredded.
- Serve with additional sauce and pickle chips on sandwiches.

Yield: 10-12 servings

Meat freezes well. Microwave to reheat.

JOY L. SUMMERS

AVOCADO SALSA

This originally came from Taste of Home. *Everyone loves it! A refreshing appetizer.*

1 (10-ounce) package frozen corn, thawed
2 cups black olives
1 sweet red pepper, chopped
1 small onion, chopped
1 teaspoon salt
1 teaspoon pepper

1 teaspoon chopped garlic
⅓ cup olive oil
¼ cup fresh lemon juice
3 tablespoons wine vinegar
1 teaspoon dried oregano
3 avocados, pitted and cubed
Scoop corn chips

- Combine corn, olives, peppers, onions, salt, pepper, garlic, oil, lemon juice, vinegar and oregano.
- Fold in avocados just before serving.
- Serve with Scoops corn chips.

Yield: 10-12 servings

STACY GUIDICE

Super Easy Salsa

1 large garlic clove, minced or
   crushed

1 handful chopped cilantro or
   to taste

½ habanero pepper, finely
   chopped

½ medium onion, finely chopped

Juice of 1 lime (2 tablespoons)

2 (14½-ounce) cans diced
   tomatoes

2 tablespoons olive oil

1 medium ripe tomato, seeded
   and coarsely chopped,
   (optional)

Scoop corn chips or tortilla
   chips

This salsa is very quick and easy to make and my whole neighborhood loves it!

- Combine garlic, cilantro, peppers, onions and lime juice in a food processor. Chop well.
- Stir in diced tomatoes with juice. Mix to desired consistency.
- Add oil and ripe tomatoes. Mix gently.
- Serve with Scoops corn chips or tortilla chips.
- Store salsa in a glass container in refrigerator.

Yield: 8-10 servings
CINDY BOUDREAU

Sausage Wontons

Wonton or egg roll wraps,
   quartered

1 pound pork sausage

Cayenne pepper to taste

1½ cups ranch dressing

¼ cup sliced black olives

¼ cup diced sweet red pepper

1½ cups shredded Monterey
   Jack cheese with jalapeños

1½ cups shredded Cheddar
   cheese

- Preheat oven to 350 degrees.
- Press wontons into greased muffin tins. Bake until browned.
- Brown sausage with cayenne. Drain well and blot dry.
- Combine meat, dressing, olives, peppers, Jack and Cheddar cheeses.
- Spoon mixture into wonton cups.
- Bake until cheese melts.

May store wonton cups in zip-top plastic bags for a few days.

Yield: 6-8 servings
LYNN KING

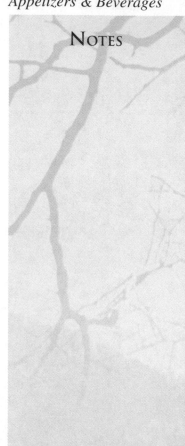

BACON WRAPPED SHRIMP

32 large shrimp, raw, shelled and deveined

1 (8-ounce) bottle French salad dressing
16 slices bacon

- Marinate shrimp in dressing in the refrigerator overnight.
- Drain shrimp.
- Wrap bacon around shrimp. Secure with a toothpick.
- Place on a broiler pan.
- Bake at 375 degrees 15-20 minutes or until bacon is crisp.

Yield: 8 servings

JANE WYETH

DAN'S SHRIMP COCKTAIL

1 large ripe tomato
1 medium bell pepper, seeded
1 small red onion
1 small ripe avocado, pitted
3 tablespoons cilantro

½ cup cocktail sauce
16-18 medium shrimp, cooked, peeled and deveined
Salt and pepper to taste

- Place tomato, pepper, onion, avocado and cilantro in a food processor.
- Process until finely chopped.
- Stir in cocktail sauce, salt and pepper. Refrigerate.
- Spoon 1½ tablespoons sauce into four large martini glasses.
- Layer 4-5 shrimp per glass over sauce. Top with more sauce and serve.

Shrimp and sauce may be prepared in advance and refrigerated until ready to serve. It has better flavor.

Yield: 4 servings

DAN KEASLER

COOGLER'S PIMIENTO CHEESE

2 cups grated Cabot's Seriously Sharp Cheddar cheese
1 cup grated smoked Gouda cheese
1 cup grated Norwegian Jarlsberg cheese

½ cup diced green salad olives or 1 (4-ounce) can diced pimientos
3-4 dashes cayenne pepper
½-1 cup Duke's mayonnaise

- Blend Cheddar cheese, Gouda cheese, Jarlsberg cheese, olives, cayenne and mayonnaise.
- Mix until smooth. Refrigerate.

Yield: 10-12 servings
CAROL COOGLER

This delicious spread is not very heart healthy. To make it healthier, eat it on celery.

GOAT CHEESE AND CARAMELIZED ONION GRATIN

3 tablespoons olive oil
3-4 garlic cloves
6 small to medium red or yellow onions, cut into small wedges
Salt and pepper to taste
Dried thyme to taste

⅛ cup balsamic vinegar
¾ cup crumbled goat cheese
¼ cup grated Parmesan cheese
2 tablespoons dry bread crumbs
Garnish: Basil, freshly chopped
Bread rounds or crackers

- Preheat oven to 350 degrees.
- Heat oil in a skillet. Sauté garlic. Add onions, salt, pepper and thyme.
- Cook over high heat 12-15 minutes.
- Reduce to low heat and cook until softened and golden browned.
- Stir in vinegar and cook another 5 minutes.
- Spoon mixture into a gratin dish. Top with goat cheese, Parmesan cheese and bread crumbs.
- Bake 15-20 minutes or until golden browned and bubbly.
- Top with basil. Serve with bread rounds or crackers.

Yield: 12 servings
SUE HAUSEMAN

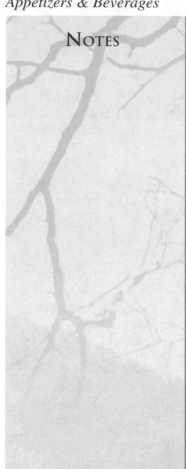

HOT REUBEN SPREAD

1 (8-ounce) package cream cheese, softened
½ cup sour cream
1 cup drained sauerkraut, chopped
½ pound lean corned beef, chopped

2 teaspoons finely chopped onions
1 tablespoon ketchup
2 teaspoons spicy brown mustard
1 cup grated Swiss cheese
Rye crackers or party rye bread

- Preheat oven to 375 degrees.
- Combine cream cheese, sour cream, sauerkraut, corned beef, onions, ketchup, mustard and Swiss cheese.
- Spoon mixture into a baking dish.
- Cover and bake 30 minutes or until bubbly.
- Uncover and bake an additional 5 minutes.
- Serve with rye crackers or party rye bread.

Yield: 10-12 servings
NANCY FARRIS

SMOKED SALMON SPREAD

1 (8-ounce) package cream cheese, softened
½ cup sour cream
1 tablespoon fresh lemon juice
1 tablespoon freshly minced dill or 1 teaspoon dried
1 teaspoon prepared horseradish, drained

½ teaspoon kosher salt
¼ teaspoon freshly ground pepper
4 ounces smoked salmon, minced
Crudités or assorted crackers

- Blend cream cheese until smooth. Add sour cream, lemon juice, dill, horseradish, salt and pepper.
- Mix well until smooth. Stir in salmon.
- Refrigerate until ready to serve with crudités or crackers.

If using a food processor, begin with salmon then add remaining ingredients.

Yield: 8-10 servings
NONA WHIPPLE

CHEESY SPINACH ARTICHOKE SQUARES

2 (8-ounce) packages
  refrigerated crescent rolls
1 (14-ounce) artichoke hearts,
  chopped
1 (10-ounce) package frozen
  spinach, thawed and
  squeezed dry

¾ cup grated Parmesan cheese
⅔ cup mayonnaise
⅔ cup sour cream
¼ teaspoon garlic powder

- Preheat oven to 375 degrees.
- Press dough into bottom and 1-inch up sides of greased 15 x 10 x 1-inch baking dish.
- Bake 12 minutes or until golden browned.
- Combine artichokes, spinach, Parmesan cheese, mayonnaise, sour cream and garlic powder.
- Spread mixture over baked crust.
- Bake an additional 12-15 minutes or until bubbly and lightly browned on edges.

Yield: 10-12 servings
ANNE PENNINGTON

SHANNY'S CRABBIES

1 (6-ounce) jar Old English
  cheese spread
4 tablespoons butter, softened
½ teaspoon seasoned salt
¼ teaspoon garlic powder

1 tablespoon mayonnaise
6 ounces lump crabmeat
1 (6 pack) package English
  muffins

- Preheat oven to 450 degrees.
- Combine cheese spread and butter. Add seasoned salt, garlic powder, mayonnaise and crabmeat.
- Spread mixture over muffin halves. Place on baking sheet.
- Bake 10 minutes or until bubbly and browned.
- Cut each half into quarters.

Yield: 48 bite-size servings
COREY TANNER

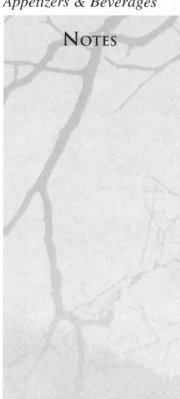

SPICY SAUSAGE TOASTS

1 pound mild sausage
1 pound ground beef
1 tablespoon Worcestershire
   sauce
1 teaspoon dried oregano

4 dashes Tabasco sauce
1 pound package Velveeta®
   processed cheese, cubed
1 package rye or pumpernickel
   party bread

- Preheat oven to 450 degrees.
- Brown sausage and beef. Drain well.
- Add Worcestershire sauce, oregano, Tabasco and cheese cubes. Heat until cheese melts.
- Spread cheese mixture over bread. Place on a baking sheet.
- May freeze at this point and store in zip-top plastic bags.
- When ready to serve, bake 5-10 minutes. Watch carefully.

Yield: 15 servings

JACKIE GILMER

SPICED PECANS

2 egg whites
1 teaspoon cold water
1 pound pecan halves

1 cup sugar
¾ teaspoon salt
1 teaspoon cinnamon

- Preheat oven to 275 degrees.
- Beat egg whites just until stiff. Fold in cold water.
- Stir in pecans until evenly coated.
- Combine sugar, salt and cinnamon. Add to pecans, stirring until thoroughly coated.
- Spread pecans on a baking sheet.
- Bake 1 hour, stirring every 15 minutes, until pecans are crunchy.
- Cool in a bowl. Store in a tightly covered container.

Yield: 1 pound

ANN HOECHSTETTER

JUST RIGHT PUNCH

1 (46-ounce) can orange juice   1 (46-ounce) can apple juice
1 (46-ounce) can pineapple juice   1 quart ginger ale

- Blend orange juice, pineapple juice and apple juice in a serving bowl.
- Add ginger ale just before serving.
- Serve with crushed ice or an ice ring.

Yield: 12 servings
MELANIE CURTIS

DELTA MINT TEA

7 tea bags   Juice of 7 lemons
12 sprigs mint   2 cups sugar
Rind of 3 lemons   8 cups water
8 cups boiling water

- Steep tea bags, mint and lemon rind in hot water 12 minutes.
- Remove tea bags, mint and rinds from tea.
- Stir in lemon juice and sugar until dissolved.
- Strain tea and add water.

Yield: 1 gallon
JUDIE BALFE

ALBERT *Einstein said, "Not everything that can be counted, counts, and not everything that counts can be counted."*

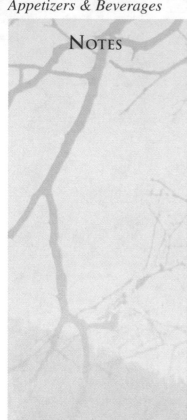

PINK LADY PUNCH

2 cups cranberry juice cocktail **1 cup canned grapefruit juice**
¾ cup sugar **1 quart ginger ale**
1 cup canned pineapple juice

- Blend cranberry juice and sugar. Stir until dissolved.
- Stir in pineapple juice and grapefruit juice. Refrigerate.
- When ready to serve, add ginger ale.

Yield: 16 servings

LENORE MORANOS

SO WHETHER *you eat or drink, or whatever you do, do it all for the glory of God.*
~ 1 Corinthians 10:31

Breads

FINAL RESTING PLACE

A place of rest, above all else,
deep within a glade,
this sanctuary looks upon
the hills where homesteads laid.

Here quietness is commonplace
and silence can be heard,
except when broken by the voice
of a small, singing bird.

Soft breezes blow gently,
limber branches slowly sway,
casting shadows on the headstones
in mottled shades of gray,

Sun glinting through the hemlock,
trumpet flowers on the vine,
the ancient oak grown skyward,
the pungent smell of pine,

All remind us of His Spirit
as it moves among these hills,
with gentle arms enfolding
as it draws us to His Will.

There is a certain presence
of God within this space,
protecting all, eternally,
in this final resting place.

Jayne Beske
Big Canoe

ASIAGO WINE CHEESE BREAD

6 tablespoons unsalted butter
6 tablespoons minced garlic
2 tablespoons active dry yeast
¼ cup warm water
1 teaspoon sugar
2 eggs, beaten

1½ teaspoons salt
1½ cups white wine
½ cup chopped green onions
6-6½ cups all-purpose flour
1 pound Asiago cheese, cut into ½-inch cubes

- Preheat oven to 375 degrees.
- Melt butter in a skillet. Sauté garlic until soft.
- Dissolve yeast in warm water and sugar.
- Combine garlic, yeast mixture, eggs, salt, wine and green onions.
- Gradually stir in flour. Add Asiago cheese cubes.
- Place dough in a greased 9 x 5-inch loaf pan.
- Bake 25 minutes. Brush top with butter.

Yield: 10 servings
SANDY FILKOWSKI

DEUTERONOMY
8:13

*Man does not
live by bread alone,
but on every word that
comes from the mouth
of the Lord.*

FAVORITE BANANA BREAD

2 sticks butter, softened
2 cups sugar
4 eggs
¼ teaspoon salt
2 teaspoons baking soda

4 cups all-purpose flour
6 large very ripe bananas, mashed
1 cup chopped pecans, raisins or dried fruit

- Preheat oven to 250-300 degrees.
- Cream butter and sugar. Add eggs, one at a time, beating well after each addition.
- Combine salt, baking soda and flour. Add to creamed mixture.
- Stir in bananas and nuts.
- Pour batter into two 9 x 5-inch loaf pans. Top with additional nuts.
- Bake 1 hour-1 hour, 30 minutes.

Yield: 2 large or 3 medium loaves
ANNE YOUMANS

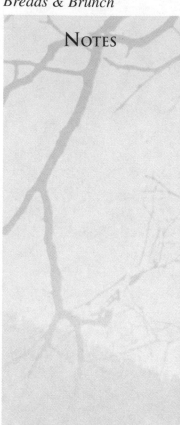

BUTTERMILK BANANA BREAD

1½ sticks butter, softened
1 cup sugar
1 teaspoon vanilla
2 eggs
3-4 ripe bananas, mashed
2¼ cups all-purpose flour

1 teaspoon baking soda
1 teaspoon salt
½ cup buttermilk
½ cup chopped walnuts
  (optional)

- Preheat oven to 325 degrees.
- Cream butter, sugar, vanilla and eggs.
- Stir in bananas until smooth.
- In a separate bowl, combine flour, baking soda and salt.
- Add dry ingredients alternately with buttermilk to creamed mixture.
- Fold in walnuts.
- Divide batter between two greased 9 x 5-inch loaf pans.
- Bake 50 minutes or until golden browned and center is set.

Yield: 16 servings
BARBARA NUNN

GLENDA'S BANANA NUT BREAD

½ cup vegetable oil
1 cup sugar
2 eggs
3 ripe bananas, mashed

2 cups self-rising flour
3 tablespoons buttermilk
½ teaspoon vanilla
½ cup chopped pecans

- Preheat oven to 350 degrees.
- Cream oil and sugar. Add eggs and mix well.
- Stir in bananas. Add flour, buttermilk, vanilla and pecans.
- Pour batter into 9 x 5-inch loaf pan.
- Bake 30-45 minutes.

Yield: 8 servings
LINDA S. WOOD

THE BEST BANANA BREAD

1 stick butter, softened
1½ cups sugar
2 large eggs
2 cups all-purpose flour
½ teaspoon salt

¼ teaspoon baking powder
¼ cup buttermilk
¾ teaspoon baking soda
1 cup ripe mashed banana
1 teaspoon vanilla

- Preheat oven to 325 degrees.
- Cream butter and sugar. Beat in eggs until smooth.
- Sift together flour, salt and baking powder. Add to creamed mixture.
- Combine buttermilk and baking soda. Add to creamed mixture.
- Stir in bananas and vanilla. Pour batter into a greased 9 x 5-inch loaf pan.
- Bake 30-45 minutes until firm.

Yield: 8 servings
LYNNE SEARFOSS

This is my grandmother's recipe and is a Chunn family favorite.

BROCCOLI CORNBREAD

1 stick butter, melted
1 (9-ounce) package Jiffy
  cornbread mix
1 cup shredded Cheddar cheese
1 large onion, chopped

4 eggs, beaten
1 (10-ounce) package frozen
  chopped broccoli, thawed and
  squeezed dry

- Preheat oven to 400 degrees.
- Pour butter into a 9 x 9-inch baking pan.
- Combine cornbread mix, Cheddar cheese, onions, eggs and broccoli.
- Pour batter into pan.
- Bake 25 minutes or until slightly browned.
- Cut into squares.

Yield: 8 servings
MELANIE CURTIS

A real family favorite!! Tastes wonderful hot or cool. People love it whether they like broccoli or not.

LOUISE'S SUPER CORNBREAD

*1½ cups self-rising cornmeal
(not cornmeal mix)*

½ cup vegetable oil

2 eggs, beaten

1 (8-ounce) carton sour cream

1 (8-ounce) can cream style corn

Combine cornmeal and oil; add eggs and stir. Add remaining ingredients, mix and pour into greased muffin pan. Bake at 400 degrees until brown, 20-25 minutes.

Makes 2 dozen cornbread muffins.

Submitted by Nona Whipple

Based on Louise's Super Cornbread recipe, submitted by Beverly Fox, Linda Travis, and Sara Naff, which appeared in A Culinary Tour of Homes. I have tweaked it a little and bake it as cornbread muffins. It's become a family favorite.

MEXICAN CORNBREAD

4 eggs
2 cups Jiffy Cornbread mix
⅔ cup olive or vegetable oil
1 teaspoon baking soda
1 teaspoon salt
1 cup milk

1 (14-ounce) can cream-style corn
1 cup shredded sharp Cheddar cheese
2 (4-ounce) cans El Paso chili peppers, diced

- Preheat oven to 350 degrees.
- Combine eggs, bread mix, oil, baking soda, salt, milk, corn, Cheddar cheese and chili peppers.
- Pour batter into a 13 x 9 x 2-inch baking dish.
- Bake 30-45 minutes.

Yield: 6-8 servings
KATHERINE CHERRY

HOLIDAY PUMPKIN BREAD

1 (15-ounce) can unsweetened pumpkin
1 cup vegetable oil
3 cups sugar
3 large eggs
3½ cups all-purpose flour
2 teaspoons baking soda

1 teaspoon baking powder
1 teaspoon cinnamon
1 teaspoon ground nutmeg
½ teaspoon salt
½ teaspoon ground cloves
1 cup chopped walnuts
1 cup raisins

- Preheat oven to 325 degrees.
- Combine pumpkin, oil, sugar, eggs, flour, baking soda, baking powder, cinnamon, nutmeg, salt and cloves.
- Beat at low speed with an electric mixer 1-2 minutes or until well blended.
- Stir in walnuts and raisins.
- Divide batter between two 9 x 5-inch greased dark nonstick loaf pans.
- Bake 50 minutes or until browned.

Yield: 16 servings
MELODY RAY

MINI PUMPKIN CRANBERRY BREADS

3 cups all-purpose flour

1 tablespoon plus 2 teaspoons
    pumpkin pie spice

2 teaspoons baking soda

1½ teaspoons salt

3 cups sugar

1 (15-ounce) can Libby's Pure
    Pumpkin

4 large eggs

1 cup vegetable oil

½ cup orange juice or water

1 cup sweetened dried, fresh or
    frozen cranberries

- Preheat oven to 350 degrees.
- Combine flour, spice, baking soda and salt.
- In a separate bowl, beat sugar, pumpkin, eggs, oil and orange juice until just blended.
- Add pumpkin mixture to flour mixture. Stir until just moistened.
- Fold in cranberries.
- Spoon batter into seven greased and floured 5 x 3-inch disposable loaf pans.
- Bake 50-55 minutes or until tester comes out clean.
- Cool in pans 10 minutes. Remove to wire racks to cool.

Yield: 7 mini loaves

ELAINE ESTILL

AND YOU shall eat there in the presence of the Lord your God, you and your households together, rejoicing in all undertakings in which the Lord your God has blessed you. ~Deuteronomy 12:7

PEPPERONI BREAD

1 (1-pound) package frozen bread dough
1 tablespoon extra virgin olive oil
½ tablespoon dried basil
½ tablespoon dried minced onion
½ tablespoon dried oregano
½ pound deli sliced pepperoni
1½ cups shredded mozzarella cheese
1 egg, slightly beaten

- Preheat oven to 350 degrees.
- Allow bread to thaw and rise.
- Roll out dough to a 12 x 18-inch rectangle on a lightly greased baking sheet.
- Brush with oil. Sprinkle with basil, onions and oregano.
- Top with pepperoni. Sprinkle with mozzarella cheese.
- Start with long edges and roll up dough into a thin cylinder. Place seam side down.
- Brush with egg.
- Bake 35 minutes or until golden browned.
- Cut into bite-sized pieces.

Publix Supermarkets carries frozen bread dough in the bakery section in a refrigerator case.

Yield: 15 servings
CHERLYNN HARRIS

POPPY SEED LOAF

BATTER

3 cups all-purpose flour
2⅓ cups sugar
1½ cups milk
3 eggs
1⅛ cups vegetable oil
1½ teaspoons salt

1½ teaspoons baking powder
1½ tablespoons poppy seeds
1½ teaspoons vanilla
1½ teaspoons almond extract
1½ teaspoon butter flavoring

GLAZE

¼ cup orange juice
¾ cup sugar
½ teaspoon vanilla

½ teaspoon almond extract
½ teaspoon butter flavoring

- Preheat oven to 350 degrees.
- Combine flour, sugar, milk and eggs. Mix well.
- Stir in oil. Add salt, baking powder, poppy seeds, vanilla, almond extract and butter flavoring. Mix well.
- Divide batter between two 9 x 5-inch loaf pans.
- Bake 1 hour to 1 hour, 30 minutes.
- Cool 10 minutes in pans on wire rack.

GLAZE

- Combine orange juice, sugar, vanilla, almond extract and butter flavoring in a saucepan.
- Cook and stir over medium heat 2 minutes or until sugar dissolves. Let cool.
- Pour glaze over bread. Let stand in pans about 1 hour before serving.

Yield: 16 servings
PAT KING

When baking sweet potatoes for dinner, bake one extra to make these muffins for the next day.

Sweet Potato Muffins

2 cups sifted all-purpose flour
1 tablespoon baking powder
½ teaspoon salt
2 eggs or ½ cup egg substitute
1 medium sweet potato, baked, peeled and mashed
⅓ cup sugar
1 cup milk

⅓ cup canola oil
2 tablespoons toasted wheat germ
2 tablespoons molasses
1½ teaspoons cinnamon
¼ teaspoon ground cloves
¼ teaspoon grated whole nutmeg
½ cup raisins

- Preheat oven to 400 degrees.
- Sift together flour, baking powder and salt.
- In a food processor, blend eggs, sweet potato and sugar.
- Add milk, oil, wheat germ, molasses, cinnamon, cloves and nutmeg. Process until smooth.
- Pour sweet potato mixture into flour mixture. Mix just until combined. Stir in raisins.
- Divide batter among 12 greased or paper-lined muffin cups.
- Place in oven and reduce heat to 350 degrees. Bake 25 minutes or until lightly browned.

Yield: 12 muffins
LAURA LINK

Tiny Herb Rolls

4 tablespoons butter
1 ½ teaspoons dried parsley
½ teaspoon dried dill
¼ teaspoon onion flakes

1 tablespoon grated Parmesan cheese
1 (8-ounce) package refrigerated buttermilk biscuits

- Preheat oven to 425 degrees.
- Melt butter. Add parsley, dill, onion flakes and Parmesan cheese. Mix well.
- Cut each biscuit into quarters with kitchen shears.
- Dip each quarter into butter mixture. Arrange in a buttered 8-inch round cake pan, sides touching.
- Bake 12-15 minutes or until lightly browned.
- Remove from pan in one piece. Serve as pull apart rolls.

Yield: 8-10 servings
DOTTIE LEASMAN

Scottish Scones

1 heaping teaspoon baking soda
1 heaping teaspoon cream of
   tartar
5 teaspoons sugar
2-3 tablespoons Lyles Syrup

1 stick butter or ½ cup
   shortening
⅓ cup scant buttermilk
Garnish: jam and whipped
   cream

- Preheat oven to 400 degrees.
- Sift together baking soda and cream of tartar. Add sugar and syrup.
- Cut in butter until crumbly. Slowly add buttermilk.
- Turn out onto a floured surface. Knead slightly.
- Roll out dough into a ½-inch thick circle. Cut into triangles.
- Bake 10-15 minutes (or cook on a 350 degree griddle).
- Cut scones in half. Serve with jam and whipped cream.

Yield: 10-12 servings
JERRIE ALEXANDER

Sour Cream Biscuits

2 cups self-rising flour
2 sticks butter, softened

1 cup sour cream

- Preheat oven to 350 degrees.
- Cream flour, butter and sour cream until smooth.
- Spoon batter into mini muffin cups, filling three-fourths full.
- Bake 15-20 minutes or until lightly browned.

Yield: 36 muffins
CAROL POWICHROSKI

This recipe is at least 100 years old and was given to Nancy Fowler (Tampa, FL) by her grandmother who brought it from Scotland.

YEAST BISCUITS

3 packages yeast, dissolved in ½ cup warm water

2 cups lukewarm buttermilk

5 cups self-rising flour

¼ cup sugar

1 tsp. salt

1 tsp. baking soda

1 cup shortening

Dissolve yeast in warm water and let sit while preparing dry ingredients (yeast should foam if active and still good). Warm buttermilk just enough to take the chill off (I do this in the microwave). Sift flour, salt, soda and sugar together into bowl which can be covered tightly. Cut in shortening with pastry cutter or two knives. Add yeast mixture and buttermilk. Mix well. Cover and refrigerate for at least 5 hours or up to 5 days.

Continued on next page

STICKY BUNS

DOUGH

4½ cups all-purpose flour, divided
2 packages active dry yeast
1 cup milk

⅓ cup sugar
1 teaspoon salt
2 eggs

TOPPING

1 cup molasses, divided
1 cup packed brown sugar, divided

1 stick butter, divided
Pecan halves

CINNAMON FILLING

1 stick butter, softened
Cinnamon/sugar mixture

Raisins (optional)

DOUGH

- In a mixer bowl with a dough hook, combine 2 cups flour and yeast.
- Heat milk, sugar and salt in the microwave until just warm (115-120 degrees) stirring often.
- Add milk to flour mixture and beat on low speed.
- Add eggs, one at a time, beating well after each addition.
- Beat 3 minutes at high speed, scraping sides as necessary.
- Reduce speed and add as much of 2-2½ cups flour.
- Knead with dough hook until dough all combines.
- Continue to knead 4-5 minutes until dough is smooth and elastic.
- Place dough in a greased bowl, turning once to coat.
- Cover and let rise in a warm place for about 1 hour or until doubled.
- Preheat oven to 350 degrees.

TOPPING

- In each of three 8-inch cake pans, place ⅓ cup molasses, ⅓ cup brown sugar and ⅓ butter.
- Place pans in oven just until butter melts. Remove and stir until well combined.
- Arrange 2 dozen pecan halves upside down in topping.

Continued on next page

STICKY BUNS *continued*

CINNAMON FILLING

- Punch down dough and divide into thirds. Roll each piece into a 12 x 18-inch rectangle
- Spread ⅓ softened butter over dough. Sprinkle with cinnamon/sugar and top with raisins.
- Roll up jelly roll fashion beginning from longest side.
- Slice into 1½-inch pieces. Place 12 slices, cut side down, in prepared pan, pressing firmly.
- Repeat with other ⅔ dough. Cover and let rise in a warm place until doubled in size.
- Bake 20 minutes or until tops are golden browned.
- Immediately invert onto a serving dish, being careful of the hot topping.
- Cool to room temperature.

May wrap in foil and freeze for several months. To serve, heat about 20 minutes at 300 degrees.

Yield: 3 dozen buns

SUE HAUSEMAN

YEAST BISCUITS
continued

Pinch off as much dough as needed, roll in flour, cut with biscuit cutter, brush with melted butter, and bake at 400 degrees in buttered pan until brown. (Or, bake until set and freeze until needed. Then place frozen biscuits in 400 degree oven to finish browning when needed.)

Makes about 70 (2-inch) biscuits.

Submitted by Nona Whipple

This recipe appeared in Served With a View.

43

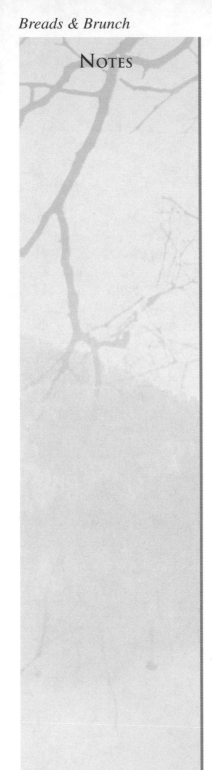

APRICOT BRUNCH CAKE

1 cup shredded coconut
⅓ cup packed brown sugar
2 tablespoons butter, melted
½ teaspoon cinnamon
1 (8-ounce) package cream
   cheese, softened
1¼ cups sugar
1 stick butter, softened

2 eggs
1 teaspoon vanilla
1¾ cups all-purpose flour
1 teaspoon baking powder
½ teaspoon baking soda
¼ teaspoon salt
¼ cup milk
½ cup apricot preserves

- Preheat oven to 350 degrees.
- Combine coconut, brown sugar, butter and cinnamon. Mix well.
- Sprinkle mixture on bottom of a greased and floured 9-inch springform pan with ring insert.
- Blend cream cheese, sugar and butter. Mix well.
- Stir in eggs and vanilla.
- Combine flour, baking powder, baking soda and salt.
- Add dry ingredients, alternately with milk, mixing well after each addition.
- Pour half batter over crust. Dot with preserves.
- Cover with remaining batter. Bake 1 hour.
- Cool 10 minutes in pan. Remove from pan.

Yield: 12 servings

COLLEEN RASH

BONNIE'S BEST COFFEE CAKE

1 (18-ounce) package yellow
    cake mix
1 (3-ounce) package instant
    vanilla pudding mix
¾ cup vegetable oil
¾ cup water
4 eggs, room temperature
1 teaspoon vanilla

1 teaspoon butter flavoring
¾ cup packed brown sugar
3 teaspoons cinnamon
1 cup chopped nuts
1 cup powdered sugar
2 tablespoons milk
¼ teaspoon vanilla
½ teaspoon butter flavoring

- Preheat oven to 325 degrees.
- Combine cake mix, pudding mix, oil and water. Mix well.
- Add eggs, one at a time, beating well after each addition.
- Stir in vanilla and flavoring.
- In a separate bowl, combine brown sugar, cinnamon and nuts.
- Place one-third of nut mixture in bottom of greased and floured Bundt pan.
- Alternate adding batter with nut mixture, ending with batter.
- Bake 1 hour. Remove from pan immediately. Cool completely.
- Blend powdered sugar, milk, vanilla and flavoring.
- Spoon glaze over cake.

Yield: 15 servings
JEANAAN KIBLER

LORD, THANK *you for the food* before us, the friends beside us and the love between us. *~Amen*

EASY CREAM CHEESE DANISH

DOUGH

2 (8-ounce) packages
  refrigerated crescent rolls
2 (8-ounce) packages cream
  cheese, softened

1 egg yolk
1 teaspoon vanilla
¾ cup sugar
1 egg white, beaten

GLAZE

1 cup powdered sugar
½ teaspoon vanilla

1 teaspoon butter, softened
2 tablespoons milk or water

DOUGH

- Preheat oven to 350 degrees.
- Press one package dough to fit a greased 13 x 9 x 2-inch baking dish. Press seams together.
- Blend cream cheese, egg yolk, vanilla and sugar. Pour filling over dough.
- Place remaining package dough over filling, pressing seams together.
- Brush with egg white.
- Bake 30 minutes. Cool completely.

GLAZE

- Blend powdered sugar, vanilla, butter and milk.
- Drizzle glaze over Danish.

Yield: 12 servings

KATHIE TAYLOR

ANN GILLESPIE'S BREAKFAST SOUFFLÉ

1½ pounds pork sausage

9 eggs, beaten

3 cups milk

1½ teaspoons dry mustard

1 teaspoon salt

3 slices white bread, torn into small pieces

1½ cups shredded Cheddar cheese

- Thoroughly cook sausage over medium heat. Stir to crumble and drain well.
- Combine sausage, eggs, milk, mustard, salt, bread pieces and Cheddar cheese. Mix well.
- Pour mixture into a greased 13 x 9 x 2-inch baking dish.
- Cover and refrigerate overnight.
- Bake at 350 degrees for 1 hour.

Yield: 8-10 large portions or 12 small

MALINDA GILLESPIE

This dish is always present at Gillespie gatherings, especially Christmas Brunch. Add a fruit salad and bread or muffins of choice and you have a great meal for any morning gathering.

BREAKFAST BRUNCH

6 eggs, beaten

2¼ cups milk

2 (4-ounce) can mushrooms, drained

1 onion, chopped

1 teaspoon dry mustard

1 teaspoon salt

8 slices buttered bread, cubed

1 cup shredded Swiss or Cheddar cheese

1-1½ pounds bratwurst or pork sausage, browned, drained and sliced

- Combine eggs, milk, mushrooms, onions, mustard and salt.
- Pour into a 13 x 9 x 2-inch baking dish.
- Gently stir in bread cubes, cheese and sausage.
- Cover and refrigerate several hours or overnight.
- Bake at 325 degrees 45-60 minutes.

Yield: 6-8 servings

JANE RAMAGE

BREAKFAST CASSEROLE

2 (7-ounce) cans chopped green chilies

1 (1-pound) package Jimmy Dean pork sausage, cooked and drained

1 (8-ounce) package shredded Cheddar cheese

1 (8-ounce) package shredded Monterey Jack cheese

2 cups evaporated milk

4 eggs

⅓ cup all-purpose flour

1 teaspoon salt

½ can chopped black olives

- Preheat oven to 350 degrees.
- In a 12 x 8 x 2-inch greased baking dish, layer green chilies, sausage, Cheddar cheese and Jack cheese.
- Combine milk, eggs, flour and salt in a blender. Process until smooth.
- Pour egg mixture over sausage. Top with black olives.
- Bake 45 minutes.

May substitute Jimmy Dean light pork sausage and low-fat cheese.

Yield: 8 servings

ANN MONTGOMERY

BREAKFAST CASSEROLE

8 slices bread, cubed

1 (8-ounce) package shredded Cheddar cheese

1 (1-pound) package Jimmy Dean sausage, browned, crumbled and drained

4 eggs

¾ teaspoon dry mustard

2¾ cups milk, divided

1 (10¾-ounce) can cream of mushroom soup

- Place bread cubes in a buttered 13 x 9 x 2-inch baking dish.
- Spread Cheddar cheese and sausage over top.
- Blend eggs, mustard and 2¼ cups milk. Pour over bread mixture.
- Cover and refrigerate overnight.
- Next morning, blend ½ cup milk and soup. Pour over entire casserole.
- Bake at 325 degrees 1 hour, 10 minutes-1 hour, 25 minutes (or 1 hour at 350 degrees.)

Yield: 10-12 servings

GAIL KOWALSKI

CHILI RELLENO CASSEROLE

1 (4-ounce) can diced green
   chilies
1 (12-ounce) package shredded
   Monterey Jack cheese,
   divided
1 (12-ounce) package shredded
   Cheddar cheese

4 eggs, separated
¾ cup instant dry milk
¾ cup water
2 tablespoons all-purpose flour
1 (7-ounce) can green chili salsa
1 (8-ounce) can tomato sauce

- Preheat oven to 350 degrees.
- Spread green chilies in the bottom of a 12 x 8 x 2-inch baking dish.
- Layer 2½ cups Jack cheese and all Cheddar cheese on top.
- Beat egg whites until soft peaks form. Beat together egg yolks, milk, water and flour.
- Fold in egg whites. Pour mixture over cheese layers.
- Bake 30 minutes.
- Combine salsa and tomato sauce. Pour over baked casserole.
- Sprinkle with remaining ½ cup Jack cheese.
- Bake an additional 20 minutes. Cool 10 minutes before serving.

Yield: 6 servings

JANET ROBERTSON

SO THAT YOU *may lead*

lives worthy of the Lord, fully pleasing him, as you bear fruit in every good work and as you grow in the knowledge of God. ~Colossians 1:10

Do not use any substitutes. Just stop worrying about your waistline and enjoy.

GOAT CHEESE, ARTICHOKE AND SMOKED HAM STRATA

2 cups whole milk
¼ cup olive oil
8 cups (1-inch) sourdough bread cubes, crust trimmed
1½ cups whipping cream
5 large eggs
1 tablespoon chopped garlic
1½ teaspoons salt
¾ teaspoon pepper
½ teaspoon ground nutmeg

12 ounces soft goat cheese
¾ pound smoked ham or turkey, cubed
3 (6½-ounce) jars marinated artichoke heart, drained and quartered
1 cup packed grated fontina cheese
1½ cups packed grated Parmesan cheese

- Whisk together milk and oil. Stir in bread cubes. Let stand 10 minutes until liquid is absorbed.
- Blend cream, eggs, garlic, salt, pepper and nutmeg.
- Add goat cheese and whisk until smooth. May take some time.
- Layer half bread cubes, ham, artichokes, fontina and Parmesan cheese.
- Pour half goat cheese mixture over all.
- Repeat all layers. Pour remaining half goat cheese mixture over top.
- Bake 50-60 minutes or until firm and browned on edges.

May be prepared a day in advance, cover and refrigerate.

Yield: 8 servings

PHYLLIS DEANE

COMPANY BAKED EGGS

1 (1-pound) package sweet
   Italian sausage
1 tablespoon butter
1 cup sliced mushrooms
1 medium red onion, chopped
12 eggs, beaten
1 cup milk

1 (8-ounce) package shredded
   mozzarella cheese
2 tomatoes, peeled and chopped
½ teaspoon salt
½ teaspoon fresh ground pepper
½ teaspoon dried oregano

- Preheat oven to 400 degrees.
- Remove casing and crumble sausage in skillet. Cook and stir until thoroughly browned. Drain well.
- Remove sausage and clean skillet. Melt butter and sauté mushrooms and onions until softened.
- Combine sausage, mushrooms, onions, eggs, milk, mozzarella cheese, tomatoes, salt, pepper and oregano.
- Pour mixture into a shallow 3-quart baking dish.
- Bake 30-35 minutes or until firm to touch.

May cook sausage, mushrooms and onions a day in advance.

Yield: 10 servings

AMANDA DAME

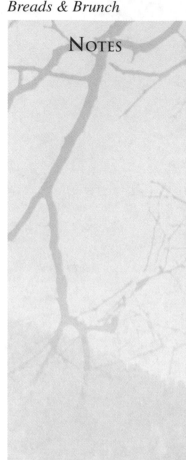

QUICHE LORRAINE

CRUST

2 cups all-purpose flour
½ teaspoon salt

1½ sticks butter or ¾ cup butter
flavored shortening
3-4 tablespoons cold water

FILLING

12 slices bacon, cooked and
crumbled
4 eggs
2 cups half & half

¼ teaspoon salt
⅛ teaspoon ground nutmeg
1¼ cups shredded Swiss cheese

CRUST

- Combine flour and salt. Cut in butter with a pastry blender until mixture resembles peas.
- Add water, a little at a time, until dough pulls away from bowl.
- Shape dough into a ball. Divide in half.
- Roll out dough on a lightly floured surface to fit into a 9-inch pie plate. Transfer to a pie plate.
- Trim and flute edges. Refrigerate. Wrap remaining dough. Refrigerate or freeze for later use.

FILLING

- Preheat oven to 425 degrees.
- Sprinkle bacon over cold crust. Beat eggs, half & half, salt and nutmeg until blended.
- Stir in Swiss cheese. Pour filling over bacon.
- Bake 15 minutes. Reduce heat to 325 degrees.
- Bake an additional 30-40 minutes or until knife inserted in center comes out clean.
- Cool 10 minutes before slicing.

Yield: 6 servings
TONYA BRIGGS

SOUTH OF THE BORDER EGG CASSEROLE

1 dozen eggs
½ cup all-purpose flour
1 teaspoon baking powder
1 stick butter, softened
1 (12-ounce) package shredded
   Monterey Jack cheese

1 (24-ounce) container cottage
   cheese
1 (4-ounce) can chopped green
   chilies, drained
Picante sauce or salsa (optional)

- Preheat oven to 400 degrees.
- Beat eggs. Stir in flour, baking powder and butter.
- Add Jack cheese, cottage cheese, chilies and salsa. Mix well.
- Pour mixture into a greased 13 x 9 x 2-inch baking dish.
- Bake 15 minutes.
- Reduce heat to 350 degrees and bake an additional 30 minutes or until bubbly and golden browned.

May prepare a day in advance. Allow 10 extra minutes for baking.

Yield: 10-12 servings
NANCY COWART

BEST PANCAKES EVER

Krusteau's Buttermilk Pancake Mix   **Club soda**

- Measure out mix to make desired number of pancakes.
- Use club soda instead of water.
- Cook batter over hot griddle.
- For thin pancakes, add more club soda.

Yield: A few-many
JEANANN MILLER

This will make the lightest best tasting pancakes you have ever eaten. Just do not tell it stated with a mix!

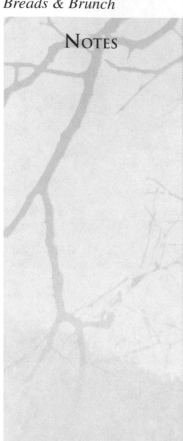

HEAVENLY PANCAKES

½ cup whole wheat flour
¼ cup wheat germ
¾ cup all-purpose flour
3 tablespoons sugar
2 teaspoons baking powder

1½ teaspoons baking soda
1 teaspoon salt
1½ cups milk or less
3 eggs
4 tablespoons butter, melted and cooled

- Combine wheat flour, wheat germ, flour, sugar, baking powder, baking soda and salt. Mix well.
- Add milk, eggs and butter. Stir just until combined.
- Pour batter on hot griddle. Serve with syrup or fruit.

For two servings, prepare dry ingredients in advance and divide into 2 portions. Store one portion in a glass or plastic container. When ready to cook, add ⅔-¾ cup milk, 1 egg and 3 tablespoons melted butter to a single portion of dry ingredients. This will make 2 servings.

Wheat germ may be found in the cereal aisle in a glass jar.

Yield: 4 servings
ANN HOECHSTETTER

GRILLED BREAKFAST SANDWICH

1 tub mascarpone cheese
Sliced Italian bread
Apricot, strawberry or
    raspberry preserves

Butter
Powdered sugar (optional)

- Spread a thin layer mascarpone cheese on one bread slice.
- Spread preserves on another bread slice. Place slices together.
- Spread butter over outside of bread.
- Grill over medium heat about 5-6 minutes until golden browned.
- Sprinkle with powdered sugar. Serve hot.

Yield: 1 serving
SANDY KIRKLEY LIPKOWITZ

CRÊPES ENSENADA

CRÊPES

12 thin slices ham
12 corn or flour tortillas
1 pound Monterey Jack cheese,
   cut into ½-inch sticks

1 (7-ounce) can green chilies, cut
   into ¼-inch slices

CHEESE SAUCE

1 stick butter
½ cup all-purpose flour
1 quart milk
1 teaspoon dry mustard

½ teaspoon salt
Dash of pepper
1 (12-ounce) package shredded
   Cheddar cheese
Paprika to taste

CRÊPES

- Preheat oven to 350 degrees.
- Place a ham slice on a tortilla. Top with cheese strips and chilies.
- Roll up tortilla and secure with toothpicks, as needed.
- Place seam side down in a greased 13 x 9 x 2-inch baking dish.

CHEESE SAUCE

- Melt butter in a saucepan. Whisk in flour.
- Add milk, mustard, salt, pepper and Cheddar cheese. Cook and stir until smooth.
- Pour sauce over crêpes. Dust with paprika.
- Bake 45 minutes.

May serve with salsa and yellow rice.

Yield: 6-8 servings

VALERIE DOLL

JOHN 21:15

When they had finished breakfast, Jesus said to Simon Peter, "Simon, son of John, do you love me more than these?" He said to Him, "Yes, Lord: you know I love you." Jesus said to him, "Feed my lambs."

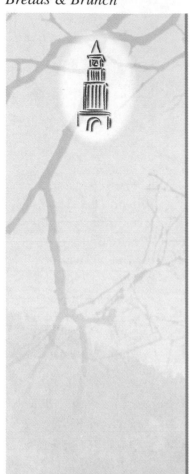

BAKED FRENCH TOAST
CASSEROLE

1 (1-pound) loaf French bread, unsliced
8 large eggs
3 cups milk
2 tablespoon sugar
1 teaspoon vanilla
¼ teaspoon salt
¾ teaspoon cinnamon, divided

¾ teaspoon ground nutmeg, divided
1 cup firmly packed brown sugar
1 cup chopped pecans
1 stick butter, softened
2 tablespoons light corn syrup

- Cut bread into 20 equal slices. Arrange bread in a buttered 13 x 9 x 2-inch baking dish in lengthwise overlapping rows.
- Blend eggs, milk, sugar, vanilla, salt, ¼ teaspoon cinnamon and ¼ teaspoon nutmeg. Pour over bread slices.
- Cover and refrigerate overnight.
- Combine brown sugar, pecans, butter, corn syrup, ½ teaspoon cinnamon and ½ teaspoon nutmeg.
- Cover and refrigerate overnight.
- Next morning, crumble sugar mixture over bread.
- Bake at 350 degrees 40 minutes or until browned.

Yield: 10 servings
DEBORAH BALL

TOMATO PIE

This pie may also be served as a side dish.

1 (9-inch) deep dish pie crust, unbaked
1 tablespoon chopped basil
4-5 large tomatoes, peeled and thick sliced

1 pound grated mozzarella cheese
Salt and pepper to taste
Olive oil

- Preheat oven to 350 degrees.
- Bake pie crust according to package directions.
- Layer in order basil, tomatoes and mozzarella cheese.
- Sprinkle with salt and pepper. Drizzle with oil.
- Bake 45 minutes or until bubbly and browned.

Yield: 8-10 servings
JERRY JUSTICE

Salads, Soups, Stews & Chili

LESSONS FROM SNOW AND SUN

Yesterday's fierce winds and swirling snow
disappear with the radiance of the morning sun
From my snug warm spot I watch, coffee cup in hand,
As the brilliance of its rays transforms my world

Stark limbed trees speak of winter's freezing touch
grasping for warmth to stave off bitter cold
Each ice covered limb catches rays of brilliant sun
Winds rip through trees creating fields of diamonds glistening briefly and beautifully

One spot gleams with intensity unmatched by its companions
Its colors shift ... red, blue, green, white ... changing
as the wind shifts the variations of reflection.

How like you, Lord, to fling your beautiful diamonds over the mountainside
While we hoard our imitations of their beauty and use them
to bolster our fading sense of worth.

How like you to choose to furnish shafts of light which
transform fragile pieces of frozen water into gems
While we think ourselves too weakly insignificant to be trusted to reflect your beauty

How like you to use yesterday's storm as raw material for today's masterpiece.
Help me to keep this scene etched in my memory when next
my world whirls with thundering winds and bitter cold.

Jimmy R. Allen

Ambrosia Salad

1 (11-ounce) can Mandarin oranges, drained

½ cup pecans, toasted and chopped

1 (3½-ounce) can sweetened coconut

⅓ cup maraschino cherries, sliced

1 (20-ounce) can chunk pineapple, drained

1 (8-ounce) container sour cream

1 cup seedless green grapes, sliced

Great salad for a summertime treat!

- Combine oranges, pecans, coconut, cherries, pineapple, sour cream and grapes. Mix well.
- Cover and refrigerate at least 8 hours.

Yield: 8 servings

CINDY BONNER

Aunt Donna's Dried Cherry Salad

1 cup vegetable oil

¾ cup sugar

½ cup red wine vinegar

2 garlic cloves, minced

½ teaspoon salt

½ teaspoon paprika

¼ teaspoon ground white pepper

1 large head romaine lettuce, torn

1 head Boston lettuce, torn

1 pint dried red cherries or dried cranberries

1 cup shredded Monterey Jack cheese

½ cup chopped walnuts, toasted

- Combine oil, sugar, vinegar, garlic, salt, paprika and white pepper in a jar. Cover tightly and shake vigorously. May refrigerate for one week.
- Combine lettuce, cherries, Jack cheese and walnuts in a large bowl.
- Shake dressing and pour over salad. Toss gently.

Yield: 12 servings

JULIE BARNARD

BEANS VINAIGRETTE

2 (14-ounce) packages frozen
  small whole green beans or
  fresh
⅓ cup sugar
⅓ cup vegetable oil
½ cup wine vinegar
2 tablespoons soy sauce
Dash of Tabasco sauce
2 tablespoons Worcestershire
  sauce

1 teaspoon salt
½ teaspoon paprika
½ cup chopped pimento
3-4 green onions, chopped
1 garlic clove, pressed
1 bell pepper, chopped
3 tablespoons sweet salad
  pickles, cubed

- Cook beans until tender crisp.
- Blend sugar, oil, vinegar, soy sauce, Tabasco, Worcestershire sauce, salt and paprika.
- Pour vinaigrette over beans.
- Combine pimentos, green onions, garlic, peppers and pickles.
- Stir into bean mixture.
- Refrigerate for at least 24 hours prior to serving.

Yield: 10-12 servings
GAYLE GILES

BLACK-EYE PEA COLD SALAD

1 (15-ounce) can black-eyed
  peas, drained
1 (15 ½-ounce) can white
  hominy, drained
1 medium tomato, chopped
1 large Vidalia onion, chopped

1 small bell pepper, chopped
2 garlic cloves, chopped
1 jalapeño pepper, chopped
  (optional)
1 (8-ounce) bottle Italian salad
  dressing

- Combine peas, hominy, tomatoes, onions, peppers, garlic and jalapeño.
- Pour dressing over salad.
- Cover and marinate in the refrigerator for at least 2 hours.
- Serve with a slotted spoon.

Yield: 6-8 servings
REGINA CHESNUT

BIBB LETTUCE SALAD WITH CRANBERRY VINAIGRETTE

CRANBERRY VINAIGRETTE

½ cup cranberry juice

2 tablespoons vegetable oil

1 tablespoon honey

1 tablespoon red wine vinegar

½ teaspoon ground allspice

Salt and pepper to taste

GLAZED PECANS

½ cup halved pecans or chopped

¼ cup sugar

SALAD

8 cups torn Bibb lettuce

½ cup sliced green onions

1 (11-ounce) can Mandarin oranges, drained

½ cup craisins

CRANBERRY VINAIGRETTE

• Combine cranberry juice, oil, honey, vinegar, allspice, salt and pepper in a blender. Process on medium speed until blended.

• Store extra vinaigrette covered in refrigerator. Makes 1 cup.

GLAZED PECANS

• Cook pecans and sugar over medium heat 5 minutes until sugar melts and pecans are lightly toasted.

• Spread out on parchment paper to cool. Break apart if needed.

• Store in an airtight container.

SALAD

• Combine lettuce and green onions in a large bowl.

• Drizzle with ½ cup vinaigrette or as desired. Toss to coat.

• Place tossed green on individual salad plates. Top with orange segments, craisins and glazed pecans.

Yield: 6-8 servings

LOUISE PRESCOTT

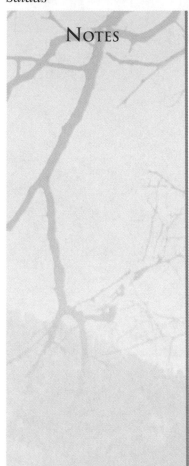

BLT SALAD

2 pounds bacon
1 (8-ounce) container sour
  cream
¾ cup mayonnaise

¼ cup bottled Italian dressing
5 cups torn romaine lettuce
4 large ripe tomatoes, diced

- Cook bacon to desired crispness. Drain, cool and crumble bacon and set aside.
- Blend sour cream, mayonnaise and dressing.
- Place lettuce in a large bowl. Arrange tomatoes over lettuce.
- Sprinkle bacon over tomatoes.
- Spread dressing mixture to cover entire salad.
- Serve immediately or cover and refrigerate up to 4 hours.

May substitute reduced-fat sour cream, mayonnaise and Italian dressing.

Yield: 12 servings

DEVON COLLINS

BLUEBERRY SALAD

2 (3-ounce) packages grape
  flavored gelatin
2 cups boiling water
1 (20-ounce) can crushed
  pineapple with juice
1 (16-ounce) can blueberry pie
  filling

1 cup sour cream
1 (8-ounce) package cream
  cheese, softened
½ cup sugar
1 teaspoon vanilla
½ cup chopped nuts

- Dissolve gelatin in hot water. Add pineapple with juice and pie filling.
- Pour mixture into 13 x 9 x 2-inch baking dish.
- Refrigerate until set.
- Blend sour cream, cream cheese, sugar and vanilla. Do not over mix.
- Spread mixture evenly over gelatin. Top with nuts.

Yield: 12-15 servings

JEAN BERRY

CHERRY MOLD

2 (3-ounce) packages black
    cherry flavored gelatin
2 cups boiling water

1 (28-ounce) can pitted Bing
    cherries, reserve juice
½ cup port wine
½ cup chopped nuts

- Dissolve gelatin in hot water. Drain cherry juice in a measuring cup. Add water to equal 1 cup.
- Add cherry juice and wine to gelatin. Refrigerate until partially set.
- Stir in cherries and nuts.
- Pour mixture into a 1½-quart mold.
- Refrigerate until set. Invert onto a serving plate and garnish.

Yield: 8 servings
JUNE TREDWAY

Pretty and warming for a cold weather table.

CHERRY SALAD SUPREME

1 (3-ounce) package raspberry
    flavored gelatin
2 cups boiling water, divided
1 (21-ounce) can cherry pie
    filling
1 (3-ounce) package lemon
    flavored gelatin
½ cup whipping cream

1 (3-ounce) package cream
    cheese, softened
½ cup mayonnaise
1 (8-ounce) can crushed
    pineapple with juice
1 cup miniature marshmallows
2 tablespoons chopped pecans or
    walnuts

- Dissolve raspberry gelatin in 1 cup hot water. Stir in pie filling.
- Pour mixture into a 13 x 9 x 2-inch baking dish. Refrigerate 2 hours or until partially set.
- Dissolve lemon gelatin in 1 cup hot water.
- Beat whipping cream, cream cheese and mayonnaise until smooth.
- Gradually add lemon gelatin to whipped mixture. Stir in pineapple with juice and marshmallows.
- Spread mixture over cherry layer. Sprinkle with nuts.
- Refrigerate until set.

Yield: 12 servings
VETIS PETWAY

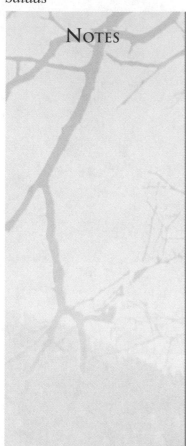

CHICKEN CAPELLINI PASTA SALAD

½ pound angel hair pasta, broken into pieces
½ package Good Seasons Garlic and Herb Dressing mix
4 cups cooked, cubed chicken
1 (14½-ounce) can artichoke hearts, coarsely chopped
1 (2¼-ounce) can sliced black olives

1 cup mayonnaise
¼ cup chopped parsley
1 cup sliced green onions
1 (8-ounce) can sliced water chestnuts
½ (4-ounce) jar pimentos (optional)

- Cook pasta al dente. Place warm pasta in a bowl and toss the dry dressing mix.
- Let cool and refrigerate overnight.
- Add chicken, artichoke hearts, olives, mayonnaise, parsley, green onions, water chestnuts and pimentos.
- Refrigerate at least 6 hours before serving.

May use marinated artichoke hearts for more flavor. This salad is a great company dish because it can be made a couple days in advance, the longer it marinates, the better it taste.

Yield: 6-8 servings
BARBIE MISBACK

CHICKEN HAYSTACK SALAD

1 cup shredded carrots
½ cup finely chopped onions
1 cup chopped celery
2 cups cooked and diced chicken

1 cup mayonnaise
1 (4-ounce) can dried shoestring potatoes
Leaf lettuce

- Combine carrots, onions, celery and chicken.
- Stir in mayonnaise. Add shoestring potatoes just before serving.
- Serve on a bed on lettuce.

May be prepared a day in advance.

Yield: 8 servings
LASSIE DYE

CHIP'S FAVORITE CHERRY SALAD

1 (¼-ounce) envelope unflavored gelatin
2 tablespoons boiling water
1 (16-ounce) can tart and pitted cherries with juice
1 (3-ounce) package cherry flavored gelatin

½ cup sugar
1 cup orange juice
Dash of lemon juice
1 (8-ounce) can crushed pineapple with juice

- Dissolve gelatin in water. Drain cherry juice in a measuring cup. Add water to equal 1 cup.
- Heat cherry juice. Stir in cherry gelatin until dissolved.
- Add unflavored gelatin, cherries, sugar, orange juice, lemon juice and pineapple with juice.
- Pour into a greased 1½-quart mold.
- Refrigerate until set.

Yield: 4-6 servings
SUSIE BROGDON

CORN AND TOMATO SUMMER SALAD

6 ears fresh corn or
   2 (10-ounce) packages frozen
3 medium-large tomatoes, diced
1 medium red onion, diced
2 tablespoons chopped basil

2 tablespoons chopped Italian parsley
2 tablespoons red wine vinegar
¼ cup olive oil
Salt and pepper to taste

- Cook corn in boiling water until tender. Drain, cool and cut corn from cob.
- Combine corn, tomatoes, onions, basil, parsley, vinegar, oil, salt and pepper.
- Refrigerate until ready to serve.

Yield: 6 servings
MELISSA LOWRIE

AMY'S SALAD

DRESSING

½ cup sugar

¼ cider vinegar

½ cup vegetable oil

1 Tbs. poppy seeds

1½ tsp. minced onion

¼ tsp. Worcestershire sauce

¼ tsp. paprika

Combine all dressing ingredients and set aside.

SALAD

2 bags spring mix greens

4 ounces crumbled blue cheese

½ bag sea salt bagel chips, slightly crushed

1 red pepper, cut in strips

½ cup salted pecans, chopped and toasted

1 Granny Smith apple, unpeeled and cut in thin strips

Mix salad ingredients and toss with dressing when ready to serve.

Hint: Dressing may be made several days ahead and refrigerated.

Submitted by Nancy Collier

A Big Canoe Favorite!

CORN, AVOCADO AND TOMATO SUMMER SALAD

DRESSING

2 tablespoons olive oil

1 tablespoon fresh lime juice

½ teaspoon lime zest

¼ cup chopped cilantro

¼ teaspoon salt

⅛ teaspoon pepper

SALAD

2 cups cooked fresh or frozen corn

1 avocado, pitted and diced into ½-inch pieces

1 pint cherry tomatoes, halved

½ cup finely diced red onions

1 (15-ounce) can black beans, drained (optional)

DRESSING

- Whisk together oil, lime juice, zest, cilantro, salt and pepper. Set aside.

SALAD

- Combine corn, avocados, tomatoes, onions and beans in a large glass bowl.
- Pour dressing over salad and gently toss to coat.

Yield: 6 servings

LOIS CARTER

CORNUCOPIA SALAD

DRESSING

2 cups mayonnaise
1 tablespoon vinegar

¼ cup sugar

SALAD

1 head iceberg lettuce, torn
½ cup diced bell pepper
½ cup diced celery
1 cup frozen green peas, thawed
2 (8-ounce) cans sliced water
    chestnuts
3 bananas, sliced tossed in
    ¼ cup lemon juice

¾ cup raisins
1 cup chopped nuts
1 cup shredded Cheddar cheese
¾ cup chopped green onions,
    green and white part
12 slices bacon, cooked crisp
    and crumbled

DRESSING

- Blend mayonnaise, vinegar and sugar. Let stand 5 minutes.

SALAD

- In a 13 x 9 x 2-inch baking dish, layer in order lettuce, peppers, celery, peas, water chestnuts, bananas, raisins and nuts.
- Spread dressing over entire top, covering salad completely.
- Sprinkle with Cheddar cheese, green onions and bacon.
- Refrigerate 4 hours before serving.

Yield: 10-12 servings
EMILY THURMAN

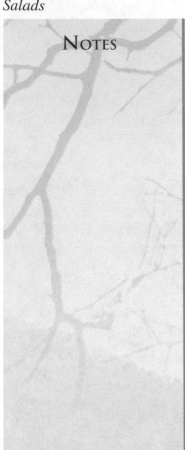

CUCUMBER SALAD À LA FINLANDAISE

4 small cucumbers, unwaxed
Fresh chopped dill
Mustard seeds
1 cup water

1 cup white vinegar, not wine vinegar
¼ cup sugar
1 teaspoon salt

- Wash and slice cucumbers. Arrange one layer cucumbers in a bowl.
- Sprinkle with dill and few mustard seeds. Continue to layer cucumber with dill and mustard seeds.
- Blend water, vinegar, sugar and salt. Slowly pour mixture over cucumbers just until covered.
- Cover with plastic wrap and refrigerate 2 hours before serving.

May adjust the salt and sugar to taste. Rice vinegar works well also.

Yield: 6-8 servings

DUSA GYLLENSVARD

FAVORITE CARROT SALAD

1 pound carrots, peeled and sliced diagonally
1 cup chopped celery
½ cup chopped bell pepper
1 medium onion, thinly sliced

1 teaspoon celery seeds
1 cup sugar
½ cup vinegar
½ cup water
⅓ cup vegetable oil

- Cook carrots in boiling water about 5 minutes until crisp-tender. Drain well.
- Combine carrots, celery, peppers, onions and celery seeds in a large shallow dish. Toss lightly.
- Blend sugar, vinegar, water and oil in a small saucepan.
- Bring to boil, stirring often.
- Pour vinaigrette over vegetables and stir to coat.
- Cover and refrigerate 8-20 hours or overnight.

May decrease amount of carrots by half and add cauliflower florets.

Yield: 6 servings

JANICE SENKBEIL

Favorite Summer Chicken Pasta Salad

1 whole chicken breast or
   2 boneless skinless breasts
⅓ cup vegetable oil
⅓ cup olive oil
¼ cup red wine vinegar
2 teaspoons Dijon mustard
2 teaspoons salt
2 teaspoons lemon pepper
2 teaspoons lemon juice
¼ teaspoon dried basil
¼ teaspoon dried oregano
¼ teaspoon dried thyme
¼ teaspoon dried marjoram
Fresh parsley
1 (8-ounce) package small pasta
   (fusilli or twisted pasta)

4 green onions, chopped plus
   2 inches green stems
1 cup large black olives, sliced
2 stalks celery, chopped
1 small bell pepper, chopped
1 small sweet red pepper,
   chopped
1 (10-ounce) package frozen
   green peas, thawed
1 (6½-ounce) jar marinated
   artichoke hearts, coarsely
   chopped
⅓ cup shredded mild Cheddar
   cheese
1¼ cups crumbled feta cheese

This looks like a ton of ingredients but it is a simple salad to make and serves 5 easily. Two people can eat dinner/lunch for a few days from it. Make it ahead so salad has time to marinate and may also play with the amounts of herbs, lemon, oil and vinegar in the dressing. It is always good. This is also delicious made without the chicken.

- Poach chicken 15 minutes. Cool to room temperature in poaching liquid. Remove skin and bones if necessary.
- Shred chicken with two forks.
- Blend vegetable oil, olive oil, vinegar, mustard, salt, lemon pepper, lemon juice, basil, oregano, thyme, marjoram and parsley until smooth.
- Pour one-third dressing over chicken.
- Add pasta, green onions, olives, celery, peppers, peas, artichokes, Cheddar cheese and feta cheese.
- Toss to evenly coat. Serve with dressing.

Yield: 5 servings
JUDY WEEMS

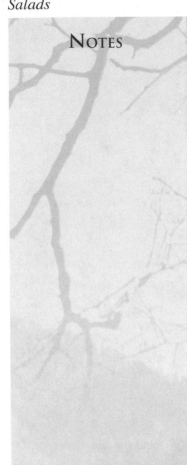

FESTIVE CRANBERRY SALAD

1 (3-ounce) package orange
  flavored gelatin
¾ cup boiling water
1 (16-ounce) can whole berry
  cranberry sauce

1 (11-ounce) can Mandarin
  oranges, drained
½ cup diced apples
½ cup chopped pecans

- Dissolve gelatin in boiling water. Stir in cranberry sauce.
- Pour mixture into an 8 x 8-inch serving dish.
- Refrigerate until partially set.
- Fold in oranges, apples and pecans.
- Refrigerate until set.

Yield: 4-6 servings
MARGARET ANDERSON

FESTIVE CRANBERRY SALAD

1 (14-ounce) can sweetened
  condensed milk
¾ cup lemon juice
1 (20-ounce) can crushed
  pineapple, drained

1 (16-ounce) can whole berry
  cranberry sauce
½ cup nuts or pecans
1 (8-ounce) container frozen
  whipped topping, thawed

- Combine milk, lemon juice, pineapple, cranberry sauce and nuts.
- Fold in whipped topping. Pour mixture into a 13 x 9 x 2-inch baking dish. Freeze.
- Remove from freezer 5 minutes before serving.

Serve this sweet salad with colorful fresh fruits garnishes such as kiwi, Mandarin oranges, cranberries or strawberries. It is also a good dessert.

Yield: 12 servings
SYBIL UNDERWOOD

FRESH GRAPE SALAD

1 (8-ounce) package cream cheese, softened
1 (8-ounce) container sour cream
½ cup sugar
1 teaspoon vanilla

1½ pounds seedless red grapes, washed and dried several hours
Brown sugar
½ cup pecans

- Combine cream cheese, sour cream, sugar and vanilla.
- Pour mixture over grapes and mix well. Sprinkle with brown sugar.
- Place pecans on top with brown sugar. Do not mix.
- Refrigerate at least 6-8 hours or overnight.

Yield: 8 servings
BARBARA FUSSELL

GRILLED CORN SALAD WITH CHERRY TOMATOES

2 teaspoons ground cumin
Juice of 3 limes (about 6 tablespoons)
1 teaspoon mild chili powder
¾ cup extra virgin olive oil
Coarse salt
Freshly ground pepper

6 ears yellow corn, shucked and brushed with oil
3 cups cherry tomatoes, halved
½ cup diced red onions
¼ cup chopped cilantro
¼ cup chopped parsley
1 cup feta cheese

- Whisk together cumin, lime juice and chili powder. Whisk in oil. Add salt and pepper.
- Grill corn about 10 minutes, turning to cook evenly, until lightly charred.
- Cool and cut kernels from cob.
- Combine corn, tomatoes, onions, cilantro, parsley and feta cheese. Pour on vinaigrette. Toss to coat.
- Transfer to a serving platter and serve immediately.

Yield: 6-8 servings
CHARLENE EHRLICH

*When as a child,
I laughed and wept,
time crept.*

*When as a youth,
I dreamed and talked,
time walked.*

*When I became a full
grown man, time ran.*

*And later, as I older
grew, time flew.*

*Soon I shall find
while traveling on,
time gone!*

*Will Christ have
saved my soul by then?*

Amen.

*From the Old Clock in
Chester Cathedral*

69

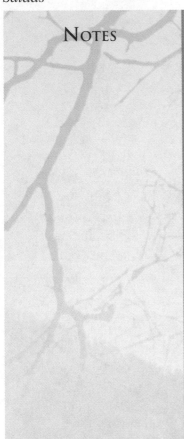

GRILLED SALMON SALAD

2 pounds salmon fillets with skin on
Olive oil
Kosher salt and freshly ground pepper to taste
Lemon juice
3 stalks celery, chopped

½ cup diced red onions
2 tablespoons minced dill
2 tablespoons capers, drained
2 tablespoons raspberry vinegar
2 tablespoons olive oil
½ teaspoon kosher salt
½ teaspoon pepper

- Cut salmon fillets crosswise into 4-inch wide slices. Rub with oil and sprinkle with salt and pepper.
- Make a boat out of aluminum foil. Place salmon, oil and lemon juice in foil boat.
- Grill fillets 5-7 minutes on each side.
- Transfer salmon to plate, cover with plastic wrap. Refrigerate until cold and firm.
- When salmon is cold, remove any skin. Break salmon into large flakes.
- Combine salmon, celery, onions, dill, capers, vinegar, oil, salt and pepper. Mix well and serve cold.

Yield: 6-8 servings
POLLY MILLS

MACARONI AND CHEESE SALAD

1 (8-ounce) package macaroni, cooked al dente
2-3 stalks celery, chopped
1 small red onion, chopped
1 cup mayonnaise

Salt to taste
1 (8-ounce) package sharp shredded Cheddar cheese
Garnish: Chopped bell pepper

- Combine macaroni, celery, onions, mayonnaise, salt and Cheddar cheese. Mix well.
- Top with peppers. Refrigerate at least 2 hours before serving.

Yield: 12 servings
FRAN SALING

MEDITERRANEAN ORZO SALAD WITH FETA VINAIGRETTE

1 cup dry orzo

2 cups bagged pre-washed spinach, chopped

½ cup chopped and drained oil-packed sun-dried tomato halves

3 tablespoons chopped red onions

3 tablespoons chopped pitted kalamata olives

½ teaspoon freshly ground pepper

¼ teaspoon salt

1 (6-ounce) jar marinated artichoke hearts, reserve marinade

¾ cup feta cheese, crumbled and divided

- Cook orzo until al dent. Drain and rinse with cold water.

- Combine orzo, spinach, sun-dried tomatoes, onions, olives, pepper and salt.

- Coarsely chop artichokes.

- Add artichokes with marinade and ½ cup feta cheese to orzo mixture. Toss gently.

- Sprinkle each serving with remaining feta cheese.

Yield: 4 servings

KATHRYN MONTGOMERY

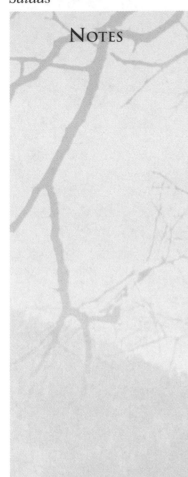

MOCK CAESAR SALAD

3 tablespoons cider vinegar
½ cup shredded Parmesan
  cheese

½ teaspoon garlic powder
⅓ cup olive oil
7 cups torn romaine lettuce

- Blend vinegar, Parmesan cheese and garlic powder in a food processor.
- While processing, add oil in a steady stream.
- Place lettuce in a salad bowl. Drizzle with dressing and toss to coat.
- Serve immediately.

Yield: 6-8 servings
BRENDA MICHEL

MY DAUGHTER'S FAVORITE FROZEN FRUIT SALAD

1 (16-ounce) container sour
  cream
¾ cup sugar
⅛ teaspoon salt
Juice of ½ lemon

2 bananas, mashed
2 (8-ounce) cans crushed
  pineapple, drained
¼-½ cup maraschino cherries
½ cup chopped nuts

- Combine sour cream, sugar, salt, lemon juice and bananas.
- Fold in pineapple, cherries and nuts.
- Spoon mixture into 12 paper-lined muffin cups.
- Freeze. When frozen, remove salad and place in a zip-top plastic bag. Return to freezer.

May use reduced-fat sour cream.

Yield: 12 servings
JEANELLE BROWN

NANA'S GERMAN POTATO SALAD

3½ pounds medium red
   potatoes, unpeeled, about 10
1 cup chopped onions
8-10 slices bacon, diced
2 tablespoons all-purpose flour
¼ cup sugar
2 tablespoons butter

1½ teaspoons salt
¼ teaspoon pepper
½ cup cider vinegar
1 cup water
½ cup sour cream
¼ cup chopped parsley

Family favorite fall dinner. Warm potato salad served with grilled bratwurst, sweet and sour red cabbage and loaf of fresh pumpernickel.

- Cook potatoes in salted boiling water 35-40 minutes until fork tender.
- Slice unpeeled warm potatoes into a bowl. Add onions.
- Cook bacon in a skillet. Remove bacon and reserve ¼ cup drippings.
- Stir flour into drippings. Add sugar, butter, salt, pepper, vinegar and water.
- Bring to boil, stirring often. Remove from heat and stir in sour cream.
- Add half bacon and dressing to potatoes. Toss gently. Sprinkle with remaining bacon and parsley.
- Serve warm or cold.

Yield: 10 servings
ALMA TONEY

NAPA SALAD

1 head Napa cabbage
1 large bunch green onions
4 tablespoons butter
1 package Ramen noodles, crushed, discard seasoning packet

1 (4-ounce) package slivered almonds
½ cup sugar
¼ cup vinegar
¾ cup vegetable oil
2 tablespoons soy sauce

- Slice, cover and refrigerate cabbage and green onions until ready to serve.
- Melt butter in a skillet. Cook noodles and almonds until browned. Cool and refrigerate.
- Blend sugar, vinegar, oil and soy sauce in a saucepan.
- Bring to boil. Boil 1 minute. Cool and refrigerate.
- When ready to serve, combine cabbage, green onions, noodle mixture and dressing. Toss to coat.

Items may be stored separately for 1 week.

Yield: 4 servings

PAMELA SCHOONMAKER

ORIENTAL SLAW

2 packages chicken flavored Ramen noodles, crushed
2 (16-ounce) packages angle hair shredded cabbage
¾ cup sliced almonds
½ cup sunflower seeds, dry roasted
1 bunch green onions, chopped

Grated carrot (optional)
Salt and pepper to taste
½ cup sugar
¾ cup canola oil
⅓ cup white vinegar
2 seasoning packets from Ramen noodles

- Combine noodles, cabbage, almonds, sunflower seeds, green onions, carrots, salt and pepper.
- Blend sugar, oil, vinegar and seasoning packets. Shake well until sugar dissolves.
- Pour dressing over cabbage mixture and toss to coat.

Yield: 6-8 servings

PHYLLIS SMITH

ORIENTAL SLAW

DRESSING

½ cup vegetable oil
¼ cup rice vinegar
¼ cup sugar

2 seasoning packets from
  Ramen noodles

SALAD

1 (16-ounce) package broccoli
  slaw
¾ cup chopped green onions
1 (4-ounce) package blanched
  slivered almonds

1 (4-6-ounce) package sunflower
  seeds
2 packages Ramen noodles,
  crushed

DRESSING

• Blend oil, vinegar, sugar and seasoning packets until smooth.

SALAD

• Combine slaw, green onions, almonds and sunflower seeds.
• Pour on dressing 1 hour before serving. Toss to coat.
• Top with noodles just before serving. Toss to coat.

*Best to add noodles just prior to serving to avoid becoming soggy.
Toss to coat. Very easy.*

Yield: 6 servings
SUSAN WILLSON

I AM *the vine, you are the branches. Those who abide in me and I in them bear much fruit, because apart from me you can do nothing. John 15:5*

ORZO FRUIT SALAD

2 (20-ounce) cans pineapple chunks
2 (15-ounce) cans Mandarin oranges
2 tablespoons all-purpose flour
¾ cup sugar

1½ teaspoons salt
2 eggs, beaten
1 (8-ounce) package orzo, cooked al dente
1 (8-ounce) container frozen whipped topping, thawed

- Drain juice from pineapple and oranges into a saucepan. Blend in flour, sugar, salt and eggs.
- Cook and stir until thickened. Let cool.
- Pour sauce over cooked orzo. Cover and refrigerate overnight.
- When ready to serve, add pineapple, Mandarin oranges and whipped topping. Mix well.

Yield: 6-8 servings
KAYE RODRIGUEZ

PHYLLIS DILLER POTATO SALAD

4 large potatoes, boiled, peeled, sliced and salted
1 large white onion, slivered
1-1½ cups mayonnaise

⅓ cup fresh lemon juice
Dash of vinegar
1½ teaspoons sugar

- Combine potatoes, onions, mayonnaise, lemon juice, vinegar and sugar.
- Mix well. Refrigerate until ready to serve.

This recipe was given by Phyllis herself during a TV Interview. Its flavor is best developed by making and refrigerating a day in advance.

Yield: 6 servings
CAROLYN OMUNDSON

Pasta Primavera Salad

Dressing

1 cup mayonnaise
1 tablespoon white vinegar
1 tablespoon apple cider vinegar
1 tablespoon Dijon mustard

1 teaspoon sugar
1 teaspoon salt
¼ teaspoon white pepper

Salad

1 pound macaroni, bowtie or
  rotini pasta
1 cup frozen sweet peas, thawed
1 cup cooked corn

¼ cup chopped Vidalia onions
1 cup thinly sliced carrots
2 tomatoes, seeded and diced

Dressing

- Blend together mayonnaise, vinegar, cider vinegar, mustard, sugar, salt and pepper until smooth.

Salad

- Cook pasta al dente. Drain and rinse in cold water. Drain and toss with few drops of olive oil.
- Combine pasta, peas, corn, onions, carrots and tomatoes.
- Pour on dressing and toss to coat. Refrigerate until ready to serve.

May add 2 cups diced ham (decrease salt in dressing) or 2 cups small cooked shrimp. Vary vegetables according to preference or season to keep it colorful.

Yield: 8-10 servings
JEAN JAMES

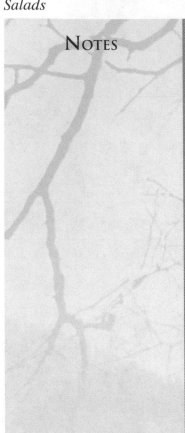

PINK ARCTIC SALAD

1 (8-ounce) package cream
   cheese, softened
2 tablespoons mayonnaise
2 tablespoons sugar
1 (8-ounce) can whole cranberry
   sauce

1 cup crushed pineapple,
   drained
1 cup chopped pecans or
   walnuts
1 cup frozen whipped topping,
   thawed

- Beat cream cheese until smooth. Stir in mayonnaise and sugar.
- Add cranberry sauce, pineapple and pecans.
- Fold in whipped topping.
- Spoon mixture into paper-lined muffin cups. Freeze.
- When frozen, transfer to a zip-top plastic bag. Return to freezer.

Yield: 10 servings
BECKY FLEMING

PRISCILLA'S GREEN BEAN SALAD

2 pounds thin green beans, cut
   into 2-inch pieces, 4 cups
¼ cup olive oil
2 tablespoons sherry vinegar
2 teaspoons Dijon mustard

¼ teaspoon salt
½ pound cherry tomatoes,
   halved or grape tomatoes
½ cup goat cheese, crumbled
Freshly ground pepper

- Cook beans in lightly salted boiling water 7-9 minutes or until tender.
- Drain and rinse in cold water.
- Whisk together oil, vinegar, mustard and salt.
- Pour dressing over beans and toss to coat.
- Fold in tomatoes and goat cheese. Sprinkle with pepper.

May also be served on individual salad plates. May prepare 2 days in advance. Store green beans, dressing, tomatoes and cheese separately in refrigerator. Combine up to 3 hours before serving.

Yield: 8 servings
PATSY WOHLWEND

POLYNESIAN CHICKEN SALAD

DRESSING

½ cup mayonnaise

⅓ cup sour cream

2 tablespoons pineapple juice
from pineapple tidbits

½ teaspoon salt

SALAD

1 (8-ounce) package macaroni,
cooked al dente

1 (15-ounce) can chicken,
drained and flaked

Chopped celery

¼-½ cup chopped onions

1 (11-ounce) can Mandarin
oranges, drained

1 (8-ounce) can pineapple
tidbits, reserve 2 tablespoons
juice

¾-1 cup walnuts

DRESSING

- Blend mayonnaise, sour cream, pineapple juice and salt until smooth.

SALAD

- Combine macaroni, chicken, celery, onions, oranges, pineapples and walnuts.
- Pour on dressing and toss to coat.

Yield: 4-6 servings

BRENDA TANNER

79

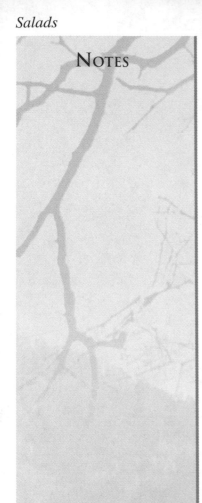

RED GRAPE SALAD

SALAD
1 (8-ounce) container sour
   cream
1 (8-ounce) package cream
   cheese, softened

½ cup sugar
1 teaspoon vanilla
1½ pounds seedless red grapes

TOPPING
1 cup chopped pecans
2 tablespoons butter

1 cup packed brown sugar

SALAD
- Combine sour cream, cream cheese, sugar and vanilla.
- Spoon mixture over grapes and toss gently. Transfer to a serving bowl.

TOPPING
- Toast pecans in butter until lightly browned. Cool.
- Combine pecans and brown sugar.
- Sprinkle over grapes. Refrigerate overnight.

May serve as a dessert.

Yield: 8 servings
BARBARA LEE

RICH'S MAGNOLIA ROOM FRUIT SALAD

1 (8-ounce) package cream cheese, softened

½ cup powdered sugar

⅓ cup mayonnaise

2 teaspoons vanilla

1 (6½-ounce) can sliced peaches, well drained

½ cup maraschino cherries, well drained

1 (30-ounce) can fruit cocktail, drained

1 (8-ounce) can crushed pineapple, drained

2 cups miniature marshmallows

½ cup whipping cream, whipped

Food coloring

- Beat cream cheese and powdered sugar until smooth.
- Blend in mayonnaise. Stir in vanilla.
- Fold in peaches, cherries, fruit cocktail, pineapple and marshmallows.
- Gently fold in whipped cream.
- Pour mixture into large paper-lined muffin cups. Freeze.
- When ready to serve, remove from freezer 10-15 minutes, but do not allow softening.
- Remove paper liners before serving.

Yield: 10-12 servings

GLADYS PERRY

SECRET SALAD

1½ tablespoons virgin olive oil

1 large tablespoon red wine vinegar

1-2 teaspoons seasoned salt

1 level teaspoon Accent

½ teaspoon dried oregano

4-6 ripe tomatoes, sliced and mashed

Chopped iceberg lettuce

Freshly chopped parsley

Freshly chopped chives

Pita bread, broken into pieces

- Combine oil, vinegar, seasoned salt, Accent, oregano and tomatoes.
- Add lettuce, parsley and chives.
- Toss salad from the bottom.
- Add 4 heaping teaspoons of pita pieces. Toss again.
- Serve in individual salad bowls.

Yield: 4-6 servings

DAN KEASLER

SAUTÉED APPLES, ONIONS, AND PEARS OVER SPINACH

2 tablespoons honey
¼ cup white wine vinegar
¼ cup dry sherry or apple juice
1 tablespoon lemon juice
⅛ teaspoon salt
⅛ teaspoon ground white pepper
⅛ teaspoon dried thyme
   (optional)

1 small onion, sliced and
   separated into rings
1 tablespoon olive oil
1 pear, cored and sliced
1 cooking apple, cored and
   sliced
1 (10-ounce) package spinach,
   washed and trimmed

- Combine honey, vinegar, sherry, lemon juice, salt, pepper and thyme.
- Sauté onions in oil, stirring constantly, until tender.
- Add pears, apples and honey mixture.
- Cook 5-6 minutes, stirring often, until fruit is tender and liquid is slightly thickened.
- Serve fruit mixture over spinach.

Yield: 4-6 servings
KATHY ELLERBE

SUMMER SALAD SUPREME PASTA

1 pound thin spaghetti, cooked
   al dente and drained
4 tablespoons McCormick's
   Salad Supreme seasoning
1 (8-ounce) bottle Wishbone
   Italian dressing

Chopped tomatoes
Chopped cucumbers
Chopped green onions
Chopped bell peppers

- Toss together spaghetti, seasoning and dressing.
- Add tomatoes, cucumbers, green onions and peppers.
- Refrigerate overnight.

May add cubed cheese and/or ham to make a main dish.

Yield: 6 servings
PAT ADAMS

SHRIMP, WATERMELON AND AVOCADO SALAD

1 pound large shrimp, cooked and peeled

4 cups bite-size watermelon pieces

1 small red onion, halved and thinly sliced

½ cup fresh cilantro leaves

2 jalapeños, seeded and finely chopped

2 avocados, peeled and cubed

Juice of 1 lime (about 2 tablespoons)

3 tablespoons extra-virgin olive oil

1 teaspoon honey

1 teaspoon salt

1 teaspoon pepper

- Combine shrimp, watermelon, onions, cilantro, jalapeños and avocados.
- In a separate bowl, whisk together lime juice, oil, honey, salt and pepper.
- Pour vinaigrette over shrimp mixture and toss gently.
- Set aside 10 minutes to allow flavors to blend.

To prevent salad from getting mushy, blot excess liquid from shrimp, watermelon and cilantro before combining.

Yield: 6 servings

SANDRA HINTZE

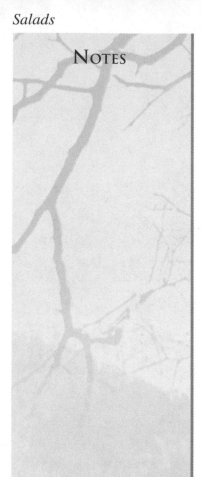

WATERMELON/SHRIMP SALAD

DRESSING

**Juice of 1 lime
(about 2 tablespoons)**
1 tablespoon honey
¾ teaspoon kosher salt

¼ teaspoon pepper
**3 tablespoons extra virgin
olive oil**

SALAD

4 cups cubed watermelon
2 avocados, cubed
1 small red onion, thinly sliced
½ cup chopped cilantro

1 pound cooked shrimp
**2 jalapeño peppers, seeded and
finely chopped**

DRESSING

- Process lime juice, honey, salt and pepper in the blender.
- Slowly add oil and blend until smooth.

SALAD

- Combine watermelon, avocados, onions, cilantro, shrimp and jalapeños.
- Pour on dressing and toss to coat.

Make a day in advance to allow flavors to blend.

Yield: 4 servings

JUDY ERICKSON

ANGIE'S OVEN STEW

1½ pounds stew meat
4 carrots, sliced
Chopped celery to taste
2 onions, quartered
Salt and pepper to taste

1 (8-ounce) can tomato sauce
½ cup chili sauce
1 (4-ounce) can mushrooms,
　　reserve juice
Cooked rice or noodles

- Combine stew meat, carrots, celery, onions, salt, pepper, tomato sauce, chili sauce and mushrooms.
- Add water to mushroom juice to equal ½ cup. Add to stew mixture.
- Place mixture in an ovenproof dish or slow cooker.
- Cover and bake 3 hours at 325 degrees or 6 hours in slow cooker.
- Serve with rice or noodles.

Yield: 4 servings
JOAN HUBER

*May my food my
body maintain,*

*May my body my
soul sustain,*

*May my soul in
deed and word*

*Give thanks for
all things to the Lord.*

*From the movie
"Babette's Feast"*

BLACK BEAN SOUP

2 (15-ounce) cans black beans,
　　drained
1 (14-ounce) can chicken broth
½ cup salsa
1 tablespoon chili powder

Garlic powder to taste
Onions, sautéed to taste
Garnish: Cheese of choice and
　　sour cream
Hot cooked rice (optional)

- Mash one can black beans. Mix with other can in a saucepan.
- Add broth, salsa, chili powder, garlic and onions.
- Bring to boil. Reduce heat and simmer 10 minutes.
- Top with cheese and sour cream. Serve over rice.

Yield: 2 servings
BRENDA LAYFIELD

Rich taste; a great dish for fall and winter.

CURRIED BUTTERNUT SQUASH SOUP

2 medium butternut squash, halved lengthwise and seeded
4 teaspoons butter
4 teaspoons brown sugar
Salt and pepper to taste
2 cups vegetable broth
1 teaspoon garlic powder
1 teaspoon onion powder
1 teaspoon curry powder
½ cup reduced-fat sour cream
¼ teaspoon lime zest
1 tablespoon lime juice
Garnish: Lime zest

- Preheat oven to 400 degrees.
- Remove all stringy pulp from squash. Place squash halves flesh side up on baking sheet.
- Place teaspoon of butter in middle of each squash.
- Sprinkle with brown sugar, salt and pepper.
- Bake 25 minutes until fork tender.
- When cool, scoop out pulp and place in a medium saucepan.
- Add broth, garlic powder, onion powder, curry, salt and pepper.
- Bring to simmer. Cook 10 minutes.
- Purée soup in batches in blender or with immersion blender until smooth. Keep warm.
- Whisk together sour cream, lime zest and lime juice until smooth.
- Ladle soup in bowls. Spoon a dollop of Lime Cream in center and garnish with lime zest.

Yield: 2 servings
JOYCE RALEY

BISQUE QUICK

2 (10-ounce) cans condensed tomato soup
½ (10¾-ounce) can condensed pea soup
1 (14-ounce) can chicken broth
1 cup heavy cream
1 (6-ounce) can crabmeat, shrimp or lobster
¾ cup sherry

- Combine tomato soup, pea soup, chicken broth, cream and crabmeat in the top of a double boiler.
- Heat thoroughly.
- Add sherry just prior to serving.

Yield: 6 servings
JOAN HUBER

CHICKEN CHILI

1 pound ground chicken
1 medium yellow onion, chopped
Olive oil
3 cups chicken broth
1 package Lawry's® chili seasoning mix
1 (10-ounce) can chopped tomatoes
1 (10-ounce) can Rotel with chilies
1 (4-ounce) can chopped green chilies
3 (15-ounce) cans white beans, drained and rinsed
Garnish: Sour cream and shredded Cheddar cheese

- Brown chicken and onions in oil over medium heat.
- Add chicken broth, seasoning mix, tomatoes, Rotel, chilies and white beans.
- Cook 10 minutes.
- Reduce heat to low and simmer 30 minutes.
- Serve with sour cream and shredded Cheddar cheese.

Do not substitute brands. Stores well for 3 days in refrigerator and freezes well too.

Yield: 3-4 servings
JEAN KEENAN

SALT IS *good but if salt has lost its saltiness, how can you season it? Have salt in yourselves, and be at peace with one another. ~Mark 9:50*

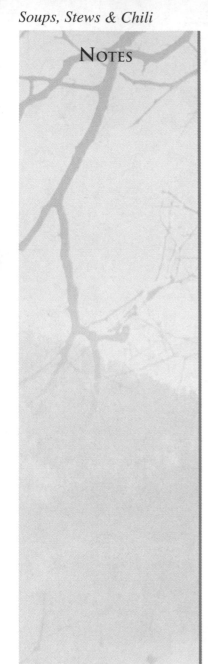

CORNBREAD CHILI

1 pound ground chuck
½ cup chopped onions
1 (15-ounce) can chili with beans
1 (15-ounce) can diced tomatoes, drained
1 (15-ounce) can chili beans
1 (15-ounce) can whole kernel corn, drained

Chili powder to taste (optional)
1½-2 cups shredded extra sharp Cheddar or Monterey Jack cheese
1 (9-ounce) package Jiffy Corn Muffin Mix

- Preheat oven to 400 degrees.
- Brown ground chuck and onions in a large stockpot. Drain drippings.
- Add chili with beans, tomatoes and chili beans. Cover and simmer 1 hour, stirring frequently.
- Stir in corn. Add chili powder.
- Pour mixture into a 13 x 9 x 2-inch baking dish. Sprinkle with cheese.
- Prepare muffin mix according to package directions except add more milk to thin mixture.
- Pour corn batter over entire casserole.
- Bake 30-45 minutes or until golden browned.

Yield: 8 servings
MARY JANE CHILDS

EASY CRAB BISQUE

1 (10¾-ounce) can Campbell's® green pea soup
1 (10¾-ounce) can Campbell's® beef bouillon

1 (10¾-ounce) can Campbell's® tomato soup
1 cup heavy cream
1 (6-ounce) can crabmeat

- Combine pea soup, bouillon and tomato soup. Do not dilute soup. Heat thoroughly.
- Cool slightly and add cream and crabmeat.
- Reheat but do not boil.

Yield: 4-6 servings
KATHY ELLERBE

CREAM OF ROASTED GARLIC SOUP

2 large heads garlic
1 tablespoon olive oil
½ cup finely chopped shallots
2 tablespoons butter, melted
1½ cups buttermilk
1 cup whipping cream

½ cup cubed and cooked red
  potatoes
½ teaspoon salt
½ teaspoon minced fresh thyme
Garnish: Homemade croutons
  (optional)

- Preheat oven to 350 degrees.
- Cut off top one-fourth of each garlic head and discard. Place garlic heads, cut side up on foil and drizzle with oil.
- Wrap foil around garlic, sealing foil at top.
- Bake 1 hour. Cool completely.
- Remove papery skin and squeeze out soft garlic into small bowl.
- Sauté shallots in butter until tender in a saucepan. Stir in buttermilk and whipping cream.
- Bring just to boil. Reduce heat and simmer 5 minutes, uncovered.
- Remove from heat and cool.
- Process garlic, buttermilk mixture and potatoes in a food processor 1 minute until smooth.
- Return to a saucepan. Stir in salt and thyme.
- Cook over medium heat until thoroughly heated, stirring often.
- Ladle soup in individual bowls. Top with croutons.

Yield: 2 servings
NANCY SHIRAH

A friend of mine, Anita Bauer, found this recipe to be a favorite of the family she stayed with as an exchange student in Australia.

CURRIED PEANUT SOUP

3 tablespoons butter
½ cup chopped onions
½ cup chopped carrots
½ cup chopped celery
1 teaspoon curry powder
2 tablespoons all-purpose flour
2 (10¾-ounce) cans cream of mushroom soup

½ cup chunky peanut butter
2 tablespoons ketchup
2 teaspoons Worcestershire sauce
1 cup cooked white rice
Garnish: Sour cream and finely chopped peanuts

- Melt butter in a large skillet. Sauté onions, carrots, celery and curry until tender.
- Stir in flour. Dilute soup and add to mixture.
- Add peanut butter, ketchup and Worcestershire sauce.
- Simmer 5 minutes. Stir in rice.
- Serve with a dollop of sour cream and peanuts.

Yield: 6 servings
ALICE EACHUS

Dad used butter but I sauté in olive oil for health and use low-fat baby Swiss cheese.

DAD'S INFAMOUS ONION SOUP

6 large onions, thinly sliced
3 tablespoons olive oil
2 tablespoons all-purpose flour
1 tablespoon Dijon mustard
2 garlic cloves, minced
¼ teaspoon thyme

1-2 beef bouillon cubes
6 cups fat-free chicken broth
1 cup white wine
2 tablespoons Brandy
Grated Swiss cheese
Slices French bread

- Sauté onions in oil until soft. Add flour, mustard, garlic, thyme, bouillon, broth, wine and brandy.
- Cook and stir until thickened.
- Ladle into soup bowls. Top with bread and Swiss cheese.
- Bake 15-20 minutes.

Yield: 6-8 servings
SANDY SCHARF

Easy Oven Chicken Chili

1 tablespoon vegetable oil
1 medium onion, chopped
3 garlic cloves, minced
1½ teaspoons ground cumin
2 large boneless skinless chicken breast halves, cut into ¾-1-inch chunks
2 (16-ounce) cans pinto beans, drained

1 (16-ounce) can corn, yellow or white, drained
2 (4-ounce) cans chopped green chilies, drained
2 teaspoons chicken bouillon granules or 2 cubes
1½ cups water
3 dashes of Tabasco sauce
1½ cups shredded Monterey Jack cheese

- Preheat oven to 350 degrees.
- Heat oil in a small saucepan. Sauté onions, garlic and cumin until tender.
- Combine onion mixture, chicken, beans, corn, chilies, bouillon and water in a 2½-quart casserole dish.
- Sprinkle with Tabasco. Bake 1 hour, 10 minutes until chicken is done.
- To serve, ladle into soup bowls. Top with Jack cheese.

Yield: 6 servings

DONNA WILLS

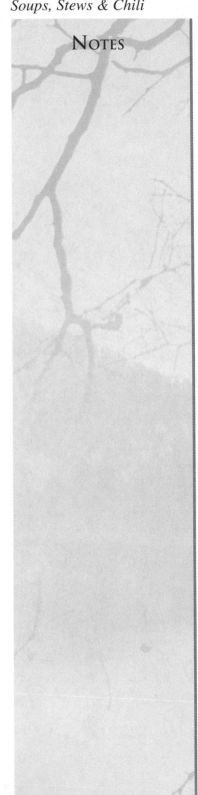

GAZPACHO

5 ripe tomatoes, peeled and quartered or 28-ounce can Italian tomatoes

1 garlic clove, mashed

1 small onion, sliced

1 small cucumber, peeled and sliced

1 small bell pepper, seeded and sliced

1 (10½-ounce) can beef consommé

2 tablespoons olive oil

3 tablespoons wine vinegar

2 tablespoons chopped parsley

⅛ teaspoon cayenne pepper

½ teaspoon salt

Dash of Tabasco sauce

Dash of Worcestershire sauce or to taste

½ teaspoon chili powder or to taste

• Combine tomatoes, garlic, onions, cucumbers, peppers, beef consommé, oil, vinegar, parsley, cayenne, salt, Tabasco, Worcestershire sauce and chili powder in a blender.

• Cover and purée until smooth.

• Refrigerate thoroughly.

• To serve, ladle cold soup into bowls.

• Serve with side dishes of finely chopped cucumbers, tomatoes and onions.

Yield: 6-8 servings

BONNIE MOORE

Grandmother Davis' Brunswick Stew (Clarence McKee's Grandmother)

6 pounds lean pork shoulder, Boston Butt

5 large Irish potatoes, peeled and cubed

7 medium-large onions, cubed

4 (14½-ounce) cans tomatoes

3 (14½-ounce) cans white cream-style corn

½ (10-ounce) bottle Lea & Perrins® Worcestershire Sauce

¾ (26-ounce) bottle ketchup

Zest of 1 lemon

Juice of 1 lemon (about 3 tablespoons)

Lemon slices

¾ cup vinegar

Salt, red and black pepper to taste

3 tablespoons cornstarch (optional)

- Boil pork shoulder until meat falls off the bone. While warm, remove as much fat as possible. Cool and cube meat.

- Boil potatoes and onions in as little water as possible in stockpot.

- Add tomatoes, corn, Worcestershire sauce, ketchup, lemon zest, lemon juice, lemon slices, vinegar, salt, red and black pepper. Heat on low heat.

- If needed, dissolve cornstarch in small amount of water. Stir into stew.

- Add meat and simmer at least 4 hours, stirring often. Do not burn.

Clarence's cousin, Little George Moreland, all 6´7˝, cooks stew outside, 100 pounds at a time and simmers for 8 hours. He sells it at his country store outside Leesburg, GA.

The lemon is the secret to the flavor. Do not leave it out. We put so much meat in this that it is a complete meal. May be served over rice or as a side dish to BBQ.

Yield: 8-10 servings
RAMONA McKEE

CHICKEN SALAD FOR SANDWICHES

2 large chicken breasts or 4 small boneless chicken breasts

Water

1½ tsp. salt

¼ tsp. pepper

Small onion

2 stalks celery

Mayonnaise to taste

Cover chicken breast with water; add 1 tsp. salt and ¼ tsp. pepper and a small onion. Bring to a boil, cover and cook until tender. Cool; remove chicken from bones and discard bones, skin, cartilage and dark portions.

Grind celery in food processor and put into medium size refrigerator bowl. Grind chicken and add to celery. Add ½ tsp. salt and a little

Continued on next page

GRILLED CHICKEN SALAD SANDWICHES

4 boneless skinless chicken breast halves
2 teaspoons Creole seasoning
¼ cup mayonnaise
¼ cup sour cream

Lettuce leaves
8 tomato slices
4 sourdough rolls, split
Vegetable cooking spray

- Coat chicken with vegetable spray. Sprinkle with Creole seasoning.
- Grill chicken, covered, 7 minutes per side until done. Cool slightly and coarsely chop.
- Blend mayonnaise and sour cream. Stir in chicken.
- Cover and refrigerate.
- Place lettuce and two tomato slices on bottom of each roll.
- Top evenly with chicken mixture. Cover with tops of rolls.

May use more mayonnaise and sour cream as desired.

Yield: 4 servings
SANDY BINGHAM

ITALIAN TORTELLINI SOUP WITH SAUSAGE

¾ pound hot Italian sausage, browned and cut into bite-size pieces
5 cups low sodium chicken broth
1 (14½-ounce) can diced Italian tomatoes, undrained

1⅓ cups cheese tortellini
1 cup zucchini, quartered and sliced
Freshly grated Parmesan cheese

- Brown sausage in a stockpot. Drain drippings. Return sausage to pot.
- Add broth and tomatoes with juice.
- Bring to boil. Scraping up any bits from bottom.
- Reduce heat and simmer 8-10 minutes.
- Return to boil and stir in tortellini.
- Cook 8 minutes or until pasta in tender. Add more broth if necessary.
- Stir in zucchini and simmer 2-3 minutes or until just tender.
- Ladle soup in bowls and sprinkle with Parmesan cheese.

Yield: 4 servings
BRENDA MATTHEWS

HOG HEAVEN CHILI

1 pound ground beef
½ pound hot pork sausage
1 large onion, chopped
1 garlic clove, slivered
1 (10-ounce) can tomato purée
1 (10-ounce) can tomatoes and chilies
1 (16-ounce) can stewed tomatoes
2-3 (16-ounce) cans kidney beans

4 cups water
1 tablespoon chili powder
½ tablespoon ground cumin
2 teaspoons salt
2 tablespoons sugar
2 tablespoons white vinegar
Dash of pepper
1 cup shredded sharp Cheddar cheese
Garnish: Sour cream and lime wedges

- Brown beef, sausage, onions and garlic in a heavy skillet until meat is crumbly. Drain well.
- Transfer meat mixture to an 8-quart stockpot.
- Add tomato paste, tomatoes and chilies, tomatoes, kidney beans, water, chili powder, cumin, salt, sugar, vinegar and pepper.
- Bring to boil. Reduce heat and simmer 3 hours, stirring often. Add more water if necessary.
- Ladle soup into bowls. Top with Cheddar cheese and sour cream. Squeeze lime over chili.

Yield: 12 servings
NANCY COLLIER

CHICKEN SALAD FOR SANDWICHES
continued

more pepper. Mix together with mayonnaise to spreading consistency. Refrigerate until needed. Will keep for 4-5 days.

If chicken salad is to be eaten as a salad entrée, cut chicken into small pieces instead of grinding and add whatever appeals to you — such as boiled eggs, pimiento, pickles or olives, almonds or pecans, etc.

Submitted by Nona Whipple

Appeared in
Served With a View

HEARTY VEGETABLE BEEF SOUP

Serve with a green salad and cornbread, it is a great winter meal.

5 pounds chuck roast, cut into bite-size chunks, fat removed
1 large beef soup bone
6 quarts water
1½ cups chopped onions
1 cup chopped celery
2 (15-ounce) cans beef broth or 2-3 tablespoons Better Than Bouillon beef base
2 (28-ounce) cans whole tomatoes, stems removed and chopped
1 (28-ounce) can crushed tomatoes
½ head cabbage, chopped
3-4 turnips, peeled and chopped

3 (1¼-ounce) envelopes dry Lipton's® onion or beefy onion soup
1-2 carrots, peeled and chopped (optional)
1 quart V-8 juice or less
1-2 tablespoons salt or to taste
½-1 teaspoon Italian seasoning or Savory
½ teaspoon black pepper
½ teaspoon cayenne pepper or to taste
4 pounds frozen soup vegetables or mixed vegetables
1 cup barley or elbow macaroni

- Place chunk roast and soup bone in water in a 12-quart stockpot.
- Bring to boil. Skim off top a couple of times.
- Add onions and celery. Cover, reduce heat and simmer 1 hour or until meat is tender.
- Add broth, tomatoes, cabbage, turnips, onion soup mix, carrots, V-8 juice, salt, Italian seasoning, pepper and cayenne.
- Bring to boil. Add frozen vegetables. Reduce heat and add barley.
- Simmer 1 hour until well cooked. Remove soup bone.
- Taste for salt and pepper.
- Cool and skim fat from top.

Yield: 8-10 servings
SYLVIA HARNESBERGER

Lentil, Barley and Kielbasa

½ pound fully cooked turkey
  kielbasa sausage, cut into
  pieces
1 large onion, chopped
2 medium celery, chopped
2 medium carrots, chopped
2 garlic cloves, finely chopped
¾ cup dry lentils, sorted and
  rinsed
½ cup uncooked pearl barley
6 cups water

1 tablespoon chicken bouillon
  granules
1½ teaspoons chopped fresh
  rosemary leaves or
  ½ teaspoon dried, crushed
1½ teaspoons chopped fresh
  oregano or ½ teaspoon dried
1 bay leaf
1 (28-ounce) can whole
  tomatoes, undrained
¼ cup chopped fresh parsley

- Cook sausage, onions, celery, carrots and garlic 8 minutes in a nonstick Dutch oven over medium heat, stirring occasionally, until vegetables are tender.

- Add lentils, barley, water, bouillon, rosemary, oregano, bay leaf and tomatoes. Break up tomatoes.

- Bring to boil. Reduce heat to medium low.

- Simmer, uncovered, about 45 minutes, stirring occasionally until lentils are tender.

- Remove bay leaf. Stir in parsley.

Yield: 6 servings

POLLY MILLS

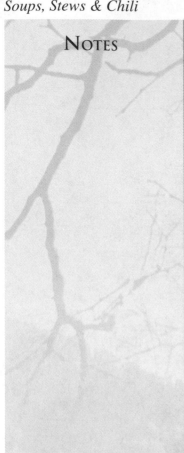

MOTHER'S POTATO SOUP

3 cups chopped potatoes
1 cup water
½ cup sliced celery
¼ cup chopped onions
Grated carrots to taste
1 tablespoon dried parsley or
   3 tablespoons freshly chopped

1 (10½-ounce) can chicken broth
½ teaspoon salt
Dash of pepper
2 tablespoons all-purpose flour
1½ cups milk
1 cup shredded Cheddar cheese
   or Velveeta® cheese, cubed

- Combine potatoes, water, celery, onions, carrots, parsley, chicken broth, salt and pepper in a large stockpot.
- Cover and simmer 15-20 minutes or until vegetables are tender.
- In a large measuring cup, whisk together flour and milk until well blended.
- Slowly stir into vegetables. Cook until thickened.
- Add cheese. Stir until cheese melts.

If soup is too thick, gradually add more milk. If too thin, add a few instant mashed potatoes to thicken soup.

May add cooked and crumbled bacon and/or homemade noodles.

Yield: 6 servings

KAY DELL KNARR

TORTELLINI AND SPINACH SOUP

1 small Vidalia onion, chopped
½ tablespoon olive oil
2 (14-ounce) cans low sodium
   chicken broth
1 (14½-ounce) can petite diced
   tomatoes, undrained
2 teaspoons lemon juice

4 ounces tortellini, cheese or
   cheese and spinach
1 (10-ounce) package baby
   spinach, washed and
   stemmed
Grated Parmesan cheese

- Sauté onions in oil. Add broth, tomatoes with juice and lemon juice.
- Bring to boil. Add tortellini and cook per package directions.
- Add spinach and simmer 1 minute until wilted.
- Serve with Parmesan cheese and crusty bread.

Yield: 2-3 servings

JEAN JAMES

PUMPKIN SOUP

1 cup finely chopped onions
4 tablespoons butter
¼ cup all-purpose flour
4-5 cups chicken broth
1 (15-ouncee) can pumpkin
4 teaspoons lemon juice

1 teaspoon salt or less to taste
¾ teaspoon ground nutmeg
2 cups whole milk or half & half
Garnish: Chopped fresh
    rosemary and sour cream
    (optional)

- Sauté onions in butter. Stir in flour until blended.
- Add broth and bring to simmer.
- Stir in pumpkin, lemon juice, salt and nutmeg.
- Slowly stir in milk. Heat thoroughly. Do not boil. Add more broth is too thick.
- Garnish with additional nutmeg and a dollop of sour cream or rosemary.

This soup is a beautiful color, especially nice for fall or holidays. I received it years ago from Lucretia Davenport's recipe published in the Atlanta paper.

Yield: 6 servings
CATHERINE CAPPS

SEVEN CAN VEGETABLE SOUP

1 (14½-ounce) can cut green
    beans
1 (15¼-ounce) can whole kernel
    yellow corn
1 (15-ounce) can black-eyed
    peas
1 (14½-ounce) can diced
    tomatoes

1 (14½-ounce) can diced new
    potatoes
1 (15¼-ounce) can lima beans
1 (14½-ounce) can sliced carrots
1 (1¼-ounce) envelope Lipton®
    Onion Soup mix
½ teaspoon salt
¼ teaspoon pepper

- Combine green beans, corn, peas, tomatoes, potatoes, lima beans, carrots, soup mix, salt and pepper with all juices in a large stockpot.
- Bring to boil, stirring occasionally.
- Reduce heat and simmer at least 1 hour, stirring occasionally.
- Add more seasoning to taste.

Yield: 8 servings
CINDY BONNER

Great soup for a cold, winter day served with homemade cornbread!

This recipe comes from the world famous Columbia Restaurant in Tampa, Florida. I have adapted it to more modern taste by leaving out the lard.

SPANISH BEAN SOUP

1 (16-ounce) package dry
   garbanzo beans or chickpeas
4 slices bacon, diced
1 onion, diced
1 ham bone, with ham meat
1 pound potatoes, diced

Pinch of saffron
Salt and pepper to taste
1 smoked chorizo, thinly sliced,
   do not use uncooked Mexican
   chorizo

- Cover beans with water and soak overnight.
- Sauté bacon and onions in large stockpot.
- Drain beans. Add beans and ham bone to pot. Cover with water.
- Bring to boil. Reduce heat and simmer 1 hour or until beans begin to soften.
- Add potatoes, saffron, salt and pepper.
- Cook until potatoes are tender.
- Remove ham bone. Add chorizo and serve.

Yield: 8 servings
SUSANNE NEWELL

As delicate as vichyssoise but with a mysterious garden fresh flavor.

SUMMER SURPRISE COLD SOUP

1 cup coarsely diced potatoes
1 cup fresh or frozen green peas
¼ cup chopped green onions
1½ cups chicken broth

⅛ teaspoon celery salt
⅛ teaspoon curry powder
½ cup whipping cream
½ cup half & half

- Combine potatoes, peas, green onions and broth in a saucepan.
- Bring to boil. Reduce heat, cover and simmer 10 minutes until vegetables are tender.
- Transfer mixture to a blender. Process until smooth about 30 seconds or press through a fine sieve.
- Add celery salt, curry, whipping cream and half & half.
- Refrigerate until cold.

Yield: 4 servings
NANCY BICKLEY

STEAK AND TWO POTATO SOUP

1½ pounds lean boneless round
   steak, cut into 1-inch pieces
¾ teaspoon salt
½ teaspoon pepper
2-3 tablespoons vegetable oil
2 stalks celery, sliced
1 medium onion, chopped
3 large garlic cloves, minced
3 cups chicken or beef broth
2 cups water, divided
3 Yukon Gold Potatoes,
   unpeeled and cut into ¾-inch
   cubes

1 medium sweet potato, peeled
   and cut into ¾-inch cubes
2 tablespoons all-purpose flour
½ cup whipping cream
1½ cups shredded sharp
   Cheddar cheese
1 tablespoon chopped parsley
   (optional)
1 tablespoon chopped chives
   (optional)

*Men fancy this soup.
Tender chunks of steak
are joined by potatoes
and Cheddar cheese
in a creamy base.*

- Sprinkle beef with salt and pepper. Brown in batches in hot oil in a Dutch oven.
- Remove beef from pan. Sauté celery and onions 5 minutes. Add garlic and sauté 30 seconds.
- Return beef to pan. Add broth and 1¾ cups water.
- Bring to boil. Cover, reduce heat and simmer 1 hour.
- Add Gold potatoes. Cover and cook 10 minutes.
- Add sweet potatoes and cook 20 minutes until beef and potatoes are tender.
- Whisk together flour and ¼ cup water until smooth.
- Gradually stir flour mixture into meat mixture. Cook, uncovered, 5 minutes.
- Stir in cream and cook an additional 5 minutes.
- Add Cheddar cheese, parsley and chives. Cook 1 minute until cheese melts.
- Sprinkle each serving with fresh ground pepper.

Yield: 6 servings
BRENDA TANNER

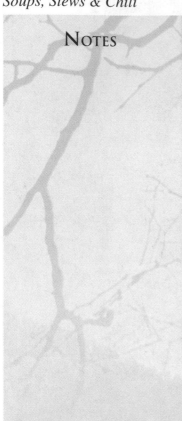

TORTILLA SOUP

1 (14-ounce) can whole kernel corn, drained
1 (14-ounce) can cream-style corn
2 (14-ounce) cans chicken broth
1 (14-ounce) can diced tomatoes
1 (15-ounce) can black beans, drained and rinsed

2-3 boneless skinless chicken breast halves, cooked and chopped
2 tablespoons taco seasoning
Garnish: Tortilla chips, sour cream and shredded Cheddar cheese

- Combine corn, cream-style corn, broth, tomatoes, beans, chicken and taco seasoning in a stockpot.
- Simmer 1 hour.
- Serve with tortilla chips, sour cream and Cheddar cheese.

Yield: 2 servings
PAT KING

TORTILLA SOUP

2 teaspoons vegetable oil
⅓ cup chopped onions
1 (4-ounce) can chopped green chilies
4 cups chicken broth
1 cup cooked and shredded chicken

1 (10-ounce) can tomatoes and green chilies
1 tablespoon lime juice
Garnish: Crushed tortilla chips and shredded sharp Cheddar cheese

- Heat oil in a large saucepan. Sauté onions until tender.
- Add green chilies, broth, chicken and tomatoes.
- Cover and simmer 20 minutes.
- Stir in lime juice.
- Serve in soup bowls with tortilla chips and Cheddar cheese.

Yield: 4 servings
NANCY POPP

VEGETABLE SOUP

1 tablespoon vegetable oil
1 pound chuck or sirloin tip
  roast, cut into ⅝-inch cubes
½ head cabbage, thinly sliced
1 small onion, chopped
3 stalks celery, chopped
6 carrots, sliced
1 (14½-ounce) can diced
  tomatoes
1 (46-ounce) can V-8 juice
3 (14-ounce) cans beef broth
1 bay leaf
2 teaspoons dried parsley
½ teaspoon Old Bay seasoning

1 beef bouillon cube
½ cup dry rice
1 (15¼-ounce) can whole kernel
  corn, undrained
1 (15¼-ounce) can peas,
  undrained
1 (15¼-ounce) can lima beans,
  undrained
1 (15¼-ounce) can cut green
  beans, undrained
1 cup fresh or frozen okra
1 teaspoon sugar
Salt and pepper to taste

*This soup takes all day
but is worth every minute
of it. Make room in the
freezer as it makes 5 quarts
of the best soup you
have ever tasted.*

- Heat oil in an 8-quart stockpot. Brown beef, stirring occasionally.
- Add cabbage, onions, celery and carrots. Cook and stir until vegetables are tender.
- Stir in tomatoes, V-8 juice and enough broth to make sufficient broth.
- Add bay leaf, parsley, Old Bay seasoning and bouillon.
- Partially cover pot, reduce heat and simmer 3 hours, stirring occasionally.
- Add more broth as needed. Stir in rice and simmer 1 hour, 30 minutes.
- Stir in corn, peas, lima beans and green beans with juice.
- Simmer an additional 30 minutes. Again add more broth as needed.
- Add okra and sugar. Simmer an additional 20 minutes. Add salt and pepper. Remove bay leaf.

Yield: 5 quarts
CATHERINE TALLEY

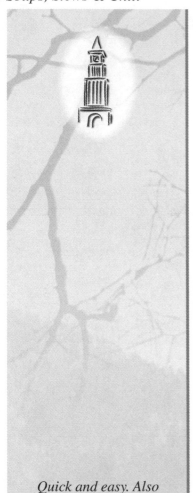

VEGETABLE SOUP

1 (10-ounce) package frozen whole kernel corn
3 (14½-ounce) cans diced tomatoes, undrained
2 (14½-ounce) cans beef broth
1 (10-ounce) can package frozen baby lima beans
2 medium baking potatoes, peeled and diced
1 large onion, chopped

2 carrots, sliced
2 stalks celery, sliced
¼ teaspoon salt
½ teaspoon pepper
½ teaspoon dried basil
¼ teaspoon dried thyme
2 bay leaves
Garnish: Grated Parmesan cheese (optional)

- Combine corn, tomatoes, broth, lima beans, potatoes, onions, carrots, celery, salt, pepper, basil, thyme and bay leaves in a 5-quart slow cooker.
- Cover and cook on high 4 hours.
- Remove bay leaves.
- Top with Parmesan cheese. Serve with crusty bread.

Yield: 3 quarts

JANE RAMAGE

WHITE BEAN CHICKEN CHILI

Quick and easy. Also low-fat and low calorie.

1 tablespoon olive oil
1 cup chopped onions
2 teaspoons chopped garlic
1¾ pounds chicken tenders, cut into bite-size pieces
1 (1½-ounce) envelope taco seasoning
1 cup water

1 (14-ounce) can artichoke hearts, drained and quartered
1 (14½-ounce) can mild Rotel
1 (15-ounce) can white beans, drained and rinsed
1 tablespoon chopped cilantro (optional)

- Heat oil over medium heat. Sauté onions until tender.
- Add garlic, chicken and ½ teaspoon taco seasoning. Cook about 5 minutes until chicken is done.
- Stir in remaining taco seasoning and water. Bring to boil.
- Add artichokes, Rotel and beans.
- Simmer, uncovered, an additional 5 minutes.
- Top with cilantro.

Yield: 6 servings

NANCY GAMBESKI

WHITE CHILI WITH SALSA

2 (14-ounce) cans chicken broth

2 (15-ounce) cans Great Northern beans, drained

3 cups cooked and chopped chicken

1 medium onion, chopped

1 (16-ounce) package frozen white corn, thawed

1 (4-ounce) can chopped green chilies

1 teaspoon ground cumin

¼ teaspoon cayenne pepper

¾ teaspoon dried oregano

1 cup shredded Monterey Jack cheese

Garnish: Sour cream and 1 cup salsa

- Place 1 cup broth and 1 cup beans in blender. Process until smooth.
- Combine bean mixture, remaining broth and beans, chicken, onions, corn, chilies, cumin, cayenne and oregano in a Dutch oven.
- Bring to boil. Cover, reduce heat and simmer 30 minutes.
- Add Jack cheese. Stir until cheese melts.
- Ladle chili into bowls and top with more cheese, sour cream and salsa.

Yield: 6-8 servings

ANN OWENS

I AM THE *true vine, and my Father is the vinegrower. He removes every branch in me that bears no fruit. Every branch that bears fruit he prunes to make it bear more fruit. ~John 15:1-2*

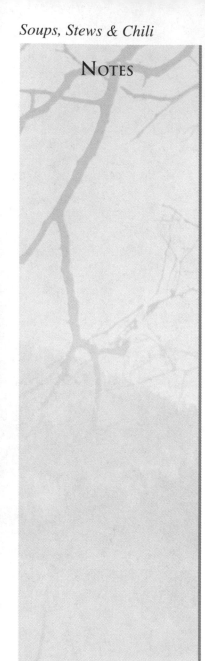

WILD RICE SOUP

¾ cup uncooked wild rice
1 tablespoon vegetable oil
4 cups water
1 onion, diced
1 stalk celery, diced
1 carrot, diced
1 stick butter

½ cup all-purpose flour
3 cups chicken broth
2 cups half & half
1 cup diced ham
1 cup diced chicken
1 teaspoon salt
Garnish: Chopped parsley

- Rinse and drain rice. Sauté rice in oil until lightly browned. Partially cook rice in water 30 minutes.
- Drain rice, reserving liquid. If necessary add water to equal 1½ cups liquid.
- Sauté onions, celery and carrots in butter. Reduce heat and blend in flour. Cook 5 minutes.
- Blend in broth and rice cooking liquid. Bring to boil and stir 1 minute.
- Add wild rice, half & half, ham, chicken and salt.
- Simmer 30 minutes. Top with parsley.

Yield: 6-8 servings
LYNNE KNAPP

Entrées

WINDOW ON LAKE PETIT

Bathed in dawn's golden glow,
Dappled by morning breeze,
The lake stirs ever so slightly.
I, too, stir — moving slowly
To shake off morning drowse.
My steps quicken
Toward a softly-lit window
Giving hint of hidden beauty
Released by a rising sun.

The lake begins its morning play.
Sparkling prisms tumble
And dance a silent ballet,
Quickly exhausting themselves
To fall back into the deep.
Jewels on wind-borne crests
Race across the sunlit stage
To exit into shaded coves.
Wisps of rising fog
Unmask an azure mirror,
Blemished only by breezy ripples
Like a horde of water sliders
Rushing to join the play.

The lake begins its day
Wrapped in Nature's beauty.
My day begins
With a prayer of thanks
That I can share this beauty
From my window on Lake Petit.

William Davenport

BAKED CHICKEN AND RICE WITH MUSHROOMS

1 (6-ounce) package original long-grain and wild rice

3 pounds boneless skinless chicken thighs or chicken breasts or a mixture

½ envelope onion soup mix

1 (8-ounce) package sliced fresh mushrooms

1 (10¾-ounce) can condensed fat-free cream of chicken soup

2¾ cups water

- Preheat oven to 325 degrees.
- Spread rice in a roasting pan. Reserve seasoning packet.
- Top rice with chicken. Sprinkle with dry onion soup mix and mushrooms.
- Spoon soup over rice and chicken.
- Sprinkle rice seasoning packet over all. Pour water over mixture.
- Cover and bake 2-2 hours, 30 minutes. Do not open or stir until cooking is complete.
- Serve immediately.

This dish freezes well and is great covered dish for gathering and also for shut-ins.

Yield: 6-8 servings
SYBIL UNDERWOOD

Lord, we ask you to bless this family with a warm place by the fire when the world is cold.

A light in the window when the day is dark.

For the blessing of this home and this food, we give thanks.

Amen

BLACKHAWK CHICKEN

Rice, green vegetables, a gelatin salad or cranberry relish will make a great meal. Bon Appetite!

12 slices prosciutto ham
6 boneless skinless chicken breast halves, sliced in two
12 slices Gruyère cheese, 1 x 3 x ¼-inch thick
½-⅔ cup all-purpose flour
Salt and white pepper to taste

3 eggs, beaten
2 cups plain bread crumbs
1 stick butter, divided
6 tablespoons cognac
2 cups heavy cream or 2% milk
1 tablespoon chicken base
1 tablespoon cornstarch

- Preheat oven to 350 degrees.
- Place a slice of ham over chicken slice. Top with cheese slice. Roll up and secure with a toothpick.
- Combine flour, salt and pepper. Dredge chicken roll in seasoned flour.
- Dip each chicken roll in egg and dredge in bread crumbs.
- Melt 3 tablespoons butter in a large skillet. Brown chicken and transfer to an ovenproof dish or pan.
- Bake 10-20 minutes or until chicken is tender.
- Remove and keep warm.
- Pour cognac into skillet. Cook 1 minute.
- Stir in cream and chicken base. Simmer 5 minutes.
- Blend cornstarch with small amount cold water. Whisk into sauce until thickened.
- Add salt and pepper as desired.
- Serve chicken with sauce on top.

Yield: 6 servings

SYLVIA HARNESBERGER

CASHEW CHICKEN

1 cup chicken broth
1 tablespoon cornstarch
2 tablespoons soy sauce
2 garlic cloves, minced
2 tablespoons vegetable oil
1 pound boneless skinless
  chicken breast halves, cut
  into bite-size pieces

½ pound broccoli, coarsely
  chopped
½ sweet red pepper, cut into
  ½-inch pieces
6 green onions, sliced diagonally
  in 1-inch slices
Hot cooked rice or Chinese
  noodles
½ cup cashews, lightly toasted

Really quick and beautiful meal if ingredients are prepared in advance.

- Blend broth, cornstarch, soy sauce and garlic in a small bowl.
- Heat wok or large nonstick skillet over medium-high heat.
- Add oil, chicken, broccoli and peppers. Stir-fry 3-5 minutes or until chicken is cooked.
- Stir broth mixture into center of pan, stirring constantly until thickened.
- Add green onions and stir-fry 1 minute.
- Serve over rice or Chinese noodles. Top with cashews.

Yield: 4 servings
LIZ DONOVAN-DAVIS

CHICKEN CASSEROLE

2 pounds boneless skinless
  chicken breast halves, cooked
  and chopped
1 (10¾-ounce) can cream of
  mushroom soup

1 (8-ounce) container sour
  cream
40 Ritz crackers, crumbled
1 stick butter

- Preheat oven to 350 degrees.
- Combine chicken, mushroom soup and sour cream.
- Pour mixture into a greased 13 x 9 x 2-inch baking dish
- Combine cracker crumbs and butter. Spoon over casserole.
- Bake 30 minutes.

May use reduced-fat Ritz crackers and fat-free sour cream. May cook chicken in fat-free chicken broth.

Yield: 6 servings
JOBETH YARBROUGH

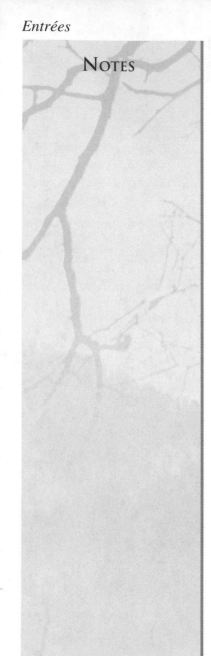

CHICKEN AND BLACK BEAN ENCHILADAS

3 slices bacon
¾ pound boneless skinless chicken breast halves, cut into short, thin strips
2 garlic cloves, minced
2 cups Pace Picante sauce, divided
1 (16-ounce) can black beans, undrained
1 large sweet red pepper, chopped

1 teaspoon ground cumin
¼ teaspoon salt
½ cup sliced green onions
12 (6-7-inch) flour tortillas
1½ cups shredded Monterey Jack cheese
Garnish: Shredded lettuce, chopped tomato, sour cream, avocado slices

- Preheat oven to 350 degrees.
- Cook bacon until crisp. Remove to paper towel. Crumble. Pour off all drippings except 2 tablespoons.
- Cook and stir chicken and garlic in drippings until done.
- Stir in ½ cup Picante sauce, beans, peppers, cumin and salt.
- Simmer 7-8 minutes until thickened, stirring occasionally.
- Add green onions and reserved bacon.
- Spoon heaping ¼ cup bean mixture down center of each tortilla.
- Top with 1 tablespoon Jack cheese.
- Roll up and place seam side down in a lightly greased 13 x 9 x 2-inch baking dish.
- Spoon remaining Picante sauce over enchiladas making sure to cover the tops.
- Bake 15 minutes.
- Top with remaining Jack cheese. Bake an additional 3 minutes.

Yield: 6 servings
PATSY WOHLWEND

CHICKEN AND DRESSING CASSEROLE

4 large chicken breasts
1 (10¾-ounce) can cream of chicken soup, undiluted
1 (10¾-ounce) can cream of mushroom soup, undiluted

1 (8-ounce) package herb seasoned stuffing mix
1 stick butter, melted

- Cook chicken in boiling water until tender.
- Remove chicken from broth. Strain off fat, reserving 2⅔ cups.
- Bone chicken and cut meat into small pieces. Set aside.
- Combine chicken soup with half broth. Mix well.
- Blend mushroom soup with remaining broth until smooth.
- Combine stuffing mix and butter. Reserve ¼ cup mixture.
- Spoon half stuffing mixture into a lightly greased 13 x 9 x 2-inch baking dish.
- Top with half the chicken. Cover with chicken soup mixture.
- Repeat stuffing and chicken layers.
- Pour mushroom soup mixture over layers.
- Top with reserved stuffing mixture.
- Cover and refrigerate overnight. May be baked at this point, if desired
- Remove from refrigerator 15 minutes before baking.
- Uncover and bake at 350 degrees 30-45 minutes.

Yield: 8-10 servings
JANICE SENKBEIL

GRANNY NELLE'S CHICKEN PIE

5 cups chopped cooked chicken
3 cups chicken broth
2 cans cream of chicken soup
3 hard-boiled eggs, chopped
2 cups self-rising flour
1 stick butter or margarine
2 cups milk

Place chopped chicken in large, ungreased (13x9x2) baking dish. Sprinkle chopped eggs over chicken. Mix soup and broth together in a small bowl and pour evenly over the chicken. (Batter will be thin.) Bake at 375 for 30 minutes.

Serves 8.

This is a good Southern comfort dish. Margarine and low-fat milk can be used to cut calories. Granny Nelle used butter and whole milk! Vegetables can be added to the dish before cooking but I prefer the vegetables on the side.

Submitted by Charlotte McCloskey

Appeared in Culinary Tour of Homes.

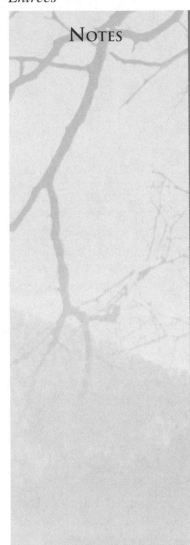

CHICKEN OPORTO

1 stick butter
1 (8-ounce) package sliced
   mushrooms
¼ cup all-purpose flour
2 teaspoons salt
¼ teaspoon pepper

¼ teaspoon ground nutmeg
8 boneless skinless chicken
   breast halves
1½ cups heavy cream
⅓ cup white wine
Hot cooked rice

- Melt butter in a large skillet. Sauté mushrooms 5 minutes.
- Transfer mushrooms to a bowl.
- Combine flour, salt, pepper and nutmeg in a pie plate.
- Dredge chicken in flour mixture. Brown chicken in butter on all sides.
- Stir in cream, wine and reserved mushrooms. Bring to boil.
- Reduce heat, cover and simmer 15 minutes or until chicken is tender.
- Serve over hot rice.

Yield: 8 servings
LYNNE SEARFOSS

CHICKEN WITH ARTICHOKES

2 (14-ounce) cans artichoke
   hearts, drained and
   quartered
3 cups diced chicken
2 (10¾-ounce) cans cream of
   chicken soup
1 cup mayonnaise

1 teaspoon lemon juice
¼ teaspoon curry powder
1¼ cups shredded sharp
   Cheddar cheese
1¼ cups bread crumbs or
   cracker crumbs
2 tablespoons butter, melted

- Arrange artichokes in a 13 x 9 x 2-inch baking dish. Spread chicken on top.
- Combine soup, mayonnaise, lemon juice and curry. Pour over chicken.
- Sprinkle Cheddar cheese on top.
- Toss bread crumbs with butter. Spread over cheese.
- Bake 30 minutes.

Yield: 8-10 servings
BARBARA LEE

CHICKEN HOT DISH

**2 cups cooked and cubed
   chicken**
**1 (15-ounce) can asparagus,
   drained and cut up**
1 cup cubed American cheese
**7 ounces narrow noodles,
   cooked and drained**
½ cup cashews, broken
1 cup diced celery
1 (4-ounce) can mushrooms
1 (4-ounce) jar pimentos

¼ cup diced onions
½ cup diced bell peppers
**1 (4-ounce) can ripe green
   olives, sliced**
½ cup mayonnaise
**1 (10¾-ounce) can cream of
   mushroom soup**
**1 (10¾-ounce) can cream of
   chicken soup**
Bread crumbs
Butter, melted

- Preheat oven to 350 degrees.
- Layer ingredients in the order in a 13 x 9 x 2-inch baking dish.
- Begin with chicken, asparagus, American cheese, noodles, cashews, celery, mushrooms, pimentos, onions, peppers and olives.
- Blend mayonnaise, mushroom soup and chicken soup. Pour over entire casserole.
- Combine bread crumbs and butter. Spoon bread crumbs over top.
- Bake 1 hour.

Yield: 10-12 servings
MICKIE SCHLUENZ

FOR THE *bread of God is that which comes down* *from heaven and gives life to the world.* ~John 6:33

113

CHICKEN LASAGNA FLORENTINE

⅔ cup chopped pecans

1 tablespoon butter, melted

1 (10-ounce) package frozen chopped spinach, thawed and well drained

2 cups cooked and chopped chicken

1 (8-ounce) package shredded Cheddar cheese

⅓ cup finely chopped onions

¼ teaspoon ground nutmeg

1 tablespoon cornstarch

½ teaspoon salt

¼ teaspoon pepper

1 tablespoon soy sauce

1 (10¾-ounce) can cream of mushroom soup, undiluted

1 (8-ounce) container sour cream

1 (4½-ounce) jar sliced mushrooms, drained

⅓ cup mayonnaise

6 dry lasagna noodles, cooked al dente

1 cup freshly grated Parmesan cheese

- Preheat oven to 350 degrees.
- Toast pecans in butter 3 minutes. Set aside.
- Combine spinach, chicken, Cheddar cheese, onions, nutmeg, cornstarch, salt, pepper, soy sauce, soup, sour cream, mushrooms and mayonnaise.
- Arrange 3 noodles in a greased 11 x 7 x 2 -inch baking dish.
- Spread half chicken mixture over noodles.
- Repeat with remaining noodles and chicken mixture.
- Sprinkle with Parmesan cheese. Top with pecans.
- Cover and bake 55-60 minutes or until hot and bubbly.
- Let stand before cutting.

Yield: 6-8 servings

NANCY SHIRAH

CHICKEN POT PIE

1 whole chicken, cooked and
de-boned
2 cups chicken broth
1 stick butter
½ cup all-purpose flour
1 (6-ounce) can evaporated milk

1 (15-ounce) can English peas,
drained
1 (15-ounce) can sliced carrots,
drained
1 (15-ounce) package Pillsbury
All-Ready pie crust
Salt and pepper to taste

- Preheat oven to 350 degrees.
- Tear chicken into bite-size pieces. Pour broth into a 2-cup measuring cup.
- Melt butter in a saucepan. Stir in flour, 2 cups broth, salt and pepper.
- Cook and stir until thickened. Stir in milk.
- Remove from heat. Add peas, carrots and chicken.
- Place one pie crust in a deep dish pie plate.
- Pour in chicken mixture. Top with second pie crust, pinching edges together.
- Cut slits in top crust.
- Bake about 1 hour or until golden browned.
- Cool 10 minutes before cutting.

Yield: 6-8 servings
MARY JANE CHILDS

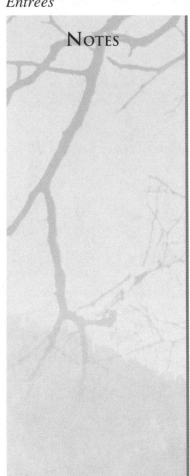

CHICKEN SPAGHETTI

¼ bell pepper, chopped
¼ onion, chopped
¼ cup chopped celery
Butter
1 (10¾-ounce) can cream of mushroom soup
½ cup sour cream
1 (15-ounce) can mild Rotel tomatoes

1 cup shredded sharp Cheddar cheese
4 boneless skinless chicken breast halves, cooked and cubed
1 (8-ounce) package spaghetti, cooked and drained

- Preheat oven to 350 degrees.
- Sauté peppers, onions and celery in butter.
- Combine soup, sour cream, tomatoes and Cheddar cheese. Add chicken broth if necessary.
- Stir in chicken, spaghetti and vegetables.
- Pour mixture into a 13 x 9 x 2-inch baking dish.
- Bake 25-30 minutes.

Yield: 8-10 servings
OUIDA AMES

GREEN BEAN CHICKEN CASSEROLE

3 cups cooked and shredded chicken
1 (6-ounce) package Uncle Ben's long-grain and wild rice, cooked
1 (10¾-ounce) can cream of celery soup

1 (4-ounce) jar chopped pimento
1 medium onion, chopped
2 (8-ounce) cans French style green beans
1 cup mayonnaise
1 (8-ounce) can chopped water chestnuts

- Preheat oven to 350 degrees.
- Combine chicken, rice, soup, pimentos, onions, green beans, mayonnaise and water chestnuts.
- Pour mixture into a 13 x 9 x 2-inch baking dish.
- Bake 45 minutes.

Yield: 8-10 servings
LYNN KING

Chicken Veronique

2 cups fine bread crumbs

2½ tablespoons salt

½ teaspoon fresh ground pepper

3 tablespoons dried tarragon

6-8 boneless skinless chicken breast halves

4 tablespoons butter

¼ cup vegetable oil

¾ cup finely chopped onions

1 cup dry white wine

1 cup chicken broth or bouillon

1 pound mushrooms, sliced

4 cups green grapes, sliced

¾ cup half & half

Hot cooked rice

- Preheat oven to 375 degrees.
- Combine bread crumbs, salt, pepper and tarragon.
- Dredge chicken in bread crumb mixture, coating well.
- Heat butter and oil in a large skillet.
- Brown chicken until golden browned on both sides.
- Transfer to a buttered 13 x 9 x 2-inch baking dish.
- Add onions to skillet. Cook until tender, not browned.
- Stir in wine and broth. Bring to boil.
- Pour sauce over chicken.
- Bake, uncovered, 30-40 minutes.
- Sauté mushrooms in butter. Pour mushrooms over chicken.
- Bake an additional 10 minutes.
- Top with grapes and half & half. Bake another 10 minutes.
- Serve with rice.

Yield: 6-8 servings

JEAN DUNN CASEY

CHICKEN WITH
ONIONS AND SHERRY GRAVY

1 (2¾-ounce) package brown
  gravy mix
¼ cup all-purpose flour
½ teaspoon garlic powder
½ teaspoon onion powder
½ teaspoon salt
¼ teaspoon black pepper

1 pound boneless skinless
  chicken tenders
1 tablespoon vegetable oil
1 large onion, sliced and
  separating into rings
⅔ cup sherry wine
1 package refrigerated mashed
  potatoes

- Prepare gravy according to package directions. Set aside.
- Combine flour, garlic powder, onion powder, salt and pepper in a zip-top plastic bag. Shake to mix.
- Drop chicken into bag and shake to coat well.
- Heat oil in a 12-inch skillet. Brown chicken 3-4 minutes on one side.
- Add onion rings.
- Turn chicken and cook 3-4 minutes until chicken is browned and onions are tender.
- Add sherry. Cook and stir, scraping to loosen bits on bottom of pan.
- Stir in prepared brown gravy. Stir well and coat chicken.
- Serve immediately with mashed potatoes and green vegetable.

Yield: 4 servings

CATHERINE TALLEY

CRESCENT CHICKEN SQUARES

1 (3-ounce) package cream cheese, softened

3 tablespoons butter, melted, divided

2 cups cooked and shredded chicken

¼ teaspoon salt

⅛ teaspoon pepper

2 tablespoons milk

1 tablespoon chopped onions

1 (8-ounce) package refrigerated crescent rolls

¾ cup seasoned croutons, crushed

- Preheat oven 350 degrees.
- Combine cream cheese and 2 tablespoons butter until smooth.
- Add chicken, salt, pepper, milk and onions. Mix well.
- Separate dough into four rectangles, sealing perforations.
- Spoon mixture into center of dough. Bring 4 corners up to the middle and twist and seal edges.
- Brush top with remaining butter. Dip dough in crushed croutons except for the bottom.
- Bake 20-25 minutes.

Crescent rolls come in two sizes. Use smaller size roll package containing 8 rolls to make 4 rectangles.

Yield: 4 servings

ELLEN FINLEY

GOLDEN RISOTTO

½ cup chopped onions

4 tablespoons butter

1 cup diced cooked chicken

1 cup diced cooked ham

1 cup cubed Little Smokie sausages

2 cups beef broth

1 (4-ounce) can sliced mushrooms, undrained

⅛ teaspoon crushed saffron

1⅓ cups rice

⅓ cup grated Parmesan cheese

- Sauté onions in butter until lightly browned.
- Add chicken, ham, sausage, broth, mushrooms with liquid and saffron.
- Bring to boil. Stir in rice and Parmesan cheese. Return to boil.
- Reduce heat and simmer 10-15 minutes.

May be served with a vegetable and fruit salad. May also be frozen and reheat in the microwave.

Yield: 6 servings

PAM EPSTEIN

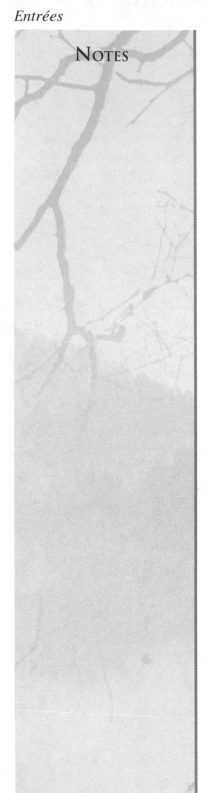

CROCKPOT MOROCCAN CHICKEN

1 pound chicken breasts, cut into chunks

1 (8-ounce) can pineapple tidbits or chunks, undrained

1 large onion, chopped

2 garlic cloves, finely chopped

2 tablespoons lemon juice

1 teaspoon salt

1 teaspoon dried marjoram

¾ teaspoon cayenne pepper

¼ teaspoon turmeric or ginger

1 tablespoon cornstarch

1 tablespoon cold water

¼ cup sliced pimento-stuffed olives

1 tablespoon chopped parsley

- Place chicken in crockpot.
- Combine pineapple with juice, onions, garlic, lemon juice, salt, marjoram, cayenne and turmeric.
- Pour mixture over chicken. Cover and cook on low 4-5 hours.
- Remove chicken and place on a serving dish. Keep warm.
- Skim fat from sauce. Blend cornstarch and water. Stir into sauce.
- Cover and cook on high 15 minutes until thickened. Stir in olives.
- Pour sauce over chicken and sprinkle with parsley.
- Serve with couscous.

Yield: 6 servings

BRENDA BEDINGFIELD

FRENCH HERBED CHICKEN

3-pound chicken fryer, cut up
1 tablespoon vegetable
   shortening
Salt and pepper to taste
1 (8-ounce) can small whole
   onions, drained
½ cup coarsely chopped carrots
1 garlic clove, crushed

2 tablespoons snipped parsley
¼ teaspoon dried thyme,
   crushed
1 (2-ounce) can sliced
   mushrooms
1 cup sauterne
2-3 stalks celery, chopped
1 bay leaf

- Preheat oven to 350 degrees.
- Brown chicken in hot shortening. Season with salt and pepper.
- Place in a 2-quart casserole. Drain excess drippings.
- Add onions, carrots, garlic, parsley, thyme, mushrooms and sauterne to skillet.
- Cook and stir, scraping up browned pieces. Pour sauce over chicken.
- Scatter celery and bay leaf among chicken.
- Cover and bake 1 hour.

Easy to prepare and tasty. A favorite for guests.

Yield: 4 servings

CAROLYN OMUNDSON

HARVEY'S CHICKEN CASSEROLE

6 large boneless skinless chicken breast halves

1 large yellow onion, sliced in half and then into thin slices

1 pound sliced mushrooms

4 garlic cloves, thinly sliced lengthwise

3 large green onions, sliced lengthwise

1 (14-ounce) can artichoke hearts

1½ cups brown rice

3 cups chicken broth

¼ cup Harvey's Bristol Crème Sherry

- Preheat oven to 350 degrees.
- Brown chicken and onions in oil. Remove to platter.
- Sauté mushrooms, garlic and green onions. Cook until tender.
- Arrange chicken in a lightly greased 13 x 9 x 2-inch baking dish.
- Pour mushroom sauce over top.
- Combine artichokes, rice, broth and sherry. Pour mixture over chicken.
- Bake 1 hour or until rice is done.

Serve with a sliced tomatoes and fresh green salad.

Yield: 4-6 servings

JEAN KEENAN

JAMBALAYA

Great supper with green salad and French bread

1 stick butter

2 cups Minute Rice

1 (14-ounce) can beef broth

1 (10¾-ounce) can French Onion Soup

1 (15-ounce) can Rotel tomatoes

1 (4-ounce) can sliced mushrooms

1 pound boneless skinless chicken breast halves, cubed

1 pound Smokey Hollow beef sausage, sliced into ¼-inch rings

1 pound shrimp, peeled

1-2 teaspoons Creole seasoning

- Preheat oven to 450 degrees.
- Melt butter in Dutch oven. Combine rice, broth, soup, tomatoes, mushrooms, chicken, sausage, shrimp and seasoning.
- Pour mixture into Dutch oven.
- Cover and bake 45 minutes. Do not open lid.

Yield: 6-8 servings

PATRICIA MCCORMICK

HOLIDAY CHICKEN

CHICKEN

8 boneless skinless chicken breast halves, cut in half
1 (14-ounce) can artichoke hearts, drained

Butter, melted
Salt and pepper to taste

HOLLANDAISE SAUCE

4 egg yolks
2 tablespoons lemon juice
2 sticks butter, melted

¼ teaspoon salt
Dash of pepper

CHICKEN

- Preheat oven to 400 degrees.
- Wrap each chicken breast around an artichoke heart. Secure with a toothpick.
- Place seam side down in a 13 x 9 x 2-inch baking dish. Pour butter over chicken.
- Sprinkle with salt and pepper.
- Bake 25 minutes, basting with butter and pan drippings.

HOLLANDAISE SAUCE

- Beat egg yolks in the top of a double boiler. Stir in lemon juice.
- Cover and cook over low heat. Add butter, little at a time, stirring constantly with a wooden spoon.
- Add salt and pepper. Cook and stir until thickened.
- Pour over cooked chicken.

Yield: 8 servings
LOUISE DODD

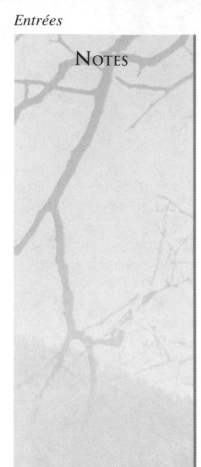

JULIE'S CHICKEN DIABLO CASSEROLE

TOPPING
1 stick butter, softened
1 cup packed brown sugar

½ cup chopped pecans

CHICKEN
2 (6-ounce) packages long-grain wild rice
2 (8-ounce) packages cream cheese, softened
1 (6-ounce) jar sliced mushrooms, drained
¼ cup dry sherry or white wine

¼ teaspoon ground nutmeg
2 tablespoons Grey Poupon mustard
2 tablespoons dried parsley
6-8 boneless skinless chicken breast halves, cooked and cut into bite-size pieces

TOPPING
• Blend butter, brown sugar and pecans. Set aside.

CHICKEN
• Preheat oven to 350 degrees.
• Cook rice according to package directions.
• Combine cream cheese, mushrooms, sherry, nutmeg, mustard and parsley.
• Stir in chicken.
• Layer rice on the bottom of a greased 13 x 9 x 2-inch baking dish.
• Spread chicken mixture on top. Top with topping mixture.
• Bake 30-45 minutes.

Yield: 12 servings
THELMA DAVIS

LEMON CHICKEN

2-4 boneless skinless chicken breast halves
Salt and pepper to taste
2 tablespoons all-purpose flour
2 tablespoons butter, divided

1 tablespoon vegetable oil
1 chicken bouillon cube
¼ cup boiling water
2 tablespoons lemon juice
Garnish: Thin lemon slices

- Flatten chicken breasts between wax paper to ¼-inch thick.
- Sprinkle with salt and pepper. Lightly dust with flour.
- Melt 1 tablespoon butter and oil in skillet. Brown chicken lightly on each side.
- Remove from skillet. Dissolve bouillon in water. Add broth and lemon juice to skillet.
- Cook and stir to deglaze pan and sauce is smooth.
- Add remaining tablespoon butter.
- Return chicken to skillet and heat 5 minutes.
- Top with lemon slices.

Especially good served with rice.

Yield: 2-4 servings
NONA WHIPPLE

JESUS SAID to them, "I am the bread of life. Whoever comes to me will never be hungry, and whoever believes in me will never be thirsty." ~John 6:35

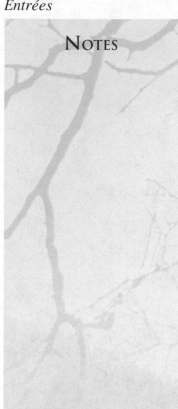

My Mom's Chicken with Red Sauce

Chicken

6 boneless skinless chicken breast halves
¼ cup all-purpose flour
½ teaspoon salt
¼ teaspoon white pepper

5 tablespoons butter, divided
1 (8-ounce) package sliced mushrooms
6 slices Swiss cheese

Red Sauce

2 tablespoons butter
½ cup chopped onions
2 garlic cloves, minced
1 (28-ounce) can Italian tomatoes

1 (6-ounce) can tomato paste
2 teaspoons crushed basil
2 teaspoons sugar
1 teaspoon salt
⅛ teaspoon white pepper

Chicken

- Preheat oven to 350 degrees.
- Pound chicken until thin. Combine flour, salt and pepper.
- Dredge chicken in seasoned flour mixture.
- Melt 4 tablespoons butter in skillet. Brown chicken on both sides.
- Transfer chicken to a glass 13 x 9 x 2-inch baking dish.
- Melt remaining tablespoon butter in skillet. Sauté mushrooms until tender.
- Spoon mushrooms over chicken and top with Swiss cheese.
- Bake 30 minutes.

Red Sauce

- Melt butter in a saucepan. Sauté onions and garlic until tender.
- Add tomatoes, tomato paste, basil, sugar, salt and white pepper.
- Simmer 30 minutes.
- Pour sauce over cooked chicken.

Yield: 6 servings

GLENDA MITCHELL

PARMESAN CHICKEN WITH LIME BUTTER

1 egg
1 tablespoon milk
1 cup grated Parmesan cheese
1 tablespoon all-purpose flour
Seasoned salt and pepper to taste
Juice of 2-3 limes (4 tablespoons)

1 stick butter
½ teaspoon dried chives
½ teaspoon dried dill
6 boneless skinless chicken breast halves
Garnish: Lime slices

- Preheat oven to 325 degrees.
- Beat egg in a shallow bowl. Mix in milk.
- In a second shallow bowl, combine Parmesan cheese, flour, salt and pepper.
- Combine lime juice, butter, chives and dill in a microwave safe dish.
- Microwave until butter melts.
- Rinse chicken and pat dry.
- Dip chicken into egg mixture. Dredge in cheese mixture.
- Place chicken in a greased 12 x 8 x 2-inch baking dish.
- Pour half lime butter over chicken.
- Bake, uncovered, 1 hour or until tender. Watch carefully to not burn dish.
- To serve, drizzle chicken with remaining lime butter.
- Top each chicken with a lime slice.

The lime butter is also good over fish.

Yield: 6 servings
JUNE TREDWAY

This recipe has become a real favorite! I use more flour and Parmesan cheese and use regular salt instead of seasoned salt. It is universally liked. It is good as chicken strips and served over romaine lettuce for protein on a salad.

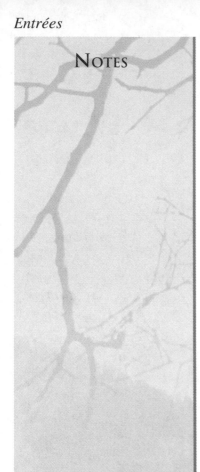

SOUTHERN CHICKEN POT PIE

1 cup chopped onions
1 cup chopped celery
1 cup chopped carrots
5⅓ tablespoons butter
½ cup all-purpose flour
2-2½ cups chicken broth
1 cup half & half
1 (8-ounce) can water chestnuts, drained

1 (6-ounce) can peas, drained
1 teaspoon salt
¼ teaspoon pepper
4 cups cooked and chopped chicken
1 (15-ounce) package Pillsbury pie crust

- Preheat oven to 375 degrees.
- Sauté onions, celery and carrots in butter 10 minutes.
- Add flour and stir constantly 1 minute.
- Combine broth and half & half. Gradually stir into vegetables.
- Stir in water chestnuts, peas, salt and pepper. If too thick add more broth or milk.
- Add chicken and mix well.
- Pour chicken mixture into 13 x 9 x 2-inch baking dish.
- Roll out pie crust to fit dish. Place over chicken mixture, sealing edges.
- Bake 40-45 minutes.

After 20-30 minutes baking, cover edges of crust with foil strips to prevent dark edges. This freezes well without the crust. Add crust prior to baking.

Yield: 8 servings

BECKY FLEMING

Hot and Spicy Turkey Spaghetti

1 small onion, chopped
1 (8-ounce) package sliced
   mushrooms
1 sweet red pepper, chopped
2 tablespoons olive oil
½ teaspoon salt
1 (8-ounce) package spaghetti,
   cooked al dente

1 (10-ounce) can diced tomatoes
   and green chilies, undrained
1 (8-ounce) package Vermont
   Cheddar cheese, cut into
   wedges
2 cups coarsely chopped turkey
1 cup frozen green peas,
   thawed

- Sauté onions, mushrooms and peppers in hot oil 3-5 minutes in a Dutch oven or until tender.
- Add salt, spaghetti, tomatoes, Cheddar cheese, turkey and peas.
- Cook over medium heat, stirring constantly, until thoroughly heated.
- Serve immediately.

This recipe freezes well. Reheat in microwave.

Yield: 6 servings
JANE GALVIN

Beef Bourguignon

2 pounds top round steak, cubed
2 tablespoons extra virgin olive
   oil
1 (1¼-ounce) package dry onion
   soup

1 (10¾-ounce) can cream of
   mushroom soup
1¼ cups red wine
1 cup water
6 cups cooked rice

- Preheat oven to 350 degrees.
- Brown beef in oil. Add onion soup mix, mushroom soup, wine and water.
- Pour mixture into a casserole dish. Cover and bake 2 hours.
- Serve over rice.

Yield: 6 servings
BARBARA E. MURPHY

ROAST PHEASANT WITH WILD RICE

1 cup wild rice
1 teaspoon salt
5 cups boiling water
1 (8-ounce) package fresh sliced
  mushrooms
3 tablespoons butter

2 pheasants (2-3 pounds)
½ cup chopped pecans
Butter, melted
1 cup dry white wine
½ cup chicken broth

- Preheat oven to 350 degrees.
- Rinse and drain rice. Add to salted boiling water. Cook 35-40 minutes or until tender.
- Strain in a colander and rinse with hot water.
- Cover with a cloth and place over steaming water.
- Sauté mushrooms in butter.
- Sprinkle pheasant cavity with salt. Stuff rice, mushrooms and pecans into cavity.
- Brush pheasant with melted butter and place in a roasting pan.
- Blend wine and broth for basting.
- Roast 30 minutes per pound.

Yield: 4 servings
VIRGINIA WHEELER

BAR-B-QUE MEAT LOAF

SAUCE

1 (15-ounce) can tomato sauce
3 tablespoons vinegar
2 tablespoons yellow mustard
3 tablespoons packed brown
   sugar

2 teaspoons Worcestershire
   sauce
½ cup water

MEAT LOAF

1½ pounds ground beef
½ cup oatmeal
½ (8-ounce) can tomato sauce
1 onion, finely chopped

1 egg
1½ teaspoons salt
¼ teaspoon pepper

SAUCE

• Blend tomato sauce, vinegar, mustard, brown sugar, Worcestershire
  sauce and water. Mix well.

MEAT LOAF

• Combine beef, oatmeal, tomato sauce, onions, egg, salt and pepper.
  Shape into a log and place in a shallow pan.
• Pour sauce over meat loaf.
• Bake 1 hour, 15 minutes.

Yield: 4-6 servings
LINDA SCHNEIDER

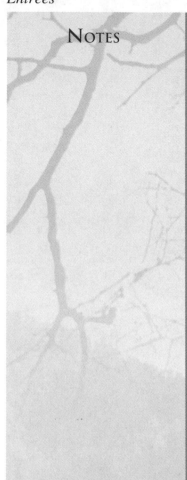

BEEF BRISKET

5-6 pounds beef brisket
⅓ cup liquid smoke
Celery salt, garlic powder, onion powder and pepper to taste

Worcestershire sauce to taste
¾ cup favorite barbecue sauce

- Place brisket in a baking dish. Pour liquid smoke over meat.
- Generously sprinkle both sides with celery salt, garlic powder and onion powder.
- Cover and marinate overnight in refrigerator.
- When ready to cook, sprinkle both sides with pepper and Worcestershire sauce. Place fat side up and cover with foil.
- Bake 1 hour per pound at 275 degrees.
- Pour barbecue sauce over brisket. Bake, uncovered, an additional hour.
- Remove brisket from drippings. Cool 1 hour before slicing diagonally across grain.
- Combine drippings with barbecue sauce. Heat and serve with brisket.

Yield: 8-10 servings
SUE BACIGALUPO

BEEF STROGANOFF

2 pounds round steak
1 medium onion, chopped
2 (4-ounce) cans mushrooms with liquid
1 (10-ounce) beef consommé

1 tablespoon ketchup
1 tablespoon soy sauce
1½ cups sour cream
Hot cooked noodles or rice

- Slice beef into strips. Brown beef and onions in a skillet.
- Add mushrooms with liquid, consommé, ketchup and soy sauce. Simmer until tender.
- If broth is too thin, thicken with flour. Add sour cream before serving, heat thoroughly.
- Serve with egg noodles or rice.

Light soy sauce and reduced-fat sour cream may be used. Mixture freezes well without sour cream.

Yield: 6 servings
KATHY BURKE

BEEF LOMBARDI

1 pound lean ground beef

1 (14½-ounce) can chopped
    tomatoes

1(10-ounce) can diced tomatoes
    and green chilies

2 teaspoons sugar

2 teaspoons salt

¼ teaspoon pepper

1 (6-ounce) can tomato paste

1 bay leaf

1 (6-ounce) package medium egg
    noodles, cooked al dente

6 green onions, chopped

1 cup sour cream

1 cup shredded sharp Cheddar
    cheese

1 cup shredded Parmesan
    cheese

1 cup shredded mozzarella
    cheese

Garnish: Fresh parsley sprigs

- Preheat oven to 350 degrees.
- Cook ground beef in a large skillet 5-6 minutes, stirring to crumble. Drain.
- Stir in tomatoes, sugar, salt and pepper. Cook 5 minutes.
- Add tomato paste and bay leaf. Simmer 30 minutes.
- Combine noodles, green onions and sour cream until blended.
- Pour noodle mixture into a lightly greased 13 x 9 x 2-inch baking dish.
- Top with beef mixture. Sprinkle evenly with Cheddar cheese, Parmesan cheese and mozzarella cheese.
- Cover and bake 35 minutes. Uncover and bake an additional 5 minutes.
- Garnish with parsley.

May freeze casserole up to 1 month. Thaw in refrigerator overnight.

May substitute low-fat or fat-free sour cream and 2% reduced-fat Cheddar cheese. Reduce amount of cheeses on top to ½ cup each.

Yield: 6 servings
NANCY COLLIER

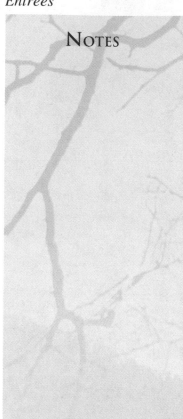

COUSIN JACKIE'S WHOLE BEEF TENDERLOIN

Whole beef tenderloin　　　**Cracked pepper**
Dale's steak seasoning

- Place trimmed whole tenderloin in large open pan.
- Pour steak seasoning over top. Marinate at least 2 hours in refrigerator, turning occasionally.
- Pour off marinade and place tenderloin in a large roasting pan.
- Cover with cracked pepper.
- Bake 20 minutes at 500 degrees. Do into open door.
- Reduce heat to 250 degrees and bake an additional 20 minutes.
- Slice and serve immediately.

This is for rare! Ends medium! Scrumptious! May also marinate in an extra-large plastic bag in pan.

Yield: 10-12 servings

BARBARA RICHARD

EASY MEATLOAF

1 pound ground turkey　　　**½ cup dry bread crumbs**
2 pounds ground chuck beef　　**1 egg**
½ jar salsa

- Preheat oven to 350 degrees.
- Combine turkey, beef, salsa, bread crumbs and egg.
- Shape mixture into two loaves. Place in two 9 x 5-inch loaf pans.
- Bake 45 minutes or until lightly browned.

May brush ketchup over tops before baking. Salsa may be mild, medium or hot. Grandkids love this!

Yield: 12 servings

BARBARA BARNETT

CROCKPOT B-B-Q

BARBECUE SAUCE

1 cup tomato juice
½ cup water
¼ cup ketchup
¼ cup vinegar
2 tablespoons Worcestershire sauce
2 tablespoons packed brown sugar

1 tablespoon paprika
1 teaspoon dry mustard
¼ teaspoon minced garlic
¼ teaspoon salt
¼ teaspoon chili powder
⅛ teaspoon cayenne pepper
2 teaspoons dry onion flakes

BEEF

3 pounds beef roast
1 onion stuffed with whole cloves

1 cup water

BARBECUE SAUCE

- Combine tomato juice, water, ketchup, vinegar, Worcestershire sauce, brown sugar, paprika, mustard, garlic, salt, chili powder, cayenne and onion flakes in saucepan.
- Simmer 15 minutes until thickened.

BEEF

- Place roast in a crockpot. Add onion and water.
- Cook on low 8-12 hours.
- Drain and discard onion, fat and bone.
- Return shredded meat to pot.
- Pour barbecue sauce over meat. Cook on low 8-10 hours.

Yield: 10-12 servings

VIRGINIA WHEELER

DAD'S HEAVENLY BEEF STEW

1¼ pounds beef chuck, cubed
All-purpose flour
3 stalks celery, chopped
2 medium onions, sliced
3 carrots, chopped
Salt to taste (optional)
½ teaspoon pepper
½ teaspoon dried oregano

½ teaspoon dried parsley
½ teaspoon paprika
1 teaspoon ground cumin
⅓-½ cup red wine
½ cup chicken broth
2 tablespoons balsamic vinegar
2 tablespoons honey
Hot cooked bow tie pasta

- Coat beef in flour. Brown in oil in a large saucepan. Remove from pan.
- Sauté celery, onions and carrots until tender.
- Return beef to saucepan. Add salt, pepper, oregano, parsley, paprika and cumin.
- Stir in red wine, broth, balsamic vinegar and honey.
- Bring to boil, stirring occasionally. Reduce heat and simmer 1 hour, 30 minutes until meat is tender.
- If necessary, blend ¼ cup water and flour to thicken stew.
- Serve over bow tie pasta.

May substitute reduced-fat and low salt chicken broth. May adjust amounts of beef, broth, vegetables, vinegar and honey to liking.

Yield: 4 servings

MARGARET SMITH

EASY STROGANOFF

1½ pounds boneless sirloin steak or chuck roast, cut into bite-size pieces
1 cup all-purpose flour
1 tablespoon Nature's Seasons seasoning mix
1 teaspoon paprika
2-3 tablespoons vegetable oil
2 medium onions, sliced
1 (8-ounce) package sliced mushrooms

3 garlic cloves, slightly chopped
1 teaspoon ground thyme or seasoning of choice
Salt and pepper to taste
1 (10¾-ounce) can cream of mushroom soup
½ cup red cooking wine
Hot cooked rice, noodles or mashed potatoes

- Combine steak cubes, flour, seasoning and paprika in a large zip-top plastic bag.
- Shake to coat. Brown meat in oil.
- Add onions, mushrooms, garlic, thyme, salt and pepper. Mix well.
- Pour mixture into a slow cooker.
- Add soup and wine. Cook on high 6 hours.
- Serve over rice, noodles or mashed potatoes.

Yield: 4 servings
ROSE FEHRENBACH

EASY YANKEE POT ROAST

1 (3-pound) rump roast
2 (10¾-ounce) cans cream of mushroom soup

1 (1¼-ounce) envelope Lipton® Onion Soup dry mix
Potatoes and carrots, chopped

- Preheat oven to 350 degrees.
- Place roast in oven safe roasting pan. Combine soup and dry onion mix.
- Pour mixture over roast. Bake 1 hour, 30 minutes.
- Add potatoes and carrots.
- Bake an additional hour, stirring occasionally. Add water as needed.

This is a great recipe because you do not have to make gravy from drippings. The gravy is perfect right out of the pot.

Yield: 6 servings
JOYCE STONEBRAKER

I love this recipe because it is so nice when we want to have steak but the weather is too bad to grill out. Even when the weather is not bad, it is great with low calorie preparations.

FILET MIGNON WITH PEPPERCORN-MUSTARD SAUCE

4 (4-ounce) beef tenderloin steaks, 1½-inches thick
¼ teaspoon salt
¼ teaspoon coarsely ground or cracked black pepper

1 teaspoon olive oil
⅓ cup minced shallots
½ cup cognac or brandy
½ cup fat-free beef broth
¼ cup Dijon mustard

- Sprinkle steaks with salt and pepper. Heat oil in a cast iron skillet over medium-high heat.
- Cook steaks 5 minutes per side or until desired degree of doneness.
- Remove steaks to pan and keep warm.
- Sauté shallots 30 seconds. Add cognac and cook 10 seconds.
- Add broth and mustard and stir well.
- Reduce heat. Cook 2 minutes, stirring constantly.
- Serve steaks with sauce.

Yield: 4 servings
KATHIE TAYLOR

FLANK STEAK TERIYAKI

¾ cup vegetable oil
¼ cup soy sauce
¼ cup honey
2 tablespoons cider vinegar
2 tablespoons chopped green onions

1 large garlic clove, minced or crushed
1½ teaspoons ground ginger
1 (2-pound) flank steak, not scored

- Combine oil, soy sauce, honey, vinegar, green onions, garlic and ginger in a zip-top plastic bag.
- Place steak in bag, turning to coat.
- Refrigerate and marinate at least 4 hours, turning occasionally.
- Grill over hot coals, turning once about 5 minutes per side for medium rare or desired doneness.
- Baste occasionally with marinade.
- Cut diagonally thin slices.

This steak may also be oven broiled.

Yield: 4 servings
AIME K. BAARS

FLANK STEAK TERIYAKI

2 garlic cloves, crushed
½ cup soy sauce
1 teaspoon sugar
½ teaspoon salt

3 teaspoons ground ginger
¼ cup vegetable oil
1½-2 pounds flank steak

- Blend garlic, soy sauce, sugar, salt and ginger. Whisk in oil.
- Pour over steak. Refrigerate and marinade 2-4 hours.
- Grill over hot heat to desired degree of doneness.
- Slice diagonally against the grain to make thin slices.

May marinate steak in a zip-top plastic bag.

Yield: 4 servings
GARY CHERRY

I received this menu from Polly and Ben Read, members of the Big Canoe Chapel.

HEAVENLY OVEN BEEF STEW

3 pounds beef stew meat
4 onions, quartered
8-10 carrots, chopped
2 bay leaves
2 cups chopped celery
2 (4-ounce) cans sliced mushrooms or 3-4 cups fresh
1 (1¼-ounce) package onion soup mix
1 (10¾-ounce) can cream of mushroom soup

1 large bell pepper, diced
1 (8-ounce) can tomato sauce
2 teaspoons dried basil
¼ teaspoon ground thyme
½ cup tapioca
Seasoned salt and pepper
Dash of cayenne pepper
2 (15-ounce) cans diced tomatoes
1 cup water

- Preheat oven to 275 degrees.
- Combine meat, onions, carrots, bay leaves, celery, mushrooms, soup mix, soup, peppers, tomato sauce, basil, thyme, tapioca, salt, pepper, cayenne, tomatoes and water in a large roasting pan.
- Seal very tightly with foil.
- Bake 5-6 hours. Do not open foil.

It makes the most gorgeous brown gravy and freezes beautifully.

May also add 1 cup red wine, green beans or peas and quartered Yukon Gold potatoes.

Yield: 12 servings
DOTTIE NIX

BIG CANOE VISITOR

*From the
corner of my eye,
I see something black
go by.
A dog, I think, then not.
Bigger, blacker than a dog.*

*Just outside my window
Lumbering up my walk
A big, black bear
Is moving toward my door.*

*I turn off the vacuum.
Catch my breath and
Watch him walk on by.
He's snubbing me today!*

*Around the house,
And back to the deck
He goes searching, sniffing,
To see what he might find.*

*To the far end of the porch
He plods, then back again.
Looking for seeds perhaps,
Put out for feathery
friends.*

Continued on next page

JANE'S FLANK STEAK MARINADE

1½ cups vegetable oil
¼ cup Worcestershire sauce
1 tablespoon ground pepper
2 garlic cloves, crushed or
    ½ teaspoon garlic salt
¾ cup soy sauce

1 tablespoon dry mustard
½ cup wine vinegar
1½ teaspoons dried parsley
½ teaspoon lemon juice
Flank steak
Bacon slices

- Blend together oil, Worcestershire sauce, pepper, garlic, soy sauce, mustard, vinegar, parsley and lemon juice.
- Trim steak and sprinkle with tenderizer. Lightly score both sides in a diagonal diamond pattern.
- Place 2-3 bacon slices on membrane side and roll up jelly roll fashion.
- Tie with string about every 1½ inches.
- Slice between each string to make filets.
- Pour marinade over meat and refrigerate about 8 hours, turning occasionally.
- Grill to desired degree of doneness.

Marinade will cover up to 5 pounds of flank steak. Unused marinade may be stored in refrigerator indefinitely. May use marinade for roasts. Do not mix used marinade and unused marinade.

Yield: 4 servings

MARY ANN WILLIAMS

KENTUCKY MEAT LOAF

½ pound sausage

1 medium-large onion, diced

1 bell pepper, diced

2 garlic cloves, minced

2½ teaspoons salt

1½ teaspoons pepper

½ teaspoon ground thyme

½ teaspoon dried oregano

2 pounds ground beef

½ cup beef broth

½ cup tomato sauce

1½ cups soft bread crumbs

2 eggs, slightly beaten

- Preheat oven to 375 degrees.
- Brown sausage in a nonstick skillet. Remove sausage and keep warm.
- Add onions, peppers, garlic, salt, pepper, thyme and oregano to skillet.
- Cook 10 minutes until vegetables are tender, stirring occasionally.
- Combine beef, broth, tomato sauce, bread crumbs and eggs in a bowl.
- Add sausage and vegetables. Mix well.
- Shape mixture into a 12 x 4-inch loaf. Place in a foil lined and greased 13 x 9 x 2-inch baking dish.
- Bake 50 minutes or until cooked in center.

Yield: 8 servings

JOE E. JOHNSON

BIG CANOE VISITOR
continued

Above him on the steps,
I focus, call out, then snap.
He pauses for a moment
Then turns away from me.

Weary and disappointed,
He leaves the deck and
Begins to cross below.
I lean out to look at him.

You're beautiful, I say.
In a voice I use for babies.
My husband keeps his
distance
And says he thinks
I'm crazy.

The old bear slowly
walks away
Toward my neighbor's
house
I'm thrilled that I've
seen him, but
He was not impressed
with me.

Joyce Reid Raley
1999

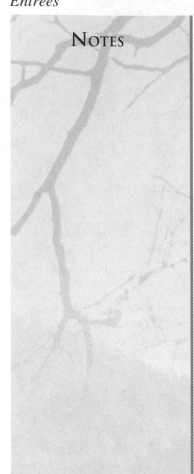

KESHY YENA

2 tablespoons all-purpose flour
¼ teaspoon salt
¼ teaspoon pepper
1 pound round steak or
   tenderloin, cut into thin strips
¼ cup vegetable oil, divided
¼ cup dry red wine
¼ cup bell pepper, chopped
¼ cup finely chopped onions
1 (8-ounce) package sliced
   mushrooms

1 medium tomato, chopped
⅛ teaspoon cayenne pepper
½ tablespoon finely chopped
   sweet pickles (optional)
1½ tablespoons seedless raisins
½ cup plus 2 tablespoons beef
   broth or ½ (10¾-ounce) can
   cream of mushroom soup
½ pound Edam or Gouda
   cheese, sliced thick or grated
3 small pimento-stuffed olives,
   drained and finely chopped

- Preheat oven to 350 degrees.
- Combine flour, salt and pepper. Dredge beef strips in mixture.
- Cook in 2 tablespoons hot oil. Add wine and cook 1 minute. Remove meat and keep warm.
- Heat 2 tablespoons oil. Sauté peppers, onions and mushrooms. Add tomatoes and cayenne.
- Cook until most of the liquid is evaporated. Remove from heat.
- Stir in pickles, raisins and broth.
- Add meat and mix well.
- Line a well-buttered 1½-quart casserole dish with cheese slices or add some grated cheese to mixture.
- Pour beef-vegetable mixture into casserole. Top with olives and additional cheese.
- Bake 20 minutes or until cheese melts and is bubbly.

This dish may be made up to one day in advance and then reheated or may be frozen. Serve as a casserole or over rice and noodles.

Yield: 6 servings

LILLIE VICK

Mama Mia Stuffed Shells

1 pound ground beef

1 pound hot or mild sausage

1 large yellow onion, sliced

1 tablespoon minced garlic

Italian seasoning to taste

2 (10-ounce) packages frozen chopped spinach, thawed

2 (12-ounce) packages shredded Italian cheese, divided

1-1½ blocks cream cheese, softened

3 (26-ounce) jars Classico Spicy Tomato Spaghetti Sauce, divided

2 (12-ounce) packages jumbo pasta shells, cooked al dente

- Preheat oven to 375 degrees.
- Brown beef and sausage with onions, garlic and seasoning. Drain and return to pan.
- Add spinach, 1 package Italian cheese, cream cheese and 2 jars spaghetti sauce.
- Stuff mixture into cooked shells.
- Spread half remaining jar spaghetti sauce in the bottom of a 13 x 9 x 2-inch baking dish.
- Arrange a single layer of shells over sauce.
- Pour remaining half sauce over shells. Top with remaining package of cheese.
- Bake 45 minutes or until cheese melts and is bubbly.

Dish freezes well and may be made in advance.

Yield: 10-12 servings

SUSAN GIBSON

Lord Jesus, be our guest, our morning joy, our evening rest

And with this food to us impart Thy love and peace to every heart, Amen

MEAT LOAF SUPREME

MOST DELICIOUS SAUCE

6 tablespoons packed brown sugar

½ teaspoon ground nutmeg

½ cup ketchup

2 teaspoons dry mustard

MEAT LOAF

2 slices toasted bread, crumbled

1 cup milk

1 pound lean ground beef

1 egg, slightly beaten

¼ cup grated onions

1 teaspoon salt

1 teaspoon pepper

1 teaspoon dried basil

1 teaspoon garlic salt

MOST DELICIOUS SAUCE

• Blend together brown sugar, nutmeg, ketchup and mustard.

MEAT LOAF

• Preheat oven to 350 degrees.

• Soak bread crumbs in milk in a large bowl.

• Add beef, egg, onions, salt, pepper, basil and garlic salt. Mix well.

• Shape mixture and place in a greased 9 x 5-inch loaf pan.

• Spoon sauce over meat loaf.

• Bake 1 hour.

Toasting the bread adds a lot of flavor, do not cheat! Leftovers make great sandwiches.

Yield: 8 servings

PATRICIA MCCORMICK

Mexican Casserole

2 pounds ground beef
1 large onion, chopped
2 (10-ounce) cans enchilada sauce
2 (4-ounce) cans green chilies

2 (10¾-ounce) cans cream of mushroom soup
½ can water
10-12 flour tortillas, quartered
1 (12-ounce) package shredded Cheddar cheese

- Preheat oven to 350 degrees.
- Brown beef and onions. Add enchilada sauce. Simmer 20 minutes.
- Heat chilies, soup and water in a separate saucepan.
- Layer in order tortillas, meat sauce, soup mixture and Cheddar cheese in a greased 13 x 9 x 2-inch baking dish, making 3-4 layers.
- Cover and allow to set 30 minutes.
- Bake, uncovered, 45 minutes.

May top with sour cream prior to serving.

Yield: 8 servings
MARGARET MORRIS

Mom's Crockpot Stroganoff

Salt, pepper and all-purpose flour
1 pound beef stew meat
1 onion, quartered
1 garlic clove, minced
1 tablespoon olive or canola oil

1 (10¾-ounce) can cream of mushroom soup
1 (4-ounce) can mushrooms, drained
½ cup red wine
1 cup sour cream

- Sprinkle salt, pepper and flour over meat. Brown meat, onions and garlic in oil in a large skillet.
- Add soup and mushrooms. Pour mixture into a crockpot.
- Cook on low 6-10 hours.
- Add wine and sour cream just prior to serving.

Serve over rice or noodles.

Yield: 4-6 servings
PATRICIA WILLIAMS

PASTITSIO

5⅓ tablespoons butter

3 tablespoons sifted all-purpose flour

3 cups hot milk

Salt and pepper to taste

Dash of ground nutmeg

1 stick butter

2 pounds ground round steak

2 medium onions, finely chopped

⅔ cup dry white wine

¼ cup tomato paste

½ teaspoon cinnamon

½ teaspoon salt

¼ teaspoon freshly ground pepper

1 pound thin macaroni or spaghetti, cooked al dente

1 cup freshly grated Parmesan cheese, divided

2 eggs, beaten

2 tablespoons bread crumbs

Butter

- Preheat oven to 400 degrees.
- To make Béchamel sauce, melt butter in a saucepan. Whisk in flour and cook 2 minutes without browning.
- Gradually add hot milk, salt, pepper and nutmeg.
- Simmer until mixture thickens. Set sauce aside.
- Heat butter and sauté meat and onions on high heat until browned, stirring constantly.
- Add wine and simmer 5 minutes.
- Place half pasta in a greased 13 x 9 x 2-inch baking dish.
- Sprinkle with ⅓ cup Parmesan cheese.
- Blend meat mixture with eggs and bread crumbs. Add small amount of remaining Parmesan cheese.
- Spread half meat mixture over pasta.
- Cover with remaining half of pasta. Sprinkle with ½ cup Parmesan cheese.
- Pour Béchamel sauce over pasta. Sprinkle with remaining Parmesan cheese.
- Dot with butter.
- Bake 30 minutes or until top is browned and bubbly. Check center of casserole to be hot.
- Cool slightly and serve.

Yield: 6-8 servings

RITA ZEILER

ROAST VEAL DIJON

1 (3-4 pound) small, boned, rolled leg of veal
1 stick butter, melted
1 (8-ounce) jar Dijon mustard

10½-ounces veal broth or 1 (10-ounce) can beef consommé
Chopped parsley

- Preheat oven to 300 degrees.
- Place meat in shallow roasting pan. Blend butter and mustard.
- Pour sauce over meat, covering all sides.
- Roast 4 hours. During last hour, baste every 20 minutes with broth.
- Keep covered with foil and cool 20-30 minutes.
- Make a sauce with pan juices. Thicken with flour.

Yield: 4 servings
SANDY FILKOWSKI

TERRY'S SPAGHETTI SAUCE RECIPE

1½-2 pounds lean ground beef
2 (28-ounce) jars Ragu Chunky Spaghetti Sauce
1 medium bell pepper, chopped into ½-inch pieces
1 medium onion, diced into ½-inch pieces

1 (7-ounce) can mushrooms, sliced
1-2 tablespoons minced garlic
3 bay leaves
½ teaspoon dried rosemary
½ teaspoon ground thyme
3-4 mild or hot Italian sausages

- Brown beef in a 6-8-quart stockpot. Drain drippings
- Add Ragu sauce, peppers, onions and mushrooms.
- Stir in garlic, bay leaves, rosemary and thyme.
- Simmer 30 minutes.
- Add Italian sausage. Simmer an additional 1 hour.

Serve with spaghetti, freshly grated Parmesan cheese and hot garlic bread. A salad can be a nice addition to a meal.

The finished sauce freezes very well in a zip-top plastic bag. It is still excellent when thawed and reheated.

Yield: 6-8 servings
R.M TERRY VALZ

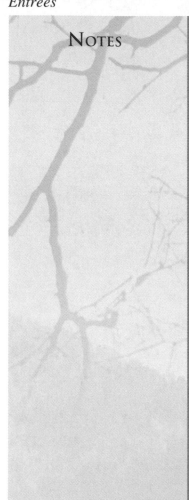

VEAL WITH ARTICHOKES

16 canned artichoke hearts
Olive oil
2 tablespoons minced parsley
Juice of 1 lemon
  (about 3 tablespoons)

2 pounds veal fillets
Garlic salt
All-purpose flour
¼ cup white wine
½ cup beef broth

- Sauté artichokes in oil very slowly. Add parsley and lemon juice.
- Sprinkle veal with garlic salt and dust with flour.
- Sauté veal in oil 5 minutes. Roast in oven 15 minutes.
- Heat wine and broth in a saucepan. Add artichokes. Sprinkle with parsley.
- Serve over pasta such as linguini or spaghetti.

Yield: 6-8 servings
SUSAN GIBSON

TEX-MEX ONE DISH MEAL

1 cup chopped onions
1 pound ground beef
2 (9-ounce) packages cornbread mix, divided
1 (15-ounce) can whole kernel corn

2 (4-ounce) cans diced green chilies, divided
3-4 cups shredded Cheddar cheese, divided
Garnish: Black beans, salsa and sour cream

- Preheat oven to 400 degrees.
- Brown onions and beef.
- Make two separate batches cornbread according to package directions, adding corn to one batch.
- Layer half of cornbread with corn in a greased 13 x 9 x 2-inch baking dish.
- Top with half meat mixture, one can chilies and 2 cups Cheddar cheese.
- Repeat layers. Pour remaining full batch of cornbread on top.
- Bake 20-25 minutes.
- Cut into squares. Top with black beans, salsa and sour cream.

Yield: 8-10 servings
JOY L. SUMMERS

TOYA LLARINE

1 medium onion, chopped
2 heaping tablespoons butter
1 pound ground chuck or round
1 (10¾-ounce) can tomato soup
1 can tomato juice
Salt, pepper, Tabasco sauce and
    Worcestershire sauce to taste
2 heaping cups uncooked
    noodles

1 (15-ounce) can cream-style
    corn
1 (4-ounce) can ripe olives,
    pitted
1 cup diced sharp Cheddar
    cheese
Butter
1 (4-ounce) can chopped olives

- Preheat oven to 350 degrees.
- Sauté onions in butter until browned. Add meat and cook until browned.
- Add tomato soup and tomato juice, salt, pepper, Tabasco and Worcestershire sauce.
- Stir in noodles and cook until al dente. Add more water if necessary.
- Remove from heat and add corn and olives.
- Alternate layers of meat mixture and Cheddar cheese in a buttered casserole dish.
- Dot with butter and sprinkle with Cheddar cheese and olives.
- Bake 45 minutes. Cool 15 minutes before serving.

Yield: 6 servings

ANN OWENS

An ideal way to enhance trout's delicacy.

BAKED TROUT PARMA

½ cup grated Parmesan cheese
½ cup cracker crumbs
2 tablespoons chopped green onions
Salt and pepper to taste, divided
4 medium trout, cleaned and heads removed

Lemon juice to taste
⅓ cup heavy cream
4 thick tomato slices
2 tablespoons butter
¼ cup dry white wine

- Preheat oven to 375 degrees.
- Combine Parmesan cheese, cracker crumbs and green onions.
- Salt and pepper trout cavities. Sprinkle with lemon juice.
- Dip fillets in cream. Roll in cracker crumb mixture. Place in a shallow baking dish.
- Place tomato slice on each fish. Sprinkle with salt and pepper. Dot with butter.
- Spoon wine over fillets. Bake 40 minutes or until tender.

Yield: 4 servings
KAREN WITZEL

ALMOND BAKED TROUT

¼ cup all-purpose flour
¼ teaspoon pepper
1½ pounds trout fillets
1 egg
3 tablespoons milk

¼ cup sliced almonds, coarsely chopped
2 tablespoons butter
¼ cup vegetable oil
Lemon wedges

- Preheat oven to 450 degrees.
- Combine flour and pepper. Coat fillets in flour mixture.
- Blend egg and milk. Dip fillets in milk mixture.
- Coat in almonds.
- Melt butter and oil in a 13 x 9 x 2-inch baking dish. Place fillets in a dish.
- Bake 5 minutes on one side. Turn fillets and bake an additional 5 minutes or until golden browned.
- Serve with lemon wedges.

Yield: 4 servings
REGINA CHESNUT

BAKED FISH WITH ARTICHOKES AND MUSHROOMS

4 (8-10 ounce) fish fillets, any thick white fillets
Melted butter
1 lemon, halved
Old Bay Seasoning
4 tablespoons butter
2 teaspoons minced garlic
2 tomatoes, diced
1 (14-ounce) can artichoke hearts, drained and quartered
1 (8-ounce) package sliced mushrooms
¼ cup capers
2 tablespoons chopped parsley
1 cup dry white wine

This is really good served over Uncle Ben's long-grain and wild rice.

- Preheat oven to 450 degrees.
- Place fillet on a baking sheet. Brush with butter.
- Squeeze lemon over top and sprinkle with Old Bay.
- Bake 10-15 minutes or until firm to the touch.
- Melt butter in a skillet. Sauté garlic 15-20 seconds. Add tomatoes, artichokes, mushrooms, capers and parsley. Sauté until vegetables are heated through.
- Add wine. Cook until reduced and slightly thickened. Spoon sauce over fillets and serve immediately.

Yield: 4 servings
JUDY WEEMS

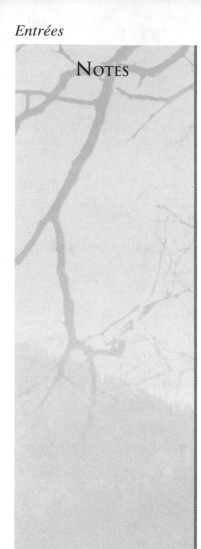

NOTES

FLOUNDER WITH DILL

**4 tomatoes, each cut into
    4 (¼-inch) thick slices**
4 (4-ounce) flounder fillets
¼ cup fine dry bread crumbs
**1 tablespoon grated Parmesan
    cheese**
1½ teaspoons chopped dill

¼ teaspoon salt
**¼ teaspoon white or black
    pepper**
⅛ teaspoon cayenne pepper
1 tablespoon butter, melted
Fresh dill sprigs (optional)

- Preheat oven to 425 degrees.
- Place tomato slices in a greased 13 x 9 x 2-inch baking dish. Arrange fillets on top.
- Combine bread crumbs, Parmesan cheese, dill, salt, pepper and cayenne.
- Stir in butter. Sprinkle bread crumbs evenly over fillets.
- Bake 13 minutes or until fish flakes easily.
- Garnish with dill.

Yield: 4 servings
CATHY CELLAMARE

CRAWFISH ÉTOUFFÉE
À LA WEESIE

3 sticks butter

3 large onions, chopped

3 stalks celery, chopped

3 garlic cloves, minced

1½ medium bell peppers, chopped

1½ teaspoons Tony Chachere's Creole seasoning

5-6 drops Tabasco sauce (optional)

2-3 pounds crawfish tails, cooked and peeled

6 tablespoons all-purpose flour

6 cups seafood broth or water

6 chicken bouillon cubes

1 cup chopped green onions

1 cup chopped parsley

Hot steamed rice

- Melt butter in a heavy stockpot. Sauté onions, celery, garlic and peppers 20 minutes.
- Add Creole seasoning and Tabasco. Stir in crawfish tails.
- Sauté 1-2 minutes. Stir in flour and cook 3 minutes, stirring constantly.
- Add broth, bouillon cubes, green onions and parsley.
- Cover and simmer 10-15 minutes.
- Serve over steamed rice.

Delicious served over steamed rice with crusty French bread! A true Cajun dish from South Louisiana. But for the faint of the heart, shrimp can be substituted for crawfish.

Yield: 12 servings

KATHY HUMPHRIES

My great aunt Weesie was the best cook in my family. She said this recipe is worth the time and trouble. It shows your family how much you love them. She was the baby in a family of 12 and I have 52 cousins. Her love of family and cooking reputation live on.

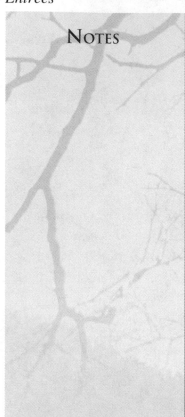

BARBECUED RIBS

5-6 pounds baby back pork spareribs
2 onions, thinly sliced
½ cup ketchup

1½ teaspoons salt
¼ teaspoon Tabasco sauce
½ teaspoon chili powder
1 cup water

- Preheat oven to 350 degrees.
- Place half spareribs in a heavy stockpot with well fitting lid.
- Cover with half the onions.
- Blend ketchup, salt, Tabasco, chili powder and water. Pour half sauce over meat and onions.
- Add another layer of spareribs, onions and remaining sauce.
- Cover and bake 2 hours.

May also use beef short ribs.

Yield: 6 servings
LOIS CARTER

CRANBERRY PORK ROAST

3-3½ pounds lean boneless pork roast
2 tablespoons olive oil
1 (16-ounce) can whole berry cranberry sauce

1 tablespoon packed brown sugar
2 teaspoons mustard, yellow or mild
2 tablespoons cornstarch
2 tablespoons water

- Trim fat from roast. Brown in olive oil
- Place roast in a greased crockpot.
- Combine cranberry sauce, brown sugar and mustard. Pour over meat.
- Cover and cook on high 1 hour
- Reduce heat to low and cook about 6 hours.
- Remove meat and keep warm. Combine cornstarch and water.
- Whisk into cranberry mixture. Cook on high until hot and thickened.
- Serve sauce over sliced pork.

Low calorie and low-fat dish.

Yield: 6-8 servings
NANCY GAMBESKI

Drunken Pork Tenderloin with Bourbon-Brown Sugar Glaze

¼ cup low sodium chicken broth
½ cup teriyaki sauce
¼ cup low sodium soy sauce
5 shallots, sliced
½ cup bourbon
¼ cup teriyaki glaze

¾ cup packed light brown sugar
2 sprigs rosemary, leaves removed and chopped
1½ pounds pork tenderloin, trimmed and cut into ½-inch slices
1 tablespoon olive oil

- Blend broth, teriyaki sauce, soy sauce, shallots, bourbon, teriyaki glaze, brown sugar and rosemary. Mix well.
- Pour half marinade over tenderloin. Refrigerate 1-2 hours.
- Drain meat and discard used marinade.
- Heat oil in a large skillet. Pan sear meat on both sides.
- Add reserved marinade and simmer 5-6 minutes or until meat is cooked.
- Serve sauce on side or over meat.

Yield: 4 servings
PATRICIA A. VALZ

Grilled Pork Tenderloin

¼ teaspoon salt
¼ teaspoon pepper
2 pork tenderloins

6 slices bacon
½ cup maple syrup

- Sprinkle salt and pepper over tenderloin. Refrigerate 30 minutes.
- Wrap bacon around tenderloin and secure with toothpicks.
- Grill and baste with maple syrup until internal temperature reaches 150 degrees.

May use more bacon slices.

Yield: 6-8 servings
MICKIE McARDLE

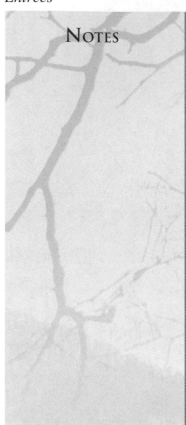

GRADE SCHOOL BUDDY SHERRY'S CENTER CUT HAM BARBEQUE

½ cup ginger ale
½ cup orange juice
¼ cup packed brown sugar
1 tablespoon vegetable oil
1½ teaspoons wine vinegar

1 teaspoon dry mustard
¼ teaspoon ground ginger
⅛ teaspoon ground cloves
1½-inch thick center cut ham

- Blend ginger ale, orange juice, brown sugar, oil, vinegar, mustard, ginger and clove.
- Cover ham with sauce. Cover and refrigerate overnight.
- Grill over hot heat 15 minutes.
- Cut into large serving pieces.

Great alternative to steaks.

Yield: 6-8 servings
PHYLLIS DEANE

MARINATED PORK TENDERLOIN

¾ cup vegetable oil
¾ cup soy sauce
¼ cup sherry
1 tablespoon dry mustard
1 teaspoon ground ginger

½ teaspoon dried parsley
½ teaspoon ground thyme
2 garlic cloves, minced
Salt and pepper to taste
2 pork tenderloins

- Combine oil, soy sauce, sherry, mustard, ginger, parsley, thyme, garlic, salt and pepper.
- Pour marinade over tenderloins. Refrigerate overnight.
- Grill to desired degree of doneness.

Yield: 6-8 servings
KATHRYN MONTGOMERY

LINDA'S PORK BARBECUE

SPICE RUB AND PORK

¼ cup salt
¼ cup black pepper
¼ cup sweet paprika
¼ cup sugar
1 tablespoon garlic powder
1 tablespoon onion powder
4 teaspoons chili powder or
   powdered ancho chilies

1 tablespoon dry mustard
1 tablespoon cayenne pepper or
   to taste
1½ teaspoons ground oregano
1 teaspoon ground cumin
8 pound Boston Pork Butt

BARBECUE SAUCE

1 (6-ounce) can tomato paste
¼ cup honey
¾ cup packed brown sugar
½ cup apple cider vinegar
½ teaspoon Tabasco sauce
½ teaspoon liquid smoke
   hickory seasoning

1 teaspoon onion powder
½ teaspoon garlic powder
1 teaspoon mustard
¾ teaspoon salt
¼ teaspoon paprika

SPICE RUB AND PORK

- Preheat oven to 250 degrees.
- Combine salt, pepper, paprika, sugar, garlic powder, onion powder, chili powder, mustard, cayenne, oregano and cumin. Rub mixture over entire Boston Butt.
- Bake 9 hours. Serve with barbecue sauce.

BARBECUE SAUCE

- Combine tomato paste, honey, brown sugar, vinegar, Tabasco, liquid smoke, onion powder, garlic powder, mustard, salt and paprika. Mix well.

Yield: 12 servings
WANDA HENDERSON

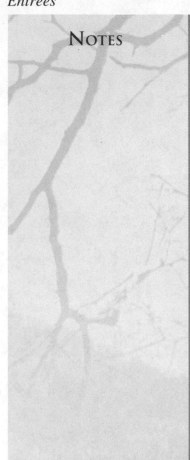

PASTA WITH PROSCIUTTO AND PEAS

1 (8-ounce) package spaghetti, cooked al dente
1 cup fresh or frozen peas
3 tablespoons olive oil

4 garlic cloves, minced
¼ pound prosciutto, trimmed
Grated Parmesan cheese

- Prepare spaghetti according to package directions. During last minute of cooking, add peas.
- Drain, reserving ¼ cup cooking liquid.
- Heat oil in a large skillet. Sauté garlic 1-3 minutes or until tender. Remove from heat.
- Add pasta and peas. Toss to coat. Stir in prosciutto.
- If dry, add tablespoon pasta water.
- Top with Parmesan cheese.

Yield: 4 servings
JOYCE STONEBRAKER

RICE-SAUSAGE CASSEROLE

1 pound pork sausage
1 onion, chopped
½ bell pepper, chopped
3 stalks celery, chopped

1 cup uncooked rice
4½ cups water
2 (1¼-ounce) envelopes Lipton's® chicken noodle soup

- Preheat oven to 350 degrees.
- Brown sausage. Add onions, peppers, celery and rice.
- Simmer until browned.
- Bring water to boil. Add soup and boil 7 minutes.
- Pour rice mixture into casserole dish. Pour on soup.
- Cover and bake 1 hour.

Yield: 8-10 servings
LOUISE PRESCOTT

SAUCY PORK CHOPS WITH CRANBERRIES

1 tablespoon vegetable oil
4-6 loin pork chops, 1-inch thick
2 leeks, white parts only, cleaned and thinly sliced
2 garlic cloves, minced
1 teaspoon salt
½ teaspoon cracked black peppercorns

½ cup port wine, Madeira or orange juice
¼ cup orange marmalade
½ cup cranberries, frozen or fresh
Hot cooked egg noodles

- Heat oil in a nonstick skillet over medium high heat. Brown pork chops on both sides, in batches, and transfer to slow cooker.
- Reduce heat to medium. Add leeks and cook, stirring until softened.
- Add garlic, salt and peppercorns. Cook and stir 1 minute.
- Stir in port wine, marmalade and cranberries. Bring to boil.
- Pour mixture over pork. Cover and cook on low 5 hours or high 2 hours, 30 minutes.
- Serve over egg noodles.

Yield: 4-6 servings
JANE GALVIN

SPANISH PORK CHOPS

6 pork chops
1½ cups chopped onions
1¼ cups chopped celery
1 cup chopped bell pepper

Salt and pepper to taste
1¾ cups cooked rice
2 (14½-ounce) cans diced tomatoes

- Preheat oven to 375 degrees.
- Brown pork chops and place in a 13 x 9 x 2-inch baking dish.
- Sauté onions, celery and peppers. Sprinkle with salt and pepper.
- Spoon vegetables over pork chops.
- Spread rice over vegetables. Cover all rice with tomatoes to keep moist.
- Bake 45 minutes.

Yield: 6 servings
GAYLE SHEAD

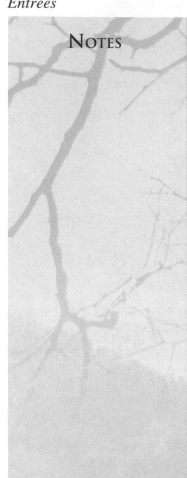

NOTES

SAUSAGE-ZUCCHINI BOATS

4 medium zucchini
¼ pound Jimmy Dean sage sausage
¼ cup chopped onions
1 egg, slightly beaten
½ cup cracker crumbs, crushed
¼ teaspoon salt

¼ teaspoon pepper
¼ teaspoon dried thyme, crushed
½ cup grated Parmesan cheese, reserve 2 tablespoons
Garnish: Paprika

- Preheat oven to 350 degrees.
- Cook whole zucchini in salted boiling water 7-10 minutes until tender.
- Cool slightly and cut in half lengthwise. Scoop out pulp and mash.
- Brown sausage and onions in skillet. Drain drippings. Add mashed zucchini.
- Stir in egg, cracker crumbs, salt, pepper, thyme and Parmesan cheese except 2 tablespoons.
- Spoon mixture into zucchini shells. Place in a shallow dish.
- Sprinkle with remaining Parmesan cheese and paprika.
- Bake 25-30 minutes.

Yield: 4 servings
BARBARA RESS

SPICY HAM BALLS

5 cups ground cooked ham
2 cups soft bread crumbs
2 eggs, slightly beaten
6 tablespoons milk

1 cup light corn syrup
¼ cup vinegar
2 tablespoons prepared mustard

- Preheat oven to 375 degrees.
- Combine ham, bread crumbs, eggs and milk. Shape mixture into twenty-four balls.
- Arrange ham balls close together in a 13 x 9 x 2-inch baking dish.
- Combine syrup, vinegar and mustard. Pour over ham balls.
- Bake, uncovered, 20 minutes.

May make two weeks in advance and freeze, unbaked. May also make the balls smaller and serve as appetizers.

Yield: 6 servings
LINDA JAMES

Spinach Stuffed Pork Tenderloin

1 small onion, diced
3 small mushrooms, diced
2 tablespoons olive oil
½-1 pound spinach, chopped
½ teaspoon ground pepper
⅓ cup shredded Parmesan cheese

3 tablespoons dried tomatoes in oil, drained and chopped
2 pork tenderloins, trimmed
Dried rosemary and pepper to taste
Garnish: Parsley sprigs

- Sauté onions and mushrooms in hot oil in a large skillet.
- Add spinach and pepper. Sauté 1 minute until spinach wilts. Remove from heat.
- Stir in Parmesan cheese and tomatoes.
- Cut tenderloin lengthwise down center, cutting to, but not through the bottom.
- Lay flat. Sprinkle with rosemary and pepper. Spoon spinach mixture down center of tenderloin.
- Fold meat over and tie with string at 1-inch intervals. Rub with rosemary.
- Wrap meat in foil and place in a roasting pan, stuffing side up.
- Bake 50-60 minutes or until thermometer reaches 170 degrees at thickest portion.
- Let rest 10-15 minutes. Slice meat on a diagonal. Arrange on a platter and garnish with parsley.

Yield: 6-8 servings

PATRICIA A. VALZ

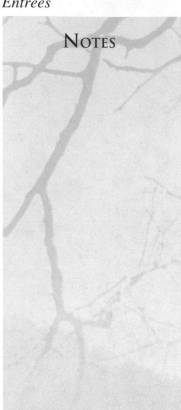

STUFFED PORK TENDERLOIN

1 Granny Smith apple, peeled
  and sliced
½ cup prunes, chopped
1 (1-pound) pork tenderloin
Salt and pepper to taste

1 teaspoon olive oil
½ cup chicken broth
½ cup white wine
½ teaspoon dried thyme
Cornstarch

- Combine apples and prunes. Butterfly cut tenderloin.
- Spoon mixture down center of meat. Sprinkle with salt and pepper.
- Fold meat together and tie with string.
- Heat oil in a skillet. Brown meat on all sides.
- Add broth, wine and thyme. Cover and bring to boil.
- Reduce heat and simmer 25 minutes, turning once.
- Remove tenderloin and keep warm.
- Whisk cornstarch into pan juices. Stir until thickened.
- Serve sliced meat with sauce.

Yield: 4 servings
SUE PIGGOTT

ZESTY PORK TENDERLOIN

¼ cup ketchup
1 tablespoon sugar
1 tablespoon white wine or
  water
1 tablespoon hoisin sauce

½ teaspoon salt
1 garlic clove, finely chopped
2 pork tenderloins, ¾-pound
  each

- Combine ketchup, sugar, wine, hoisin sauce, salt and garlic. Pour over pork, turning to coat.
- Cover and refrigerate at least 1 hour, no longer then 24 hours.
- Place pork on a rack in a shallow roasting pan.
- Bake, uncovered, at 375 degrees 35-45 minutes or until thermometer reaches 160 degrees for medium.

Yield: 6-8 servings
KAAREN ARTHURS

ANGEL HAIR PASTA WITH BASIL

**1 pound package angle hair
    pasta**
2 garlic cloves
¼ cup olive oil

**Salt and pepper to taste
    (optional)**
**1 package fresh basil leaves, cut
    into strips**

- Cook pasta until al dente. Sauté garlic in oil until tender. Discard or mash garlic.
- Combine pasta, garlic, oil, salt, pepper and basil. Toss to coat.

If using minced garlic, do not discard.

Yield: 4 servings
SANDY BINGHAM

CHARCOAL-GRILLED SALMON WITH VIDALIA ONIONS

Salt and pepper to taste
**1 large Vidalia onion, peeled
    and cut into thick slices**

¼ cup light olive oil
2 pounds salmon fillets

- Sprinkle salt and pepper on onion slices. Brush with oil.
- Grill on a cool spot 5 minutes. Turn and grill another 5 minutes.
- Sprinkle salt and pepper over salmon. Brush with oil.
- Grill over medium-hot heat 3 minutes per side or until firm to touch.
- Serve salmon topped with onions.

May slice Vidalia into thin slices.

Yield: 6 servings
MICKIE McARDLE

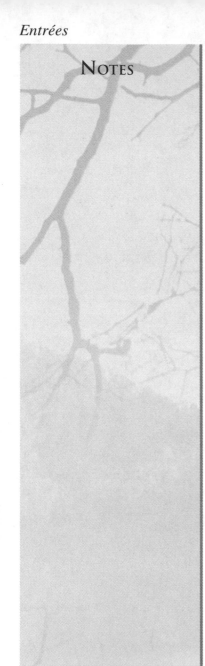

CAJUN SHRIMP AND GRITS

GRITS

4 cups water
½ teaspoon salt
1 tablespoon butter

1 cup stone ground yellow grits
½ cup heavy or whipping cream
1 tablespoon butter

SHRIMP

3 slices bacon
4 ounces country ham, julienne
4 ounces smoked pork sausage, cut into rounds
1 teaspoon butter
8 large sea scallops, quartered or bay scallops (optional)

24 jumbo shrimp, peeled and deveined
⅛ teaspoon minced garlic
Pinch or more Cajun spice
¼ cup diced seeded tomatoes
¼ cup minced green onions
1 tablespoon water
1 tablespoon butter

GRITS

- Combine water, salt and butter in a saucepan. Bring to boil.
- Stir in grits. Reduce heat and simmer 40 minutes until creamy and thickened.
- Remove from heat. Stir in cream and butter. Keep warm.

SHRIMP

- Cook bacon. Remove bacon from skillet.
- Sauté ham and sausage in drippings.
- Add butter, scallops and shrimp. Sauté 3-4 minutes.
- Stir garlic and Cajun spice. Sauté 30 seconds.
- Add tomatoes, green onions, water and butter. Cook and stir until butter melts.
- Return bacon. Spoon grits on a plate and top with shrimp mixture.

Yield: 4 servings

CAROL POWICHROSKI

CRAB QUICHE

Pastry for 9-inch pie
2 tablespoons minced green
**   onions**
1 tablespoon butter, melted
4 eggs, beaten
1½ cups whipping cream

2 (6-ounce) packages frozen
**   crabmeat, thawed and**
**   drained**
1 cup shredded Swiss cheese
2 tablespoons sherry
¾ teaspoon salt
⅛ teaspoon cayenne pepper
Garnish: Parsley sprigs

- Preheat oven to 400 degrees.
- Roll dough to ⅛-inch thickness on a lightly floured surface.
- Place in a 9-inch quiche dish, trim excess pastry along edges.
- Pierce bottom and sides of pastry with fork.
- Bake 3 minutes. Remove from oven and gently pierce with fork.
- Bake an additional 5 minutes.
- Sauté green onions in butter until tender. Blend eggs and cream in a large bowl.
- Stir in green onions, crabmeat, Swiss cheese, sherry, salt and cayenne.
- Pour filling into crust. Bake at 425 degrees 15 minutes.
- Reduce heat to 325 degrees. Bake 25-30 minutes or until set.
- Let stand 10 minutes before serving.
- Garnish with parsley.

Note the two different oven temperatures for the quiche. May make a day in advance and refrigerate in a tightly covered container.

Yield: 6 servings
FRANKIE REHG

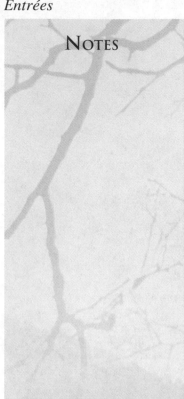

CRABMEAT LASAGNA

4 tablespoons butter
1 cup shredded carrots
½ cup finely chopped celery
½ cup finely chopped onions
⅓ cup chopped yellow bell pepper
⅓ cup chopped sweet red pepper
3 garlic cloves, minced
1 teaspoon coriander seeds, crushed
1 (8-ounce) container plain yogurt

¼ cup chopped cilantro
¼ teaspoon salt
⅛ teaspoon white pepper
⅛ teaspoon ground nutmeg
1 pound fresh lump crabmeat
1 cup shredded mozzarella cheese
1 cup shredded Cheddar or American cheese
6 lasagna noodles, cooked al dente

- Melt butter in a large skillet. Add carrots, celery, onions, peppers, garlic and coriander seeds.
- Cook and stir 4-5 minutes until tender.
- Blend yogurt, cilantro, salt, white pepper and nutmeg. Pour into vegetable mixture.
- Gently stir in crabmeat. Combine mozzarella cheese and Cheddar cheese.
- Arrange three noodles in the bottom of a lightly greased 13 x 9 x 2-inch baking dish.
- Top with half crabmeat mixture. Sprinkle with half cheese mixture.
- Repeat layers of remaining noodles and crabmeat mixture.
- Cover and bake 30 minutes until thoroughly heated.
- Sprinkle with remaining cheese mixture.
- Bake uncovered an additional 5 minutes until cheese melts.

Yield: 6 servings
DOLLY BLAKE

EASY SAUTÉED SHRIMP

2 tablespoons olive oil
3 garlic cloves, minced
1 green onion, finely chopped
1 teaspoon favorite seasoning

1 pound large shrimp,
  uncooked, peeled and
  deveined

- Combine oil, garlic, green onions and seasoning in a nonstick skillet. Sauté 2-3 minutes.
- Add shrimp and sauté 3-5 minutes until shrimp are pink.

Great dish with rice pilaf and a salad. Quick and easy.

Yield: 3-4 servings
SUSAN ROLADER

PASTA WITH LOBSTER (SHRIMP) AND TARRAGON

2 tablespoons virgin olive oil
½ cup finely chopped yellow
  onions
1 (2 pound 3 ounce) can
  chopped Italian plum
  tomatoes
2 teaspoons dried tarragon
Salt and pepper to taste
1 cup heavy cream

2 tablespoons salt
Cayenne pepper to taste
½ pound lobster, about
  1½ cups or ½-¾ pounds
  medium shrimp
1 pound spaghetti
Garnish: Sprigs of parsley, basil
  or tarragon

- Heat oil in saucepan. Add onions, reduce heat and cook covered 25 minutes until tender.
- Add tomatoes, tarragon, salt and pepper. Cover and simmer 30 minutes, stirring often.
- Remove from heat and cool slightly. Purée in food processor.
- Return purée to saucepan. Stir in cream. Simmer 15 minutes until slightly reduced.
- Add salt, cayenne and lobster. Simmer 5 more minutes.
- Arrange pasta on warm plates. Spoon lobster mixture on top.
- Garnish with parsley, basil or tarragon.

Yield: 6 servings
FRANCES SMITH

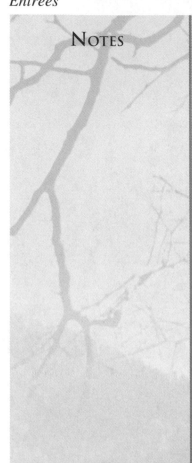

KING AND PRINCE MARINATED SHRIMP

½ cup ketchup
½ cup chili sauce
1 cup tartar sauce
1 cup mayonnaise

3 large onions, shredded
5 pounds shrimp, cooked, deveined and chilled
Salt to taste

- Combine ketchup, chili sauce, tartar sauce, mayonnaise, onions, shrimp and salt.
- Refrigerate 2 hours.

Yield: 8 servings
FRANCK COLLIER

PASTA WITH SHRIMP, ASPARAGUS AND BASIL

1 cup basil leaves
2 garlic cloves
½ cup lemon juice
1 tablespoon olive oil
¾ teaspoon salt, divided
1 tablespoon sun-dried tomatoes, chopped

1 pound asparagus, cut into 2-inch pieces
¾ pound large shrimp, peeled and deveined
⅛ teaspoon cayenne pepper
1 (8-ounce) package spaghetti, cooked al dente

- Process basil, garlic, lemon juice, oil and ½ teaspoon salt in a food processor or blender until smooth.
- Cook asparagus in a greased 10-inch skillet 5 minutes, stirring frequently, until crisp-tender.
- Add shrimp, cayenne and ¼ teaspoon salt.
- Cook, stirring frequently, about 4 minutes until shrimp turn pink.
- Toss pasta with basil mixture in a large serving bowl. Stir in shrimp and asparagus.

Yield: 4 servings
ANN BURTON

PAT'S PASTA

½-1 pound angel hair pasta, cooked al dente and drained

½ (8-ounce) bottle Paul Newman Original Oil and Vinegar Salad dressing

1 (15-ounce) can LeSeur peas, drained

1 (4-ounce) container crumbled blue cheese

1-2 bunches green onions, chopped

1-1½ pounds shrimp, cooked and peeled or grilled chicken breast

Grated Parmesan cheese

- Combine pasta, half bottle dressing, peas, blue cheese, green onions and shrimp or chicken.
- Add more dressing if desired. Toss to coat. Refrigerate overnight. Serve with Parmesan cheese.

Yield: 4 servings
PAT GIRDLER

SHRIMP ALFREDO PENNE

4 tablespoons butter

1 pound medium mushrooms, sliced

1 large onion, chopped

4 large garlic cloves, crushed

3 (10-ounce) packages spinach

2 pounds shrimp, peeled and drained

1 pound penne pasta, cooked al dente

2 (8-ounce) jars Bertolli alfredo sauce

1 (8-ounce) package shredded mozzarella cheese

- Preheat oven to 350 degrees.
- Melt butter in skillet. Sauté mushrooms, onions and garlic. Stir in spinach.
- Cover and cook until spinach wilts.
- Stir in shrimp and cook 2 minutes. Combine spinach mixture with pasta and alfredo sauce.
- Pour mixture into a casserole dish. Top with mozzarella cheese.
- Bake 30 minutes.

Yield: 10 servings
LOUISE PRESCOTT

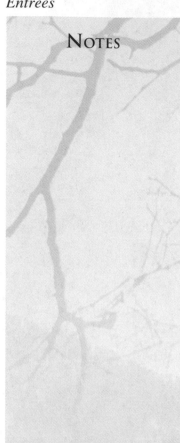

SALMON LOAF
WITH SHRIMP SAUCE

SHRIMP SAUCE

1 (10¾-ounce) can condensed
   cream of shrimp soup

¼ cup milk

SALMON

2 (1-pound) cans salmon

¼ cup finely minced onions

¼ cup chopped parsley

¼ cup lemon juice

½ teaspoon salt

½ teaspoon pepper

½-1 teaspoon ground thyme

2 cups coarse cracker crumbs

½ cup milk

4 tablespoons butter, melted

4 eggs, well beaten

SHRIMP SAUCE

• Heat soup according to package directions. Add milk and stir until smooth.

SALMON

• Preheat oven to 350 degrees.

• Drain salmon, reserving liquid. Flake salmon into a bowl.

• Add onions, parsley, lemon juice, salt, pepper, thyme and cracker crumbs. Mix lightly.

• Measure salmon liquid and add enough milk to equal 1 cup.

• Add milk mixture, butter and eggs and mix lightly.

• Spoon mixture into a greased 2-quart loaf pan.

• Bake 1 hour or until center is set.

• Spoon Shrimp sauce onto hot salmon loaf.

Yield: 8 servings

FRANCES D. SMITH

SEAFOOD LASAGNA

1 onion, chopped
1 tablespoon butter
1 (8-ounce) package cream cheese, softened
1 (15-ounce) container ricotta cheese
1 egg
1½ teaspoons dried basil
½ teaspoon pepper
2 (10¾-ounce) cans cream of mushroom soup

⅔ cup white wine
½ pound shrimp, cooked and peeled
½-¾ pound scallops
½ pound crabmeat or lobster
½ cup grated Parmesan cheese
9 lasagna noodles, cooked al dente
¾-1 cup grated mozzarella cheese

- Preheat oven to 325 degrees.
- Sauté onions in butter. Combine onions, cream cheese, ricotta cheese, egg, basil and pepper.
- Blend soup, wine, shrimp, scallops, lobster and Parmesan cheese.
- Arrange 3 noodles on the bottom of a 13 x 9 x 2-inch baking dish.
- Cover with seafood mixture. Layer three more noodles on top.
- Cover with onion/cheese mixture. Top with three more noodles.
- Sprinkle with mozzarella cheese. Bake 1 hour, 15 minutes.

Yield: 10-12 servings
MARY FULLER

Our heavenly Father, Master of Life, thou has given us work to do.

Give us strength to do it well, on time, and cheerfully, for thy name sake, Amen

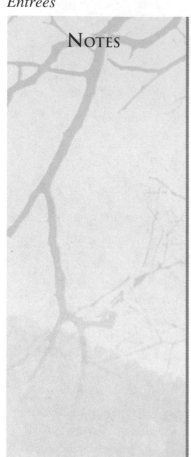

SHRIMP AND SAUSAGE JAMBALAYA

1 onion, chopped
1 bell pepper, chopped
2 garlic cloves, finely chopped
4 stalks celery, finely chopped
¼ cup olive oil
Salt and pepper to taste
Chili powder to taste

1 (28-ounce) can crushed
   tomatoes
1 pound shrimp, peeled, tail on
6 links spicy sausage, cooked on
   grill, cut into bite-size pieces
2 cups cooked rice

• Sauté onions, peppers, garlic and celery in oil until tender. Add salt, pepper and chili powder.
• Add tomatoes and simmer 5-10 minutes.
• Stir in shrimp and sausage. Cook until shrimp are pink.
• Spoon shrimp mixture over ½ cup rice on individual plates.

Yield: 4 servings
DANIEL MACARI

SHRIMP SAMUELS

3 sticks butter
¼ cup packed brown sugar
2 tablespoons chopped thyme
1 tablespoon chopped rosemary
½ teaspoon Tabasco sauce
1 tablespoon Worcestershire
   sauce

1 tablespoon minced garlic
24 large shrimp, unpeeled
1 tablespoon lemon juice
Salt and pepper to taste
¼ teaspoon cayenne pepper
½ cup Maker's Mark
Hot cooked rice

• Melt butter in a large skillet. Cook brown sugar, thyme, rosemary, Tabasco, Worcestershire sauce and garlic 2 minutes.
• Add shrimp and cook 3 minutes or until pink.
• Stir in lemon juice, salt, pepper, cayenne and Maker's Mark. Flame mixture and simmer 2 minutes.
• Serve on a bed of rice.

Allow ¾-1 pound unpeeled shrimp to serve as a main dish.

Yield: 6 servings
SANDRA HINTZE

SHRIMP, PEPPERS AND CHEESE GRITS

½ cup chopped Canadian bacon
1 cup sweet red pepper strips
1 cup bell pepper strips
1 (10-ounce) can Rotel diced
   tomatoes
1½ pounds medium shrimp,
   peeled

½ cup chopped green onions
4 cups chicken broth
1⅓ cups stone ground white
   grits
1 (8-ounce) package shredded
   sharp Cheddar cheese

- Cook bacon over medium heat 3 minutes or until lightly browned, stirring frequently.
- Add pepper strips and cook 10 minutes
- Stir in tomatoes and cook 5 minutes.
- Add shrimp and cook 3 minutes. Stir in green onions and keep warm.
- Bring broth to boil. Add grits, cover and cook abut 20 minutes.
- Stir in Cheddar cheese.
- Serve shrimp mixture over grits.

Low-fat dish!

Yield: 4 servings
LINDA MOORE

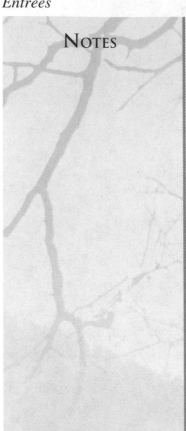

SPICY GRILLED SHRIMP

1 teaspoon chili powder
1 tablespoon vinegar
¼ teaspoon pepper
1 garlic clove, minced or mashed
1 teaspoon salt
1 teaspoon dried basil

1 tablespoon finely chopped mint
¾ cup vegetable oil
2 pounds medium size shrimp or 1½ pounds frozen

- Blend chili powder, vinegar, pepper, salt, basil and mint. Stir in oil until well blended.
- Pour marinade over shrimp. Cover and refrigerate at least 4 hours or overnight.
- Thread shrimp onto skewers. Grill 6-10 minutes, depending on size of shrimp.

May also broil shrimp off the skewers.

Yield: 4 servings
SANDY GEIBEL

TERRI T'S SHRIMP FETTUCCINE

6 tablespoons butter
¾ cup chopped green onions
2 tablespoons minced garlic
1 tablespoon Tony Chachere's original seasoning
1-2 pounds shrimp, peeled and deveined

1 pint half & half
1 pound fettuccine, cooked al dente
Grated Parmesan and Romano cheese to taste

- Melt butter in a skillet. Sauté green onions, garlic and seasoning. Add shrimp and cook until pink.
- Stir in half & half. Cook 5-10 minutes.
- Add fettuccine and toss to coat.
- Top with Parmesan and Romano cheese.

If Tony's Chachere's seasoning is not available, use salt, pepper and cayenne.

Yield: 4 servings
MELISSA LOWRIE

Vegetables

MY MORNING PRAYER

This is the day the Lord as made; let us rejoice and be glad in it. Psalm 118:24

O God, for another day, for another morning,
for another hour, for another minute,
for another chance to live and serve Thee,
I am truly grateful.

Do Thou this day free me
from all Fear of the future,
from all Anxiety about tomorrow,
from all Bitterness towards anyone,
from all Cowardice in the face of danger,
from all Laziness in the face of work,
from all Failure before opportunity,
from all weakness when Thy power is at hand.

But fill me
with Love that knows no barrier,
with Sympathy that reaches to all,
with Courage that cannot be shaken,
with Faith strong enough for the darkness,
with Strength sufficient for my tasks,
with Loyalty to Thy Kingdom's goal,
with Wisdom to meet life's complexities,
with Power to lift me to Thee.

Be Thou with me for another day,
And use me as Thou will.

For Christ's sake I pray. Amen.

Wallace Fridy

APPLE CHEESE CASSEROLE

1 stick butter, softened
1 cup sugar
**1 cup shredded sharp Cheddar
 cheese**

¾ cup self-rising flour
**4 large Granny Smith apples,
 sliced**

- Preheat oven to 350 degrees.
- Cream butter and sugar. Stir in Cheddar cheese and flour.
- Arrange apple slices in a buttered casserole dish.
- Spread mixture over apples.
- Bake 35-40 minutes.

Yield: 8-10 servings
EMILY THURMAN

*This dish is great
with any kind of pork.
It can be served as a
side dish or dessert.*

CANDIED APPLES

**10 large Golden Delicious
 apples, cut into eighths**
2 cups sugar
1 teaspoon salt
4 tablespoons butter

**1 teaspoon cinnamon or
 1 cup cinnamon red hots**
¼ cup water
2 tablespoons cornstarch
2 tablespoons water

- Combine apples, sugar, salt, butter, cinnamon and water in a large skillet.
- Cook slowly over medium heat until apples are transparent. Be careful not to break up apples.
- Blend cornstarch and water. Move apples to side of skillet.
- Stir in cornstarch mixture until thickened.
- Transfer apples into a bowl and pour sauce over apples.

Yield: 6-8 servings
JUDY LACEY

*A family-favorite
served every Thanksgiving
and Christmas.*

This is a traditional Monday dinner in New Orleans. Monday is wash day while the beans simmer all day! We left New Orleans 18 years ago and my family still looks forward to Monday's Red Beans and Rice. Best with cornbread.

RED BEANS AND RICE

1 tablespoon vegetable oil
1 large onion, chopped
1-2 garlic cloves, chopped
1-2 stalks celery, chopped
2 bay leaves
1 pound sausage, sliced

Salt and pepper to taste
1 pound package dry red kidney beans, rinsed
6-8 cups water
Hot cooked rice

- Heat oil in a Dutch oven. Add onions, garlic, celery, bay leaves, sausage, salt and pepper.
- Cook until onions are tender.
- Add beans and 6 cups water. Bring to boil.
- Reduce heat and cook about 4 hours, stirring occasionally. Add more water if necessary.
- Remove bay leaves. Serve over cooked rice.

Yield: 8 servings

LISA JENNINGS

LARRY'S FAMOUS BEANS

10 slices bacon, diced
3 medium onions, chopped
1 medium bell pepper, chopped
1 (28-ounce) can pork and beans, drained
¾ cup ketchup

½ cup firmly packed brown sugar
½ cup molasses
1 teaspoon liquid smoke
5 drops beano

- Preheat oven to 425 degrees.
- Sauté bacon, onions and peppers over medium heat until lightly browned and tender. Drain.
- Combine bacon mixture, pork and beans, ketchup, brown sugar, molasses, liquid smoke and beano.
- Pour mixture into a 12 x 8 x 2-inch baking dish.
- Bake, uncovered, 30-45 minutes or until bubbly.

Yield: 6 servings

LARRY BROGDON

RUTH CRISP'S BROCCOLI CASSEROLE

2 (10-ounce) packages frozen chopped broccoli, thawed
1 cup rice
1 onion, chopped
1 stick butter
1 (10¾-ounce) can cream of chicken soup
1 cup grated Cheddar cheese, divided
½ cup milk
1½ teaspoons Paul Prudhomme's Poultry Magic

- Preheat oven to 350 degrees.
- Steam broccoli. Drain well. Cook rice according to package directions.
- Sauté onions in butter in a large skillet until tender.
- Add broccoli and rice to onions. Stir in butter, soup, ¾ cup Cheddar cheese, milk and seasoning.
- Spoon mixture into greased casserole dish. Top with remaining ¼ cup Cheddar cheese.
- Bake 30 minutes.

Yield: 4-6 servings
KATHY HUMPHRIES

AUNT EMILY'S CORN PUDDING

¼ cup self-rising flour
¼ cup sugar
1 egg
Dash of salt
¾ cup milk
1 (15-ounce) can cream-style corn
Butter
Garnish: Ground nutmeg

- Preheat oven to 350 degrees.
- Combine flour and sugar. Add egg and salt. Mix well.
- Stir in milk and corn. Pour mixture into a greased casserole dish.
- Dot with butter and sprinkle with nutmeg.
- Bake about 1 hour or until set.

Yield: 4-6 servings
JACKIE GILMER

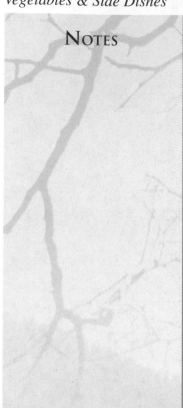

FAVORITE CORN CASSEROLE

¼ cup sugar
3 tablespoons all-purpose flour
2 teaspoons baking powder
2 teaspoons salt

6 eggs
2 cups whipping cream
1 stick butter, melted
6 cups frozen corn, thawed

- Preheat oven to 350 degrees.
- Combine sugar, flour, baking powder and salt.
- In another bowl, beat eggs. Stir in whipping cream and butter. Gradually add dry mixture, stirring until smooth.
- Stir in corn. Pour mixture into a lightly greased 13 x 9 x 2-inch baking dish.
- Bake 45 minutes.

May substitute fat-free half & half for whipping cream.

Yield: 8 servings
JAN CATES

GRANDMA'S SCALLOPED CORN

¼ cup minced onions
2 tablespoons minced celery
6 tablespoons butter, divided
2 (15-ounce) cans cream-style corn
2 tablespoons all-purpose flour

½ cup milk
½ cup crushed saltine crackers
2 eggs, beaten
½ teaspoon salt
¼ teaspoon pepper
10-12 Ritz crackers, crushed

- Preheat oven to 325 degrees.
- Sauté onions and celery in 4 tablespoons butter until tender.
- Combine vegetables, cream-style corn, flour, milk, cracker crumbs, eggs, salt and pepper.
- Pour mixture into a greased 1½-quart casserole dish.
- Melt remaining 2 tablespoons butter in a skillet. Stir in Ritz crumbs until coated and lightly browned.
- Spread over casserole. Bake 40-45 minutes or until center is set.

Yield: 8 servings
BARBARA NUNN

GRILLED CHEESY CORN ON THE COB

6 ears corn
1 cup mayonnaise
1 cup shredded Parmesan cheese

Chili powder, salt and pepper to taste

- Place each corn cob on an individual piece of foil to cover.
- Spread mayonnaise over all ears of corn. Sprinkle Parmesan cheese over all ears.
- Sprinkle with chili powder, salt and pepper.
- Tightly wrap each cob in foil.
- Grill 20 minutes, turning every 2-3 minutes.

May add chopped chives for more flavor.

Yield: 6 servings

BILL, CAROLYN AND MEGAN STRANSKY

FAVORITE CORNBREAD DRESSING

1 stick butter, cut into pieces
6 cups crumbled cornbread
6 cups soft bread crumbs
½ cup bacon drippings
1 cup diced celery (optional)
1 cup minced onions

2 teaspoons salt
½ teaspoon pepper
2 teaspoons ground sage
2 eggs, beaten
1½-2 cups broth or water

- Preheat oven to 350 degrees.
- Combine butter pieces, cornbread and bread crumbs.
- Heat bacon drippings. Sauté celery and onions 5 minutes. Add to crumb mixture.
- Add salt, pepper, sage, eggs and enough broth to moisten.
- Pour mixture into a 13 x 9 x 2-inch baking dish.
- Bake 20 minutes or until bubbly.

Yield: 10 servings

MILLANN FUNK

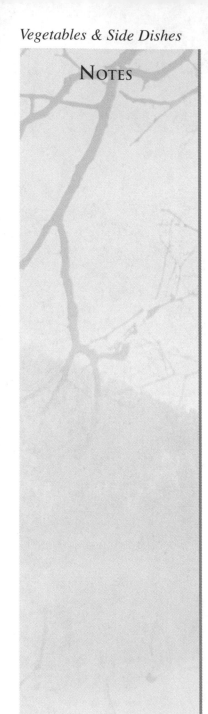

EGGPLANT CASSEROLE

1 medium eggplant
⅓ cup chopped bell pepper
⅓ cup chopped onions
⅓ cup chopped celery
1 tablespoon butter
½ cup bread crumbs
1 tablespoon bacon drippings (optional)

1 egg, slightly beaten
2 tablespoons milk
1 tablespoon sugar or sugar substitute
1 cup shredded Cheddar cheese, divided
½ teaspoon salt
Pepper to taste

- Preheat oven to 350 degrees.
- Peel and cut eggplant into 1-inch cubes. Soak in cold salted water about 30 minutes.
- Drain and rinse thoroughly with clear water. Cook eggplant in slightly salted water until tender.
- Drain well and mash in a bowl.
- Sauté peppers, onions and celery in butter until tender. Add to eggplant.
- Stir in bread crumbs, bacon drippings, egg, milk, sugar, ½ cup Cheddar cheese, salt and pepper.
- Mix well and pour into a greased 1-quart casserole dish. Top with remaining ½ cup Cheddar cheese.
- Bake 30 minutes.

Yield: 4 servings

BARBARA MOORE

EGGPLANT PERLE

Eggplant, peeled or unpeeled sliced ¼-inch slices

Butter

Salt and freshly ground black pepper to taste

Seasoned bread crumbs

Grated extra sharp Cheddar cheese

Onion, sliced into ¼-inch rings

Bell pepper, sliced into ¼-inch rings

Tomatoes, sliced

- Preheat oven to 350 degrees.
- Arrange a layer of eggplant slices in a buttered 13 x 9 x 2-inch baking dish, filling spaces with broken pieces.
- Dot with butter and sprinkle with salt and pepper.
- Top with some bread crumbs and Cheddar cheese.
- Place a layer of onion rings. Repeat butter, salt, pepper, bread crumbs and cheese.
- Arrange a layer of peppers. Top with layers of butter through cheese again.
- Place a layer tomatoes, filling any open spaces. Top with layers of butter through cheese.
- Cover and bake 30 minutes. Uncover and bake another 30 minutes.

May prepare in advance and refrigerate. Bring to room temperature and bake. It is delicious with beef, pork, chicken or fish.

Yield: 8-10 servings

RITA ZEILER

FRUIT COMPOTE

1 (20-ounce) can pineapple chunks

1 (16-ounce) can pears, quartered

1 (17-ounce) can apricot halves

1 (18-ounce) can peach slices

2 (21-ounce) cans cherry pie filling

½ cup sweet red wine (optional)

- Preheat oven to 350 degrees.
- Drain fruit thoroughly and towel dry. Place pineapples, pears, apricots and peaches in baking dish.
- Spread pie filling over fruit. Pour wine over fruit.
- Bake 25-30 minutes.

Yield: 4-6 servings

LYNN ROBERTS

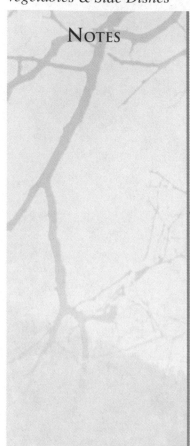

HORSERADISH GREEN BEANS

3 (16-ounce) cans whole green
   beans, undrained
1 large onion, chopped
1 cup mayonnaise
2 tablespoons creamed
   horseradish

1½ teaspoons dried parsley
1 teaspoon Worcestershire sauce
Garlic salt, celery salt, pepper
   and salt to taste
Juice of 1 lemon
   (about 3 tablespoons)

- Cook green beans and onions in saucepan 1 hour. Drain.
- Blend mayonnaise, horseradish, parsley, Worcestershire sauce, garlic salt, celery salt, pepper, salt and lemon juice.
- Spoon over beans. Serve hot or cold.

Yield: 10-12 servings
JANE BROOKS

CHEESY GRITS
AND SHRIMP CASSEROLE

4 cups chicken broth
½ teaspoon salt
1 cup regular grits, not instant
1 cup shredded sharp Cheddar
   cheese, divided
1 cup shredded Monterey Jack
   cheese with peppers
2 tablespoons butter
6 green onions, chopped

1 bell pepper, chopped
1 garlic clove, minced
1 pound small fresh or frozen
   shrimp, peeled and cooked
1 (10-ounce) can diced tomatoes
   with chilies, drained
¼ teaspoon salt
¼ teaspoon pepper

- Preheat oven to 350 degrees.
- Bring broth and salt to boil. Stir in grits. Cover, reduce heat and simmer 20 minutes.
- Add ¼ cup Cheddar cheese and Jack cheese.
- Melt butter in a large skillet. Add green onions, peppers and garlic. Sauté 5 minutes.
- Combine green onion mixture, grits, shrimp, tomatoes, salt and pepper.
- Pour mixture into a lightly greased 2-quart baking dish.
- Top with remaining Cheddar cheese. Bake 30-45 minutes.

Yield: 10 servings
BARBARA FUSSELL

MARTHA'S GRITS

1 cup quick grits, not instant
1 quart whole milk
Pinch of cayenne pepper

Minced garlic to taste (optional)
4 tablespoons butter, melted
Shredded Parmesan cheese to taste

Wonderful side with a steak.

- Combine grits, milk, cayenne and garlic in a saucepan.
- Simmer over medium-high heat until thickened. Do not boil.
- Pour mixture into a greased 8 x 8 x 2-inch square baking dish.
- Refrigerate overnight.
- Cut into squares. Place back into dish in a layered shingle style
- Pour butter over all. Sprinkle with Parmesan cheese.
- Bake at 350 degrees until golden browned.

Yield: 6-8 servings
PAT GIRDLER

CROCKPOT MAC N CHEESE

1 (8-ounce) package elbow macaroni
1 (12-ounce) can evaporated milk
½ cup whole milk
1 teaspoon salt
1 cup grated medium Cheddar cheese

1(8-ounce) package shredded Cheddar cheese
4 tablespoons butter, melted
2 eggs, beaten
Black pepper to taste
Thinly sliced Cheddar cheese

This is easy for kids to make. Kids of all ages love it!!

- Combine macaroni, evaporated milk, whole milk, salt, medium and sharp Cheddar, butter, eggs and pepper in a greased crockpot. Mix well.
- Place Cheddar cheese slices on top.
- Cook on low 3 hours, 30 minutes without removing lid or stirring.

Yield: 8-10 servings
MALINDA GILLESPIE

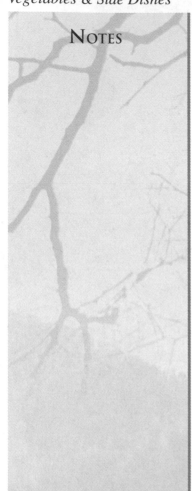

FRENCH FRIED ONIONS

¾ **cup all-purpose flour**
¼ **teaspoon salt**
⅓ **cup milk**
¼ **cup heavy cream**

1½ **tablespoons vegetable oil**
1 **egg white, beaten**
Vidalia onion, cut into rings

- Sift flour and salt into a bowl. Add milk, cream and oil.
- Gently fold in egg white. Dredge onion rings in batter. Fry in hot oil until golden browned.

Yield: 4-6 servings
BARBARA WEAGLY

PINEAPPLE CASSEROLE

1 **(20-ounce) can pineapple**
    chunks, drained and
    reserving 3 tablespoons
½ **cup sugar**
3 **tablespoons all-purpose flour**

1 **cup grated extra sharp**
    Cheddar cheese
1½ **tablespoons butter, melted**
½ **cup crushed Ritz crackers**
1½ **tablespoons butter, melted**

- Preheat oven to 350 degrees.
- Place pineapples in a bowl.
- In a separate bowl, combine sugar, flour and pineapple juice to make a paste.
- Stir into pineapples. Add Cheddar cheese and butter. Mix well.
- Pour mixture into a buttered 1-quart casserole dish.
- Combine cracker crumbs and butter. Sprinkle over pineapple mixture.
- Bake 30 minutes.

To make 8 servings, use 3 cans pineapple chunks and double all other ingredients. Pour into a medium size casserole dish.

Yield: 4 servings
JUDY BERGIN

PINEAPPLE CASSEROLE

1 stick butter, softened
1½ cups sugar
½ cup milk
3 eggs

1 (8-ounce) can crushed
   pineapple, undrained
4 cups bread cubes, may
   use day old

- Preheat oven to 350 degrees.
- Cream butter and sugar. Beat together milk and eggs.
- Combine creamed mixture, egg mixture, pineapples and bread cubes.
- Pour mixture into a 2-quart casserole dish.
- Bake 45-50 minutes or until lightly browned

Yield: 6-8 servings
JANET ROBERTSON

*Delicious with
chicken or ham.*

CHEESY HASH BROWN POTATOES

1 (26-ounce) package frozen
   hash brown potatoes, thawed
1 (8-ounce) package shredded
   Colby cheese
¼ cup minced onions
1 cup half & half or milk
½ cup beef broth

2 tablespoons butter, melted
1 teaspoon salt
¼ teaspoon pepper
⅛ teaspoon garlic powder
Garnish: Crisply cooked and
   crumbled bacon

- Preheat oven to 425 degrees.
- Combine potatoes, Colby cheese and onions in a large bowl.
- Add half & half, broth, butter, salt, pepper and garlic powder. Mix well.
- Spoon mixture into a greased 13 x 9 x 2-inch baking dish.
- Bake 45-60 minutes. Top with bacon.

Yield: 8-10 servings
GAIL KOWALSKI

COMPANY POTATOES

8 potatoes
1 onion, diced
½ (16-ounce) package Velveeta® cheese, cubed

¾-1 cup mayonnaise
4 slices bacon, cooked and crumbled
6-8 olives, sliced

- Preheat oven to 350 degrees.
- Cook potatoes, peel and dice. Combine potatoes, onions, cheese and enough mayonnaise to moisten.
- Pour mixture into a 13 x 9 x 2-inch baking dish.
- Top with bacon and olives. Bake 45 minutes.

Yield: 8-10 servings
BARBARA WEAGLY

SWEET POTATO AND APPLE BAKE

This dish is great with pork. Everyone seems to love it.

2 pounds sweet potatoes
1½ pounds Granny Smith apples, cored, peeled and thinly sliced
⅔ cup packed dark brown sugar

6 tablespoons butter
½ cup apple cider
3 tablespoons maple syrup
1 tablespoon lemon juice
2 teaspoons cinnamon

- Preheat oven to 350 degrees.
- Cook potatoes in boiling water. Cool, peel and slice potatoes.
- Arrange potatoes and apples in a lightly greased 2-quart casserole dish.
- Combine brown sugar, butter, apple cider, maple syrup, lemon juice and cinnamon in a saucepan.
- Bring to boil. Pour over potatoes and apples.
- Bake 25-30 minutes.

Yield: 8 servings
CHARLOTTE MCCLOSKEY

Easy and Delicious Rice and Mushroom Casserole

6 tablespoons butter
1 cup long-grain rice
1 (10-ounce) can beef bouillon soup

1 (10-ounce) can onion soup
1 (4-ounce) can mushrooms

- Preheat oven to 350 degrees.
- Melt butter in 1½-quart casserole dish. Add rice, beef soup, onion soup and mushrooms.
- Bake 1 hour, 15 minutes.

Yield: 6 servings
JEANELLE BROWN

This casserole is an excellent accompaniment to beef.

Green and Gold Rice Casserole

1 medium onion, chopped
1 tablespoon butter
1 (10¾-ounce) can cheese soup
1 (6-ounce) roll nippy cheese
½ teaspoon garlic powder
1 (8-ounce) can mushroom pieces with liquid

1 (10-ounce) package frozen chopped broccoli, cooked and drained
2½ cups hot cooked rice
1 (3-ounce) can French fried onions

- Preheat oven to 350 degrees.
- Sauté onions in butter until tender but not browned.
- Add soup, cheese and garlic powder. Cook and stir until cheese melts.
- Stir in mushrooms with liquid, broccoli and rice.
- Pour mixture into a shallow casserole. Top with French fried onions.
- Bake 15-20 minutes or until hot and bubbly.

Yield: 8 servings
SUSIE BROGDON

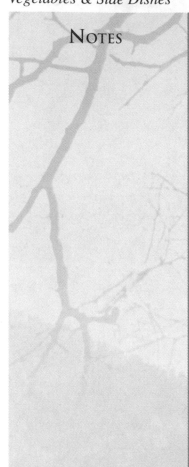

GREEN RICE

1⅓ cups instant rice
1 (8-ounce) jar Cheez whiz
1 (10¾-ounce) can cream of
   mushroom soup, undiluted
1 (10-ounce) package frozen
   chopped broccoli, thawed

½ cup chopped celery
½ cup chopped onions
1 stick butter
1 (4-ounce) can chopped
   mushrooms

- Preheat oven to 350 degrees.
- Cook rice according to package directions. Add cheese and soup.
- Pour boiling water over broccoli. Drain. Add to rice.
- Sauté celery and onions in butter. Stir into rice mixture.
- Pour mixture into a casserole dish.
- Bake 40 minutes.

Yield: 4-6 servings
GAYLE SHEAD

SPINACH ARTICHOKE
CASSEROLE

1 onion, chopped
1 stick butter
2 (10-ounce) packages frozen
   chopped spinach, thawed and
   drained
1 (14-ounce) jar artichokes,
   drained

1 (8-ounce) package cream
   cheese, softened
Salt and pepper to taste
¼ cup Italian Bread crumbs
¼ cup grated Parmesan cheese

- Preheat oven to 350 degrees.
- Sauté onions in butter. Combine onions, spinach, artichokes, cream cheese, salt and pepper.
- Pour mixture into a 9 x 9 x 2-inch baking dish. Top with bread crumbs and Parmesan cheese.
- Bake 30 minutes.

Yield: 6 servings
LYNNE KNAPP

TOMATO BACON PIE

3 medium tomatoes, cut into
   ¼-inch slices
1 (9-inch) deep dish pie crust,
   baked

10 slices bacon, cooked and
   crumbled
1 cup shredded Cheddar cheese
1 cup mayonnaise

- Preheat oven to 350 degrees.
- Arrange tomatoes in bottom of crust. Sprinkle with bacon.
- Blend Cheddar cheese and mayonnaise.
- Spoon over bacon in the center, leaving 1-inch around edge.
- Bake 30-40 minutes or until golden browned, covering edges with foil.

May substitute reduced-fat or fat-free mayonnaise for regular mayonnaise.

Yield: 6 servings
BRENDA MICHEL

TOMATO PIE

1 (9-inch) deep dish pie crust,
   baked and cooled
5 large tomatoes, peeled and
   thickly sliced, drain well on
   paper towels
½ teaspoon salt
½ teaspoon pepper or more to
   taste

3 teaspoons dried basil
¾ cup mayonnaise
1¼ cups grated sharp Cheddar
   cheese
Dash of Tabasco sauce
   (optional)

- Preheat oven to 350 degrees.
- Layer half tomatoes in pie crust. Sprinkle with half salt, pepper and basil.
- Repeat tomato layer and seasonings.
- Blend mayonnaise, Cheddar cheese and Tabasco.
- Spread mixture over tomatoes.
- Bake 35-40 minutes. Cool 5 minutes before cutting.

Yield: 6 servings
JOY BOEKE

MARINATED VEGETABLES

MARINADE
1 cup sugar
1 cup cider vinegar

½ teaspoon Tony's seasoning
   or McCormick's Creole
   seasoning
Salt and pepper to taste

VEGETABLES
1 (15-ounce) can cut green beans
1 (15-ounce) can cut wax beans
1 (2-ounce) jar chopped pimento
3 large stalks celery, chopped
1 (15-ounce) can shoe peg corn

1 (15-ounce) can Leseur English
   peas
1 (15-ounce) can dark red
   kidney beans
1 large onion, chopped
½ bell pepper, chopped
   (optional)

MARINADE
- Combine sugar, vinegar, seasoning, salt and pepper in a saucepan.
- Bring to boil. Set aside.

VEGETABLES
- Drain all vegetables.
- Combine both beans, pimentos, celery, corn, peas, kidney beans, onions and peppers in a bowl.
- Pour marinade over vegetables. Mix to coat.
- Refrigerate at least 12 hours.

Yield: 10-12 servings
TEAGUE MATTERN

LEMON BASIL BOW-TIE PASTA

1 pound bow-tie or other short pasta
¼ cup extra-virgin olive oil
¾ cup pine nuts, toasted
1½ cups cottage cheese or ricotta cheese

½ cup packed basil leaves, chopped
Zest of 2 lemons
Salt to taste

- Cook pasta in salted boiling water until al dente.
- Drain and place in a large serving bowl. Toss with oil.
- Stir in pine nuts, cottage cheese, basil, zest and salt.

Yield: 4-6 servings

SHERRY MISHKIN

BOW-TIE PASTA

1 (8-ounce) package bow-tie pasta, cooked al dente with 1 teaspoon olive oil
1 (8½-ounce) jar sun-dried tomatoes with herbs, chopped
1 (4-ounce) jar roasted pepper, chopped

½-1 cup chopped bell peppers
Greek olives to taste
Garnish: Shredded Parmesan cheese

- Combine pasta, tomatoes, peppers, bell peppers and olives. Mix well. Top with Parmesan cheese.

May add cooked and chopped chicken or shrimp.

Serve warm or at room temperature.

Yield: 4-6 servings

JEAN DUNN CASEY

191

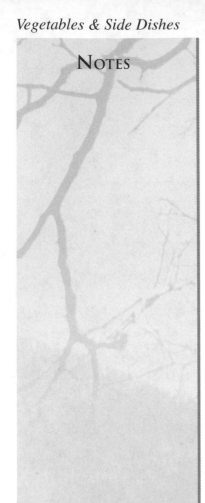

ZITI CASSEROLE

1 (26-ounce) jar Ragu Pasta Sauce
1½ cups water
1 (15-ounce) container ricotta cheese

1 (8-ounce) package shredded mozzarella cheese, divided
¼ cup grated Parmesan cheese
1 (8-ounce) package ziti pasta

- Preheat oven to 400 degrees.
- Combine pasta sauce and water. Stir in ricotta cheese, 1 cup mozzarella cheese and Parmesan cheese.
- Add pasta. Spoon mixture into a 13 x 9 x 2-inch baking dish.
- Cover with foil. Bake 55 minutes.
- Uncover and top with remaining mozzarella cheese. Bake an additional 5 minutes.

May add other ingredients such as Italian sausage, mushrooms or peppers.

Yield: 8 servings

GARY CHERRY

Desserts

SPRING DAY

When the sky is a deep clear blue
And breezes play among the leaves,
While the sun illuminates every dark place,
My spirit soars and believes
In possibilities.

The hours are rich with the promise
Of adventures and discoveries —
Options galore.
And I will choose them all;
Overlook no treasure.

In this day's golden light,
Night seems far away —
More a memory than a reality.
No cobwebs of pain or sadness
Can survive such a glorious day.

Joyce Reid Raley - 2006

CHEESECAKE

CRUST
1½ cups graham cracker crumbs

3 tablespoons butter, melted
2 tablespoons sugar

FILLING
2 (8-ounce) packages cream cheese, softened
6 eggs, room temperature and separated

1 (8-ounce) container sour cream
3 tablespoons all-purpose flour
2 teaspoons vanilla
1 cup sugar

CRUST
- Combine cracker crumbs, butter and sugar. Press into the bottom of a 9-inch springform pan.

FILLING
- Preheat oven to 350 degrees.
- Blend cream cheese, egg yolks, sour cream, flour, vanilla and sugar. Mix well.
- Beat egg whites until slightly stiff.
- Fold egg whites into batter. Pour filling over crust.
- Bake 1 hour. Cool completely.
- Remove sides of pan. Serve plain or top with fruit of choice. Store in refrigerator.

Yield: 12-15 servings
ROSE FEHRENBACH

Now let us from this table rise, renewed in body, mind and soul.

With Christ we die and live again; his selfless love has made us whole.

To fill each human house with love, it is the sacrament of care.

The work that Christ began to do, we humbly pledge ourselves to share.

Fred Kaan 1964

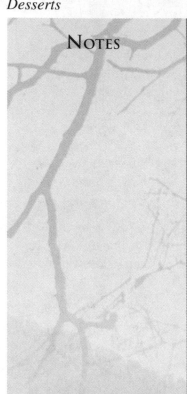

MOTHER'S FRESH APPLE CAKE

CAKE

**4 cups unpeeled and
chopped apples**
2 cups sugar
2 eggs, separated
1 cup vegetable oil

2½ cups all-purpose flour
1 teaspoon salt
2 teaspoons baking soda
2 teaspoons cinnamon
1 cup chopped pecans

GLAZE

**1 (16-ounce) package powdered
sugar, sifted**

**Juice of 1 lemon
(about 3 tablespoons)**

CAKE

- Preheat oven to 350 degrees.
- Combine apples and sugar. Set aside.
- Beat egg whites into soft peaks. Fold in egg yolks and oil.
- Sift together flour, salt, baking soda and cinnamon. Stir into egg mixture.
- Fold in sugared apples and pecans.
- Pour batter into a well greased and floured Bundt pan.
- Bake 1 hour-1 hour, 10 minutes. Cool. Remove from pan.

GLAZE

- Beat powdered sugar and lemon juice. Add milk if necessary to reach spreading consistency.
- Drizzle glaze over top and sides of cake.

Yield: 12 servings

JAN CATES

CHOCOLATE CAKE

1 (18-ounce) package Devil's
   Food cake mix
1 (14-ounce) can sweetened
   condensed milk
1 (18-ounce) jar caramel
   topping

1 (8-ounce) container frozen
   whipped topping, thawed
3-4 chocolate toffee bars,
   crushed

- Preheat oven to 350 degrees.
- Bake cake according to package directions in a 13 x 9 x 2-inch baking dish. Cool 10 minutes.
- Pierce cake with handle of wooden spoon.
- Pour milk over entire warm cake. Cover with caramel topping.
- Cool completely. Spread whipped topping over cake.
- Sprinkle with crushed chocolate toffee pieces.

Yield: 8-10 servings
LYNN ROBERTS

DEEP DARK CHOCOLATE CAKE

1¾ cups all-purpose flour
2 cups sugar
¾ cup Hershey cocoa powder
1½ teaspoons baking powder
1½ teaspoons baking soda
1 teaspoon salt

2 eggs
1 cup milk
½ cup vegetable oil
2 teaspoons vanilla
1 cup boiling water

- Combine flour, sugar, cocoa, baking powder, baking soda and salt.
- Add eggs, milk, oil and vanilla. Beat at medium speed 2 minutes.
- Stir in hot water. Batter will be thin.
- Pour batter into two greased and floured 9-inch or three 8-inch round pans or one 13 x 9 x 2-inch baking dish.
- Bake 30-35 minutes for round pans or 35-40 minutes for oblong dish until tester comes out clean.
- Cool 10 minutes in pan. Cool completely and frost with favorite frosting.

Yield: 10-12 servings
RUBY STIRZAKER

MOUNTAIN EXCHANGE

*If I could talk with
animals, I'd say,
"Don't eat my pansies.
Don't devour my
winter cabbages.
Don't nibble away my Hostas
Or munch on my Gaillardias.
My shrubbery is landscaping —
Not your salad bar!*

*Dear squirrels,
at gathering time,
Try to be neater when you
Bury your winter food supply
In flower pots on my deck.
I tire of cleaning after you.*

*Chubby ground hog,
you're cute,
Waddling across my porch,
Until you make your way to
To the side of the house and
Decimate Dianthus en masse
In little more than an instant.*

*I can only talk to animals
By spraying my plants with
Egg and Tabasco.
They clearly respond
by finding
The plants I overlook.*

*If animals could talk to me,
They might say, "Lady,
You planted your garden
Inside my domain,
And I must shop for food
In different ways than you."*

Continued on next page

CHOCOLATE MOUSSE CAKE

**7 (1-ounce) squares semi-sweet
chocolate**
1 stick butter
1 cup sugar

7 eggs, separated
Heavy cream, whipped
Chocolate shavings

- Preheat oven to 325 degrees.
- Melt chocolate and butter in saucepan. Gradually add sugar.
- Add egg yolks, one at a time, beating well after each addition. Beat 3 minutes on high speed.
- In a separate bowl, beat egg whites until stiff.
- Fold into chocolate batter. Pour three-fourths batter into an ungreased springform pan.
- Bake 35 minutes. Cool completely.
- Run knife around edges and remove frame.
- Pour remaining batter on top. Refrigerate.
- Serve with whipping cream and top with chocolate shavings.

Yield: 8 servings
SUE PIGGOTT

BUTTERNUT POUND CAKE

3 cups sugar
1 cup vegetable shortening
3 cups all-purpose flour
6 eggs

**1 (½-pint) container whipping
cream**
**1 tablespoon vanilla butternut
flavoring**

- Preheat oven to 325 degrees.
- Cream sugar and shortening. Stir in flour.
- Add eggs, one at a time, beating well after each addition.
- Stir in whipping cream and flavoring. Beat until smooth.
- Pour batter into a greased and floured Bundt pan.
- Bake 1 hour, 10 minutes.

Yield: 15 servings
MELBA SLATON

INDIVIDUAL MOLTON CHOCOLATE LAVA CAKES

1 stick unsalted butter
1 (8-ounce) package semi-sweet
   chocolate chips
4 large eggs
1 large egg yolk
1 teaspoon vanilla

¼ teaspoon salt
½ cup sugar
2 tablespoons all-purpose flour
Garnish: powdered sugar,
   whipped cream or vanilla ice
   cream

- Preheat oven to 400 degrees.
- Melt butter and chocolate in glass bowl in microwave at 30 second intervals, stirring each time until smooth.
- Pour mixture in large bowl.
- In a separate bowl, beat eggs, egg yolk, vanilla, salt and sugar on high speed 5-7 minutes until volume triples and light in color.
- Pour egg mixture over chocolate mixture. Sprinkle with flour.
- Gently fold in until mixture is well blended.
- Divided batter among 8 greased ramekins, filling three-fourths full. Place on baking sheet.
- At this point, may cover ramekins with plastic wrap and refrigerate up to 8 hours. Bring to room temperature before baking.
- Bake 10-12 minutes until puffed with a thin crust and slightly moist in center
- Run a knife around inside of each ramekin. Invert onto individual plates.
- Cool 1 minute and lift off ramekin.
- Sprinkle with powdered sugar or top with whipped cream or vanilla ice cream. Serve warm.

Yield: 8 servings
CINDY BOUDREAU

MOUNTAIN EXCHANGE
continued

Oh, but one morning,
Outside my window,
A mother bear with three cubs
Comes romping down the
mountainside,
And transforms the day.

A discovery of a
dozen wild turkeys,
Gathered in the middle
of a road,
Called Wild Turkey Bluff,
Presents a kaleidoscope
of plumage,
Intensified by the setting sun.

At nightfall I drive
to the crest of a knoll,
Where a deer stands
frozen in my headlights,
Posed as if for a
woodland photo,
Focused on the sleek
beauty of his form.

And at these times,
I must admit
The animals give me more
value than pansies,
Purple cabbages,
and shrubbery.
They intrigue, delight
and inspire me
As we pass the days
and seasons together
In our uncommon
mountain home.

Joyce Reid Raley
2000

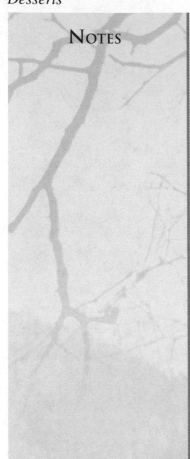

CARAMEL CAKE

1 (18-ounce) package yellow cake mix
1 (16-ounce) package light brown sugar

1½ sticks butter
9 tablespoons evaporated milk
1 teaspoon vanilla

- Bake cake according to package directions.
- Combine brown sugar, butter and milk in a large saucepan. Bring to boil.
- Boil exactly 3 minutes once boiling begins. Cool. Stir in vanilla.
- Spread caramel frosting over cake.

Yield: 10-12 servings
CATHY SMITH

COCONUT PECAN BUNDT CAKE

1 (18-ounce) package butter pecan cake mix
1¼ cups water
⅓ cup vegetable oil

3 eggs
1 (16-ounce) can coconut pecan frosting

- Preheat oven to 350 degrees.
- Beat cake mix, water, oil and eggs about 2 minutes with an electric mixer.
- Add frosting and blend well.
- Pour batter into a well greased Bundt cake pan.
- Bake 45-55 minutes. Cool 15 minutes in pan.
- Remove from pan.

Yield: 12-15 servings
OUIDA AMES

FRESH COCONUT CAKE

1 (18-ounce) package yellow
   cake mix
1 (16-ounce) container sour
   cream
1 cup sugar

Coconut milk
2 cups grated coconut
   (fresh or frozen), divided
1 (12-ounce) container frozen
   whipped cream, thawed

- Prepare cake according to package directions. Cool. Slice each layer in half, making 4 layers.
- Combine sour cream, sugar and 1 cup coconut. Reserve 1 cup mixture in refrigerator.
- Place one cake layer on a cake platter. Drizzle with coconut milk.
- Spread with sour cream frosting. Sprinkle with coconut.
- Repeat with each layer.
- Blend reserved sour cream frosting and whipped cream.
- Frost top and sides of cake. Press remaining coconut on top and sides.

Yield: 10-12 servings
NANCY COWART

MANDARIN ORANGE CAKE

1 (18-ounce) package butter
   cake mix
½ cup vegetable oil
4 eggs
1 (11-ounce) can Mandarin
   oranges with juice

1 (3-ounce) package instant
   vanilla pudding mix
1 (20-ounce) can crushed
   pineapple with juice
1 (8-ounce) container frozen
   whipped topping, thawed

- Preheat oven to 350 degrees.
- Beat together cake mix, oil, eggs and oranges with juice.
- Divide batter into three greased and floured 9-inch cake pans.
- Bake 20-25 minutes. Cool completely.
- Blend pudding mix, pineapple with juice and whipped topping.
- Spread frosting between cake layers, top and sides.

Yield: 12 servings
MELODY RAY

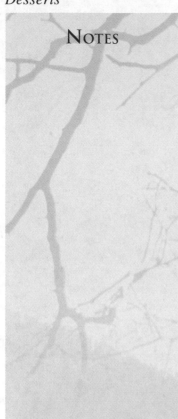

FRESH CRANBERRY CAKE WITH HOT RUM SAUCE

CAKE

4 tablespoons butter, softened	**2 cups all-purpose flour**
1 cup sugar	**1 teaspoon salt**
2 eggs	**1 teaspoon baking soda**
½ cup water	**2 cups whole cranberries**
½ cup evaporated milk	**1 cup chopped walnuts**

HOT RUM SAUCE

2 sticks butter	**1 cup evaporated milk**
2 cups sugar	

CAKE

- Cream butter and sugar. Add eggs, one at a time, beating well after each addition.
- Stir in water and milk.
- Add flour, salt and baking soda. Mix well.
- Stir in cranberries and nuts.
- Pour batter into a well greased 13 x 9 x 2-inch baking dish.
- Bake 30 minutes.

HOT RUM SAUCE

- Heat butter, sugar and milk until butter melts and sugar dissolves.
- Serve with cake.

Yield: 8-10 servings

JANE BROOKS

Easy Sour Cream Cheesecake

Crumb Crust

30 vanilla or chocolate wafers
2 tablespoons sugar

6 teaspoons cinnamon or nutmeg
5⅓ tablespoons butter, melted

Filling

2 eggs
½ cup sugar
2 teaspoons vanilla
1½ cups sour cream

2 (8-ounce) packages cream cheese, softened, cut into pieces
2 tablespoons butter, melted

Crumb Crust

- Break half of wafers in a blender. Cover and blend on high speed 6 seconds.
- Transfer to a bowl. Repeat with remaining wafers.
- Combine all crumbs with sugar, cinnamon and butter. Refrigerate.
- Press mixture onto bottom and up sides of 9-inch springform pan.

Filling

- Preheat oven to 325 degrees.
- Beat eggs, sugar, vanilla and sour cream about 30 seconds.
- Add cream cheese and butter. Blend 15 seconds or until smooth.
- Pour filling into crust.
- Bake 30-40 minutes or until set in center.
- Cool completely.

May top with strawberry or blueberry pie filling.

Yield: 15 servings
PATRICIA APPEL

This was my daughter's favorite cake to make when she was in the Girl Scouts.

JANE ANN'S CAKE

1 (8-ounce) can crushed
    pineapple
1 (18-ounce) package butter
    pecan cake mix

1 stick butter, cut into pieces
Garnish: Ice cream

- Preheat oven to 300 degrees.
- Pour pineapple in a greased deep 8 x 8 x 2-inch baking dish.
- Sprinkle with cake mix. Dot with butter.
- Bake 1 hour. Top with ice cream.

Yield: 8 servings
BOBBIE GARNER

SOUR CREAM COFFEE CAKE

2 cups sugar
2 sticks butter, softened
3 eggs
1 teaspoon vanilla
2 cups sifted all-purpose flour
1 teaspoon baking powder

¼ teaspoon salt
1 cup sour cream
1 cup packed brown sugar
1½ teaspoons cinnamon
1 cup chopped pecans
Garnish: Powdered sugar

- Preheat oven to 350 degrees.
- Cream sugar and butter until light and fluffy. Add eggs and vanilla. Beat well.
- Combine flour, baking powder and salt. Add flour mixture, alternately with sour cream, to creamed mixture.
- Spread half batter in a greased and floured tube pan.
- Mix together brown sugar, cinnamon and pecans.
- Sprinkle half of topping over batter.
- Cover with remaining batter. Sprinkle with remaining topping.
- Bake 1 hour until tester comes out clean.
- Dust with powdered sugar.

Cake may be frozen for weeks.

Yield: 12 servings
FRANKIE REHG

COFFEE CAKE

TOPPING
⅓ cup all-purpose flour

¼ cup packed brown sugar

2 tablespoons butter, softened

CAKE
1 stick butter, softened

1 cup sugar

2 egg yolks

1½ cups all-purpose flour

2 teaspoons baking powder

¼ teaspoon salt

½ cup milk

2 egg whites, stiffly beaten

TOPPING
- Combine flour and brown sugar. Cut in butter until crumbly.

CAKE
- Preheat oven to 350 degrees.
- Cream butter and sugar. Beat in egg yolks.
- Sift together flour, baking powder and salt.
- Add dry ingredients, alternately with milk, to creamed mixture. Beat well after each addition.
- Fold in egg whites.
- Pour batter into a greased 9 x 9 x 2-inch baking dish.
- Sprinkle topping over batter.
- Bake 30-40 minutes.

Yield: 8-10 servings

AIME K. BAARS

GRANNY CAKE

The Granny Cake is best when served warm.

CAKE

2 cups sifted all-purpose flour
1½ cups sugar
1 teaspoon salt
1 teaspoon baking soda

2 eggs
1 (20-ounce) can crushed pineapple, undrained
Garnish: Brown sugar and chopped pecans

GLAZE

1 stick butter, melted
1 teaspoon vanilla
½ cup sugar

1 (14-ounce) can sweetened condensed milk

CAKE

- Preheat oven to 350 degrees.
- Combine flour, sugar, salt and baking soda.
- Beat together eggs and pineapple. Add flour mixture to pineapple mixture.
- Pour batter into a greased and floured 13 x 9 x 2-inch baking dish.
- Sprinkle with brown sugar and pecans.
- Bake 20 minutes. Do not over bake.
- Pierce holes in cake with fork.
- Pour warm glaze immediately over cake.

GLAZE

- Combine butter, vanilla, sugar and milk in a saucepan.
- Bring to just boil, stirring constantly. Keep warm.

Store cake in refrigerator.

Yield: 15 servings
MELANIE McCABE

HARVEY WALLBANGER CAKE

1 (18-ounce) package yellow
  cake mix
1 (3-ounce) package instant
  vanilla pudding mix
1 cup vegetable oil
4 eggs

¼ cup vodka
¼ cup Galliano
¾ cup orange juice
2 cups powdered sugar
Galliano and orange juice

- Preheat oven to 350 degrees.
- Combine cake mix, pudding mix, oil, eggs, vodka, Galliano and orange juice. Beat until smooth.
- Pour batter into a well greased and floured Bundt pan.
- Bake 45-50 minutes. Cool 10 minutes. Invert cake onto cake platter.
- Blend powdered sugar and enough Galliano and orange juice until smooth.
- Pour glaze over warm cake.

Yield: 12-15 servings
MARTHA ELKINS

For a beautiful dessert, put flowers in center of cake. My family's all-time favorite cake. Freezes beautifully.

HUMMINGBIRD CAKE

3 cups all-purpose flour
2 cups sugar
1 teaspoon baking soda
1 teaspoon salt
1 teaspoon cinnamon
3 eggs, beaten

1 cup vegetable oil
1½ teaspoons vanilla
1 (8-ounce) can crushed
  pineapple, undrained
1 cup chopped pecans
2 cups chopped bananas

This is a great cake!

- Preheat oven to 350 degrees.
- Combine flour, sugar, baking soda, salt and cinnamon.
- Stir in eggs and oil until moistened. Do not beat.
- Add vanilla, pineapple, pecans and bananas.
- Divide batter among three 8-inch round cake pans.
- Bake 25-30 minutes.
- Frost with favorite frosting.

Yield: 8-12 servings
KAREN O'NEIL

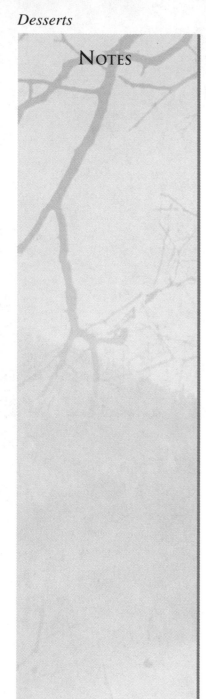

KAHLÚA CAKE

1 (18-ounce) package Devil's food cake mix, no pudding in mix
2 eggs
¼ cup vegetable oil
1 (16-ounce) container light sour cream
½ cup Kahlúa

1 (3-ounce) package instant vanilla pudding
1 cup semi-sweet chocolate chips, freeze and mix with some flour
1-1½ cups semi-sweet chocolate chips
Milk

- Preheat oven to 350 degrees.
- Combine cake mix, eggs, oil, sour cream, Kahlúa, pudding mix and floured chocolate chips by hand.
- Place batter in a greased and floured Bundt pan.
- Bake 45-50 minutes or until tester comes out clean.
- Cool 10 minutes in pan.
- Invert onto serving platter.
- Heat chocolate chips and milk in saucepan until smooth.
- Drizzle chocolate sauce over top.
- Serve warm with ice cream.

Yield: 12-15 servings
BLOSSOM HOLYOAK

WHIPPING CREAM CAKE

3 cups sugar
1¼ cups vegetable shortening
6 large or 7 medium eggs
3 cups sifted cake flour

½ pint whipping cream
1½ tablespoons lemon flavoring
1 teaspoon butter flavoring

- Cream sugar and shortening. Add eggs, one at a time, beating well after each addition.
- Add cake flour alternately with cream to creamed mixture.
- Stir in lemon and butter flavoring.
- Pour batter into a wax paper lined 10-inch tube pan.
- Place in a cold oven. Bake at 325 degrees 1 hour, 45 minutes.
- Invert to cool.

Yield: 12-15 servings
LAURA WALKER

TEXAS SHEET CAKE

CAKE

2 cups all-purpose flour
2 cups sugar
1 teaspoon baking soda
½ teaspoon salt
2 sticks butter

¼ cup cocoa powder
1 cup milk
2 eggs, beaten
½ cup buttermilk
1 teaspoon vanilla

ICING

1 stick butter, softened
1 teaspoon vanilla
¼ cup cocoa powder
2 tablespoons buttermilk

**1 (16-ounce) package powdered
  sugar**
1 cup chopped pecans

CAKE

- Preheat oven to 350 degrees.
- Combine flour, sugar, baking soda and salt.
- Heat butter, cocoa and milk in a saucepan until smooth. Stir into flour mixture.
- Blend eggs, buttermilk and vanilla. Add to flour mixture. Mix well.
- Pour batter into a 13 x 9 x 2-inch baking dish.
- Bake 20-30 minutes.

ICING

- Blend butter, vanilla, cocoa, buttermilk, powdered sugar and pecans.
- Pour icing over cake while warm.

Yield: 12-15 servings
CLAIRE CRONK

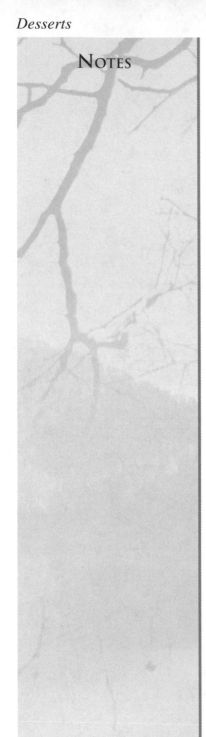

PUMPKIN GEMS

CAKE

1 (18-ounce) package yellow cake mix
3 eggs
½ cup vegetable oil

1 teaspoon baking soda
2 teaspoons cinnamon
1 (20-ounce) can solid packed pumpkin

FROSTING

1 (3-ounce) package cream cheese, softened
1½ sticks butter, softened

½ teaspoon vanilla
1 tablespoon milk
2 cups powdered sugar

CAKE

- Preheat oven to 350 degrees.
- Beat together cake mix, eggs, oil, baking soda, cinnamon and pumpkin about 2 minutes.
- Spoon batter evenly into miniature muffin cups.
- Bake 15 minutes.

FROSTING

- Blend cream cheese, butter, vanilla, milk and powdered sugar until smooth.
- Spread frosting over mini cupcakes.

Yield: 48 mini cupcakes
COREY TANNER

WHIPPING CREAM POUND CAKE

3 cups sugar
2 sticks butter, softened
6 eggs

3 cups cake flour
½ pint heavy cream
1 teaspoon vanilla

- Preheat oven to 325 degrees.
- Cream sugar and butter with electric mixer.
- Add eggs and flour alternately, beating well after each addition.
- Stir in cream and vanilla. Beat on low speed until smooth.
- Pour batter into a greased and floured Bundt pan.
- Bake 1 hour, 25 minutes.
- Cool 30 minutes in pan. Turn out onto wire rack to cool completely.

Yield: 12 servings
JUDY LACEY

An old Southern recipe that is truly moist with great flavor!

CHERRY PIE

2 (16-ounce) cans tart red
   cherries, drained
1 teaspoon vanilla or ½ teaspoon
   vanilla and ½ teaspoon
   almond extract
1 teaspoon salt

¼ cup all-purpose flour
1 cup sugar
4 tablespoons unsalted butter
Pillsbury double pastry crust
Butter

- Preheat oven to 425 degrees.
- Combine cherries, vanilla, salt, flour and sugar.
- Place pie pastry in a 9-inch pie pan. Pour cherry filling into crust.
- Dot with butter. Place second pastry on top and pierce with fork.
- Bake 45 minutes.

Yield: 8 servings
SALLY REED

NOTES

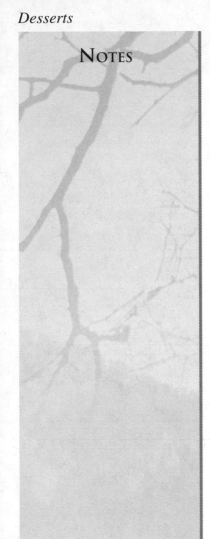

MINIATURE
KENTUCKY DERBY TARTS

CRUST
2 sticks butter, softened
**2 (3-ounce) packages cream
   cheese, softened**

2 cups sifted all-purpose flour

FILLING
2 eggs
**1½ cups packed light brown
   sugar**
½ teaspoon salt

2 tablespoons butter, melted
¼ teaspoon vanilla
**¾ cup mini semi-sweet chocolate
   chips**
½ cup chopped nuts

CRUST
- Cream butter and cream cheese until smooth. Blend in flour.
- Shape dough into small balls. Press balls into bottom and up sides of greased mini-muffin cups.

FILLING
- Preheat oven to 350 degrees.
- Lightly beat eggs. Add brown sugar, salt, butter and vanilla. Stir in mini chips.
- Sprinkle bottom of each cup with nuts. Spoon 1-1½ teaspoons filing into each cup.
- Top with nuts.
- Bake 20-25 minutes. Cool and carefully remove from pan.

Yield: 48 tartlets
CONNIE McKINNEY

FRENCH SILK CHOCOLATE PIE

1 stick butter, softened	2 eggs
¾ cup sugar	1 (8-inch) pie crust, baked
2 (1-ounce) squares unsweetened chocolate, melted	Whipping cream, whipped and sweetened
1 teaspoon vanilla	German Chocolate shavings

- Cream butter and sugar until light and fluffy.
- Add chocolate and vanilla. Beat until smooth.
- Add eggs, one at a time, beating at least 3 minutes after each addition.
- Pour filling in pie crust.
- Refrigerate at least 3 hours before serving.
- Just before serving, spread a thick layer of whipped cream.
- Sprinkle with chocolate shavings.

Yield: 8 servings

SANDY GEIBEL

This pie is so rich and sweet that it needs the final touch of bitterness as an accent.

OLD TIMEY CHOCOLATE PIE

1 cup sugar	1 cup milk
2 rounded tablespoons all-purpose flour	2 rounded tablespoons butter
2 rounded tablespoons cocoa powder	½ teaspoon vanilla
2 eggs, separated	1 (9-inch) pie crust, baked
	4 tablespoons sugar
	1 teaspoon lemon juice

- Preheat oven to 400 degrees.
- Blend sugar, flour and cocoa. Beat egg yolks until lemon colored.
- Beat in milk. Melt butter in a cast iron skillet on medium low heat.
- Stir dry ingredients into butter and mix lightly.
- Gradually stir in egg mixture. Cook and stir with a wooden spoon until thickened.
- Add vanilla. Pour filling into pie crust.
- Beat egg whites to form stiff peaks. Gradually beat in sugar and lemon juice.
- Spread meringue over filling.
- Bake 5 minutes until golden browned.

Bake only in iron skillet.

Yield: 6 servings

MARTHA QUINN

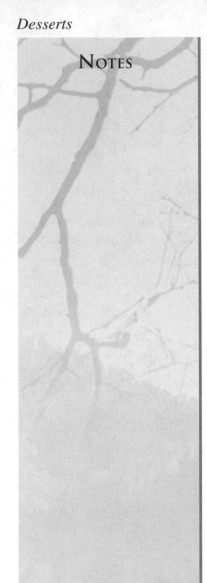

CREAM CHEESE PIE

FILLING

2 (8-ounce) packages cream
    cheese, softened
¾ cup sugar

⅛ teaspoon salt
½ teaspoon almond extract
3 eggs

TOPPING

1 (8-ounce) can crushed
    pineapple, drained
1 cup sour cream

3 tablespoons sugar
1 teaspoon vanilla

FILLING

- Preheat oven to 350 degrees.
- Beat cream cheese, sugar, salt and almond extract.
- Add eggs one at a time, beating well after each addition.
- Pour filling into a buttered 9-inch pie plate.
- Bake 25 minutes. Cool 20 minutes on rack. Refrigerate until cool.

TOPPING

- Spoon pineapple over filling. Blend sour cream, sugar and vanilla.
- Pour over pineapple. Bake an additional 10 minutes.
- Cool and refrigerate.

May eliminate pineapple to make a plain pie or use fresh fruit of choice.

Yield: 6-8 servings

MARILYN HUGHES

CHRISTMAS PIE

1 (14-ounce) sweetened
   condensed milk
¾ cup lemon juice
1 (8-ounce) can crushed
   pineapple, drained
1 cup diced pecans

1 (12-ounce) container frozen
   whipped topping, thawed
1 (3½-ounce) can flaked coconut
2 (9-inch) graham cracker pie
   crusts
Garnish: Miniature
   marshmallows and
   maraschino cherries

- Combine milk, lemon juice, pineapple, pecans, whipped topping and coconut.
- Divide filling between two pie crusts.
- Top with marshmallows and cherries.
- Refrigerate overnight.

Yield: 12 servings
SARAH KELLY

COFFEE-FUDGE ICE CREAM PIE

18 chocolate sandwich cookies,
   crushed
5⅓ tablespoons butter, softened
2 quarts coffee ice cream,
   softened
1½ ounces unsweetened
   chocolate

½ cup sugar
1 teaspoon butter
1 (5-ounce) can evaporated milk
1 (8-ounce) container frozen
   whipped topping, thawed
1 cup chopped pecans

- Combine cookie crumbs and butter. Press into bottom of a 13 x 9 x 2-inch baking dish. Freeze.
- Spread ice cream over frozen crust.
- Combine chocolate, sugar, butter and milk in a saucepan.
- Cook and stir until thickened. Cool. Pour over ice cream.
- Top with whipped topping. Sprinkle pecans on top.
- Refreeze. Cut into squares.

Yield: 8-10 servings
GLENDA MOLTON

LEMON TOPPED
ICE CREAM PIE

CRUST

¾ cup vanilla wafer crumbs

2 tablespoons sugar

4 tablespoons butter, melted

½ cup chopped pecans

FILLING

1½ pints vanilla ice cream, softened

3 tablespoons lemon juice

½ teaspoon lemon zest

½ cup sugar

3 tablespoons butter

1 egg, slightly beaten

CRUST

- Combine wafer crumbs, sugar, butter and pecans.
- Press mixture into bottom of a buttered 9-inch pie plate. Freeze.

FILLING

- Spoon ice cream into frozen crust. Freeze.
- Heat lemon juice, zest, sugar and butter over low heat until butter melts and sugar dissolves.
- Remove from heat and cool. Slowly whisk in egg, stirring vigorously.
- Return to heat. Cook until thickened and coats back of spoon.
- Spread filling over ice cream. Freeze.

Yield: 8 servings

NANCY BARR

Sour Cream Lemon Pie

⅔ cup sugar
3 tablespoons cornstarch
3 egg yolks
1 cup milk
4 tablespoons butter, melted

¼ cup lemon juice
1 teaspoon lemon zest
1 cup sour cream
1 (9-inch) pie crust, baked
1 cup whipping cream, whipped and sweetened

- Combine sugar and cornstarch in a heavy saucepan. Whisk in egg yolks and milk.
- Add butter, lemon juice and zest.
- Cook over medium heat until thickened, stirring constantly.
- Cool in refrigerator. Fold in sour cream.
- Spoon filling into pie crust. Refrigerate 2 hours. Serve with whipped cream.

Yield: 8 servings
DONNA WILLS

Frosty Margarita Pie

2½ cups finely crushed small pretzels
4 tablespoons reduced calorie butter, melted
1 tablespoon sugar
6 cups nonfat frozen yogurt, softened

¼ cup tequila
3 tablespoons frozen limeade concentrate, do not dilute
1 teaspoon lime zest
1 tablespoon lime juice
Garnish: Lime slices and lime curls

- Combine pretzels, butter and sugar. Mix well.
- Press mixture into bottom and up sides of 9-inch pie plate.
- Blend yogurt, tequila, limeade, zest and lime juice.
- Spoon filling into crust. Cover and freeze until firm.
- Let stand at room temperature 5 minutes before slicing.
- Garnish with lime slices and lime curls.

The recipe filling is for two pies. May make additional crust. May top with whipped topping, a slice of twisted lime and sprig of mint.

Yield: 8 servings
CHARLENE EHRLICH

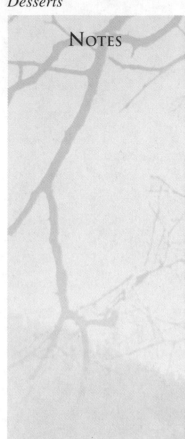

KEY LIME PIE

CRUST

1 wrapped package graham
  crackers

5 tablespoons unsalted butter,
  melted
⅓ cup sugar

FILLING

3 egg yolks
Zest of 2 limes
1 (14-ounce) can sweetened
  condensed milk

⅔ cup fresh Key lime juice
Garnish: whipped cream

CRUST

- Preheat oven to 350 degrees.
- Place broken crackers in food processor. Pulse to make crumbs.
- Add butter and sugar. Pulse until combined.
- Press mixture into bottom and up sides of a buttered 9-inch pie plate.
- Bake 8 minutes until golden browned. Cool on wire rack.

FILLING

- Beat egg yolks and zest about 5 minutes with wire whisk of electric mixer until very fluffy.
- Gradually beat in condensed milk about 3-4 minutes until thickened.
- Slowly add lime juice on low speed just until combined.
- Pour mixture into crust.
- Bake 10 minutes until filling is set.
- Cool on wire rack. Refrigerate.
- Freeze 15-20 minutes prior to serving.
- Garnish with dollop whipped cream.

Yield: 8 servings
CYNTHIA JUNGER

PECAN PIE
FOR THE HOLIDAY CROWD

CRUST

2 cups all-purpose flour
2 sticks butter, softened

¾ cup loosely packed brown sugar

FILLING

5 eggs, beaten
1 cup loosely packed brown sugar
1 stick butter, melted
1½ cups light corn syrup

¾ teaspoon salt
1½ cups coarsely chopped pecans
2 tablespoons all-purpose flour

CRUST

- Preheat oven to 350 degrees.
- Blend flour, butter and brown sugar. Mix well.
- Press 3 cups crumb mixture into a greased 13 x 9 x 2-inch baking dish.
- Bake 15 minutes.

FILLING

- Combine eggs and brown sugar. Stir in butter. Add corn syrup, salt and pecans.
- Stir in flour until well blended. Pour filling over crust.
- Top with reserved crumb mixture.
- Bake 30-35 minutes. Cool on wire rack. Refrigerate until ready to serve.

May garnish with whipped cream or ice cream. Serve at Thanksgiving.

Yield: 16 servings

MARY ANN WILLIAMS

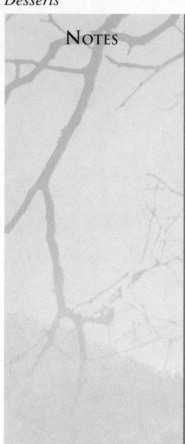

STRAWBERRY-RHUBARB PIE

2 cups washed, hulled and halved strawberries
4 cups chopped rhubarb. ½-inch thick slices
⅓ cup seedless raisins
1⅓ cups sugar

6 tablespoons all-purpose flour
¼ teaspoon ground ginger
Pastry for 9-inch double crust
1 egg white, slightly beaten
1½ tablespoons unsalted butter

- Preheat oven to 425 degrees.
- Combine strawberries, rhubarb, raisins, sugar, flour and ginger. Let stand 15 minutes.
- Line a 9-inch pie plate with one pastry sheet.
- Brush bottom of pie crust with egg white.
- Pour filling into crust. Dot with butter.
- Brush rim of crust with water. Cover with second pastry sheet, sealing edges.
- Place on a rimmed baking sheet.
- Bake 20 minutes.
- Decrease temperature to 400 degrees. Bake an additional 40 minutes, covering edges with foil.

Yield: 8 servings
PEGGY DICKEY

TUTTI-FRUTTI PIE

1 (8-ounce) container frozen whipped topping, thawed
1 (14-ounce) can sweetened condensed milk
¼ cup lemon juice

1 (11-ounce) can Mandarin oranges, drained and halved
½ cup maraschino cherries, halved
½ cup chopped pecans
1 (9-inch) graham cracker crust

- Combine whipped topping, milk and lemon juice.
- Add oranges, cherries and pecans. Pour filling into pie crust.
- Refrigerate at least 1 hour before serving.

May use blueberries or fruit of choice.

Yield: 6-8 servings
FRAN SALING

CHERRIES JUBILEE

1 (16-ounce) can Bing cherries
1 tablespoon powdered sugar
1 tablespoon cornstarch

¼ cup Kirshwasser or other cherry brandy
1 quart vanilla ice cream, hard frozen

- Drain liquid from cherries into saucepan. Blend powdered sugar and cornstarch.
- Heat cherry liquid and stir in cornstarch mixture until clear and thickened.
- Add cherries and bring to boil. Pour warm Kirshwasser on top.
- Ignite and spoon flaming sauce over cherries until flames die.
- Pour cherries and sauce over ice cream. Serve immediately.

Yield: 4 servings
NICK BROWN

MY SISTER'S FLAN

¾ cup sugar
1 (14-ounce) can sweetened condensed milk

1¾ cups milk
2 eggs
2 teaspoons vanilla

- Preheat oven to 325 degrees.
- Caramelize sugar in heavy skillet over high heat, stirring constantly.
- Pour sugar into a round glass bowl. Rotate dish to cover sides and bottom. Cool.
- Blend condensed milk, milk, eggs and vanilla. Pour mixture over sugar.
- Place bowl in a second pan filled with 1-inch cool water.
- Bake 1 hour until knife inserted comes out clean.
- Cool and refrigerate.

May substitute no fat condensed milk, no fat milk and egg beaters substitutes. Refrigerated flan can be unmolded onto a platter and served. Caramelized sugar makes a beautiful syrup topping.

Yield: 6 servings
TONI WOODS

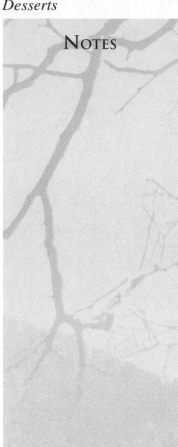

ALMOST MARSHALL FIELD'S PEPPERMINT FRANGOS

2 sticks butter
2 cups sifted all-purpose flour
4 squares unsweetened chocolate, melted
4 eggs

2 teaspoons vanilla
2 teaspoons peppermint flavoring
1 cup vanilla wafer crumbs

- Cream butter and flour until light and fluffy. Add chocolate.
- Add eggs, one at a time, beating well after each addition.
- Stir in vanilla and peppermint.
- Sprinkle half cookie crumbs in 24 cupcake liners.
- Spoon peppermint filling in each cup. Top with remaining crumbs.
- Freeze until firm. Serve frozen or just cold.

May also be made in a 13 x 9 x 2-inch baking dish and cut into small squares.

Yield: 24 cupcakes
KAY DELL KNARR

CHOCOLATE DELIGHT

2 (6-ounce) packages instant French vanilla pudding mix
1 (12-ounce) container frozen whipped topping, thawed

1 (16-ounce) package graham crackers, crushed
1 (16-ounce) can fudge frosting

- Make pudding according to package directions.
- Stir in whipped topping and mix well.
- Spread a layer of cracker crumbs in bottom of 13 x 9 x 2-inch baking dish.
- Spoon a layer of pudding over top.
- Repeat layers starting and ending with cracker crumbs.
- Top with frosting.

Yield: 12-16 servings
NANCY POPP

CHOCOLATE TRIFLE

1 (18-ounce) package brownie
   mix

¼ cup Hershey's chocolate
   syrup or Kahlúa or Amaretto

2 (6-ounce) packages instant
   chocolate pudding mix

1 (8-ounce) package Heath
   bar chips

1 (12-ounce) container frozen
   whipped topping, thawed

- Prepare brownies according to package directions in a 13 x 9 x 2-inch baking dish.
- While warm, pierce holes into brownies. Pour syrup over top. Cool and crumble.
- Prepare chocolate pudding according to package directions. Do not refrigerate.
- Layer half crumbled brownies, pudding, Heath chips and whipped topping in a glass bowl.
- Repeat all layers. Top with Heath chips.

Yield: 8-10 servings

BRENDA MATTHEWS

BLUEBERRY CRUNCH

1 (20-ounce) can crushed
   pineapple

1 (15-ounce) can blueberries
   (not pie filling)

1 (18-ounce) package yellow
   cake mix

1 cup chopped pecans

1 stick butter, melted

Garnish: Whipped topping or
   vanilla ice cream

- Preheat oven to 350 degrees.
- Combine pineapples and blueberries with juice in a 13 x 9 x 2-inch baking dish.
- Sprinkle cake mix over fruit. Top with pecans.
- Drizzle with butter.
- Bake 35-40 minutes or until lightly browned and bubbly.
- Serve with whipped topping or ice cream

Yield: 12-15 servings

LINDA JAMES

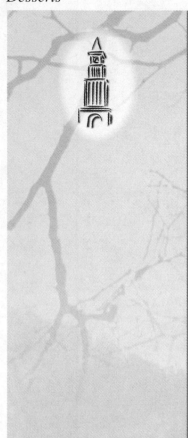

SMASHING MYSTERY DESSERT

2 cups firmly packed brown
  sugar
2 eggs
1 cup chopped pecans
⅔ cup all-purpose flour

1 teaspoon baking soda
2 cups well-chilled whipping
  cream
2 tablespoons brandy

- Preheat oven to 350 degrees.
- Combine brown sugar, eggs, pecans, flour and baking soda. Batter will be thick.
- Spoon batter into a lightly greased 13 x 9 x 2 -inch baking dish.
- Bake 25 minutes or until tester comes out clean.
- Cool completely at least 2 hours.
- Whip cream in a large bowl until soft peaks form. Fold in brandy.
- Break cake into small pieces, reserving some for topping.
- Fold cake pieces into whipped cream. Spread mixture into a clean 13 x 9 x 2-inch baking dish.
- Freeze at least 4 hours or overnight.
- Spoon dessert into goblets to serve. Top with reserved crumbs.

For a quick preparation, use almond or amaretto cookies and break into small pieces to substitute for pecan cake. Use amaretto liqueur instead of brandy.

Yield: 10 servings
DOTTIE NIX

APPLE AMBROSIA

1 (6-ounce) can orange juice
  concentrate, undiluted
3 apples, peeled and grated
1 (15-ounce) can crushed
  pineapple, thawed and
  undiluted

1 (7-ounce) package frozen
  coconut or (3½-ounce) can
1 orange juice can water

This ambrosia is guaranteed to fool even a purist!

- Combine orange juice, apples, pineapples, coconut and water.
- Refrigerate at least 2 hours.

Yield: 8 servings
BRENDA BEDINGFIELD

PEACH COBBLER

2 cups sliced peaches, fresh or
frozen
½ cup sugar
1 stick butter
¾ cup all-purpose flour

2 teaspoons baking powder
1 cup sugar
¼ teaspoon salt
¾ cup milk

- Preheat oven to 350 degrees.
- Combine peaches and sugar. Melt butter in a 9 x 9 x 2-inch baking dish in oven.
- Mix flour, baking powder, sugar, salt and milk. Pour batter over butter. Do not mix.
- Place peaches over batter. Do not stir.
- Bake 35-45 minutes until lightly browned.

Yield: 4-6 servings
LYNDA CASE

BUTTERSCOTCH BROWNIES

1 stick butter
2 cups packed light brown sugar
2 eggs
2 cups sifted all-purpose flour

½ teaspoon salt
2 teaspoons baking powder
1½ cups chopped pecans
2 teaspoons vanilla

- Preheat oven to 350 degrees.
- Heat butter and brown sugar in a saucepan until butter melts and sugar dissolves. Cool.
- Beat in eggs. Sift together flour, salt and baking powder. Stir into sugar mixture.
- Add nuts and vanilla.
- Spread batter into a greased ad floured 13 x 9 x 2-inch baking dish.
- Bake 30-35 minutes. Score brownies while hot.
- Cool slightly and cut through and remove from dish.

Yield: 5½ dozen brownies
ARDIS McCAIN

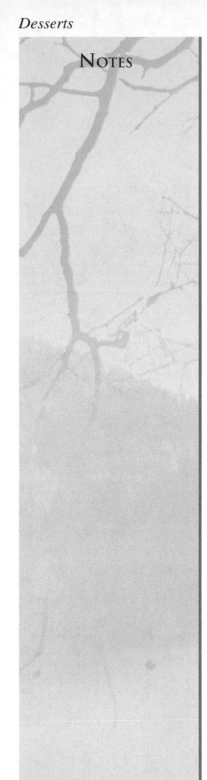

BABOON BROWNIES

1 (18-ounce) package German chocolate cake mix

1 stick butter, salt or unsalted, melted

1 (5-ounce) can evaporated milk

1 (14-ounce) package caramel candies

1 (12-ounce) package mini dark chocolate chips

¾ cup chopped walnuts (optional)

Sifted powdered sugar

- Preheat oven to 325 degrees.
- Combine cake mix, butter and half can evaporated milk. Mixture will be crumbly.
- Spread half mixture in bottom of a 13 x 9 x 2-inch baking dish.
- Bake 7-10 minutes.
- Melt caramels and remaining evaporated milk over low heat, stirring often.
- Pour caramel sauce over baked crust. Do not spread as cake may tear.
- Sprinkle chocolate chips evenly over sauce. Scatter walnuts on top.
- Crumble remaining cake mixture evenly over top.
- Bake 17-20 minutes.
- Dust with sifted powdered sugar. Cool completely before cutting.

Yield: 15 servings

MIMI ZENTGRAF

MISSISSIPPI MUD BARS

BATTER

2 sticks unsalted butter, softened
2 cups sugar
4 eggs
1 teaspoon vanilla
1½ cups all-purpose flour

3 tablespoons cocoa powder
1½ cups flaked coconut
1 cup chopped pecans
1 (7-ounce) jar marshmallow
  creme

FROSTING

1 stick butter, softened
1 teaspoon vanilla
4 cups powdered sugar

⅓ cup cocoa powder
½ cup evaporated milk

BATTER

- Preheat oven to 350 degrees.
- Cream butter and sugar. Beat in eggs and vanilla.
- In a separate bowl, combine flour and cocoa. Beat into creamed mixture.
- Fold in coconut and pecans.
- Spoon batter into a greased 13 x 9 x 2-inch baking dish.
- Bake 25-40 minutes or until tester comes out clean.
- Remove from oven and immediately spoon marshmallow creme over brownies. Spread gently.
- Cool completely.

FROSTING

- Cream butter and vanilla.
- In a separate bowl, combine powdered sugar and cocoa.
- Gradually beat into creamed mixture, alternately with milk.
- Beat 3-5 minutes until light and fluffy.
- Spread over brownies.

Yield: 18 servings
GLENDA MITCHELL

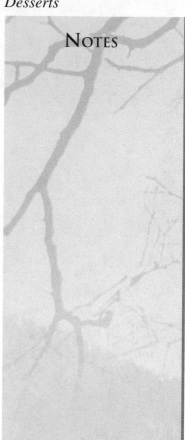

MARBLED MOCHA SQUARES

1 cup graham cracker crumbs
¼ cup Hershey's cocoa powder
¼ cup sugar
4 tablespoons butter, melted
4 teaspoons powdered instant coffee
1 tablespoon hot water

1 (14-ounce) can sweetened condensed milk
⅔ cup plus ¼ cup Hershey's chocolate syrup, divided
1 cup chopped walnuts
1 pint cold whipping cream, whipped

- Combine cracker crumbs, cocoa, sugar and butter. Mix well.
- Press crumbs firmly into bottom of 9-inch square pan.
- Dissolve coffee in hot water. Stir in milk and ⅔ cup chocolate syrup.
- Fold in nuts and whipped cream.
- Pour batter over crust. Drizzle with ¼ remaining chocolate syrup.
- Using a knife or spatula, gently swirl chocolate syrup for a marbled effect.
- Cover and freeze at least 6 hours or until firm.
- Cut into squares and serve immediately.

May substitute chocolate graham crackers, crushed, for graham crackers and cocoa.

Yield: 8-10 servings
ELLEN FINLEY

CHOCOLATE CHIP MERINGUE COOKIES

2 egg whites
¾ cup sugar

½ teaspoon vanilla
1 cup semi-sweet chocolate chips

- Beat egg whites until stiff. Gradually beat in sugar.
- Stir in vanilla and chocolate chips.
- Drop batter by small spoonfuls onto baking sheet.
- Preheat oven to 375 degrees.
- Turn off heat. Place cookies in oven. Leave several hours or overnight.

Very easy. Follow steps exactly in order.

Yield: 3 dozen cookies
ARDIS McCAIN

COUSIN GERRY'S BISCOTTI

6 eggs
1 cup sugar
1 cup vegetable oil
2 teaspoons anise oil

3 cups all-purpose flour
3 teaspoons baking powder
1½ cups toasted almonds
   (optional)

- Preheat oven to 350 degrees.
- Beat eggs until thick. Gradually add sugar.
- Fold in vegetable oil and anise oil. Combine flour and baking powder. Fold into creamed mixture.
- Fold in almonds. Shape mixture into a 3-inch wide log on a greased and floured baking sheet.
- Bake until firm and lightly browned.
- Cut into slices. Lay flat on baking sheet.
- Reduce heat to 300 degrees. Bake until lightly browned.

Yield: 8-10 servings
JOYCE DMETRUK

The meaning of biscotti: Cotti in Italian means cooked, bis means twice. These are twice baked.

CARAMEL COOKIES

36 caramel candies, unwrapped
2 tablespoons milk
1 cup corn flakes
1 cup crispy rice cereal

1 cup pecan pieces
1 cup flaked coconut
Powdered sugar

- Preheat oven to 350 degrees.
- Place caramels in top of double boiler with milk. Cook and stir until caramel melts.
- Stir in corn flakes, rice cereal, pecans and coconut. Mix well to coat.
- Spread butter over hands. Roll mixture into balls.
- Roll balls in powdered sugar.
- Bake 10 minutes.

Yield: 8-10 servings
BARBARA MURPHY

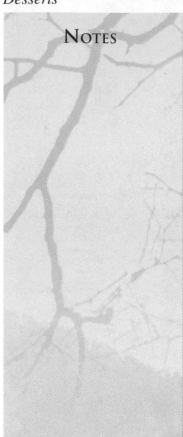

CHEWY OATMEAL RAISIN COOKIES

1 cup sugar
2 cups packed dark brown sugar
2 eggs
½ cup water
2 teaspoons vanilla
1½ cups vegetable shortening

2 cups all-purpose flour
2 teaspoons salt
1 teaspoon baking soda
5½ cups uncooked oats
1 cup dark raisins
1 cup golden raisins

- Preheat oven to 350 degrees.
- Cream sugar, brown sugar, eggs, water, vanilla and shortening until creamy.
- Combine flour, salt, baking soda, oats and raisins. Add to creamed mixture. Mix well.
- Drop by rounded teaspoonfuls onto baking sheet.
- Bake 10-12 minutes.

Yield: 5 dozen
PAT CONNELLY

PRALINE COOKIES

Graham crackers
2 sticks butter

1 cup packed light brown sugar
1 cup chopped pecans

- Preheat oven to 350 degrees.
- Line a 15 x 11 x 1-inch jelly roll pan with foil. Fit graham crackers in bottom of pan.
- Combine butter and brown sugar in a saucepan. Bring to a rolling boil. Boil 2 minutes.
- Remove from heat. When bubbling stops, add pecans.
- Spread mixture over crackers.
- Bake 10 minutes. Cool and cut into rectangles.

Yield: 15 servings
NANCY ROBINSON

THREE CEREAL COOKIES

2 large eggs
1 cup sugar
1 cup packed brown sugar
1 cup vegetable oil
1 teaspoon vanilla
1¾ cups all-purpose flour

½ teaspoon baking powder
1 teaspoon baking soda
2 cups oatmeal
2 cups crispy rice cereal
1 cup corn flakes, slightly
   crushed

- Preheat oven to 350 degrees.
- Beat eggs, sugar, brown sugar, oil and vanilla until smooth.
- Combine flour, baking powder and baking soda. Stir into creamed mixture.
- Stir in oatmeal, rice cereal and corn flakes.
- Mix by hand and drop batter by teaspoonfuls. Press with a wet fork.
- Bake 10 minutes until edges are slightly browned.
- Cool and store in a tight container.

May use canola oil and Splenda brown sugar for healthy cookies.
May also add raisins, nuts or coconut.

Yield: 3-4 dozen cookies
CAROL COOGLER

DELICIOUS BANANA PUDDING

1 (3-ounce) package banana
   cream pudding mix
1 cup milk
1 (14-ounce) can sweetened
   condensed milk
1 (8-ounce) container sour
   cream

2 cups whipped cream
1 (12-ounce) package vanilla
   wafers
6 bananas, sliced
1 (16-ounce) can chocolate
   syrup

- Blend pudding mix and milk. Add condensed milk, sour cream and whipped cream.
- Layer half in glass bowl in order: vanilla wafers, banana slices, pudding mixture, drizzled chocolate syrup.
- Repeat layers. Refrigerate until ready to serve.

May use low-fat pudding mix, condensed milk, sour cream and vanilla wafers.

Yield: 8 servings
GAIL COOPER

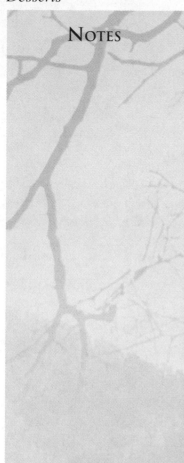

MAMA'S BANANA PUDDING

¾ cup sugar, divided
⅓ cup plus 2 tablespoons all-purpose flour
Dash of salt
4 eggs, separated

2 cups whole milk
1 teaspoon vanilla
6 ripe medium bananas, sliced
Vanilla wafers

- Preheat oven to 425 degrees.
- Combine ½ cup sugar, flour and salt in top of double boiler.
- Stir in egg yolks and milk. Mix well.
- Cook, uncovered, stirring constantly until thickened.
- Reduce heat. Cook and stir 5 minutes.
- Remove from heat. Add vanilla.
- Spread small amount pudding on bottom of 1½-quart baking dish.
- Top with a layer of bananas and layer of wafers.
- Spread remaining pudding over wafers.
- Beat egg whites and remaining ¼ cup sugar until stiff.
- Spoon over pudding.
- Bake 5 minutes or until lightly browned.

May double recipe to plan for a crowd. Do not substitute ingredients.

Yield: 8 servings

CHARLENE TERRELL

MARRIAGE PROPOSAL BANANA PUDDING

6-8 large bananas, sliced
1 (12-ounce) package vanilla wafers, reserve a few wafers
1 (6-ounce) package instant vanilla pudding mix

1 (14-ounce) can sweetened condensed milk
1 teaspoon vanilla
1 (16-ounce) container frozen whipped topping, thawed and divided

- Layer half bananas and half wafers in a large bowl.
- Prepare pudding according to package directions.
- Add milk, vanilla and half whipped topping. Mix well.
- Spoon half pudding over wafers. Repeat banana, wafer and pudding layers.
- Top with remaining whipped topping and wafer crumbs.

Yield: 12-15 servings

THELMA DAVIS

Lagniappe

NORTH GEORGIA FOOTHILLS

Within the rolling countryside
Of northern Georgia land,
Interwoven among farms,
Tall southern pine groves stand.
The mountains rise majestically,
Create a distant view
In misty shades of purple,
Gray and greens of every hue.

Hazy peaks form waves as far as the eye can see.
Eagles soaring overhead convey tranquility.
They are a mere reminder,
If we pause for just a minute,
Of the magnitude of God's great world
And everything that's in it.

Deep within the forest, soft, green fern
Protect the ground
And twisting roots of trees and laurel
Keep it firmly bound.
High ridges and crevasses
Transverse the rough terrain.
Waterfalls and rippling creeks
Move swiftly, swollen with fresh rain.

Indians lived in these hills
Before the white man came.
Then settlers moved throughout the land
To occupy their claim.
Rich history embraced these hills,
And remnants linger still,
Of homesteads, and tales
Of a people with strong zeal.

Gold mining was alluring
And settlers left behind
Log cabins, mills, moonshine stills,
And quarries not yet mined.
As you walk along the trails,
Remembering how life grew,
Gather up the richness
That these foothills bring to you.

Jayne Beske

Bob's Deer Cocktail

~~2~~ 1 eggs
~~1 gallon water~~ 1 Qt

½ ~~1~~ teaspoon liquid detergent
1 ~~2~~ tablespoons fine garlic powder

- Combine eggs and 1 cup water until foamy.
- Add detergent to 2 cups water. Stir in garlic powder.
- Beat garlic water until foamy and free of clumps.
- Add egg mixture to remaining water and mix well.
- Stir garlic water into egg mixture.
- Pour mixture into a gallon sprayer. If clumpy, beat again or remove clumps.
- Spray on plants and enjoy the Italian smell. Deer will not like it.

Powdered garlic is available at Harry's.

Yield: 1 gallon
MICKIE SCHLUENZ

LAGNIAPPE

In Louisiana, lagniappe is a little present given to customers by shop owners. It's a little something extra just like a baker's dozen.

Canine Cookies

1¼ cups whole wheat flour
½ cup quick rolled oats
1 egg, slightly beaten
½ cup all-purpose flour
1 teaspoon sugar
¾ cup dry powdered milk

¼ cup yellow cornmeal
½ cup hot water
⅓ cup vegetable oil
1 tablespoon chicken or beef bouillon granules or ¼ cup grated American cheese

- Preheat oven to 350 degrees.
- Combine wheat flour, oats, egg, flour, sugar, milk, cornmeal, water, oil and bouillon.
- Roll mixture out on floured board. Cut out treats with dog bone cookie cutter.
- Bake 15-20 minutes or until dry. May also microwave at 50 percent power 5-10 minutes, turning every 2 minutes.

Yield: 3 dozen biscuits treats
MARY PORTER

I have been making these treats for the Tour of Homes Bake Sale the last few years. My neighbor's dogs just love them.

231

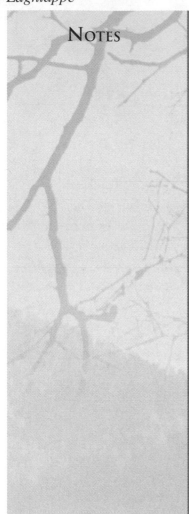

CARAMEL CORN

6 quarts popped corn
2 sticks butter
2 cups packed brown sugar
½ cup light corn syrup

Pinch of salt
¼ teaspoon cream of tartar
½ teaspoon baking soda

- Preheat oven to 200 degrees.
- Place popped corn in a lightly greased foil lined roasting pan or deep baking dish.
- Melt butter in a large saucepan. Add brown sugar, corn syrup, salt and cream of tartar.
- Bring to boil and cook 5 minutes.
- Remove from heat. Add baking soda. Pour mixture over popped corn, stirring to coat.
- Bake 1 hour. Cool and store in sealed containers.

Yield: 6 quarts
NANCY FARRIS

CHOCOLATE BARK

One sleeve saltine crackers
2 sticks butter
1 cup packed brown sugar

1 (12-ounce) package semi-sweet chocolate chips

- Preheat oven to 400 degrees.
- Line a baking sheet with foil and spray with cooking spray.
- Lay saltine crackers over entire baking sheet.
- Heat butter and brown sugar in a saucepan. Bring to boil. Cook 3 minutes.
- Pour mixture over crackers.
- Bake 7 minutes. Pour chips on top and spread as chocolate melts.
- Refrigerate 30 minutes or more.
- Tear off foil and break bark into cookie size pieces.

Yield: 12 servings
SHERRY RUSSO

CRANBERRY CHUTNEY

1 package fresh cranberries
2 Granny Smith apples, peeled, cored and diced
1 pear, peeled, cored and diced
1 cup raisins
¼ cup minced onions

1 cup sugar
1 tablespoon orange zest
1 teaspoon cinnamon
⅛ teaspoon ground nutmeg
½ cup orange juice
2 tablespoons Grand Marnier

- Combine cranberries, apples, pear, raisins, onions, sugar, zest, cinnamon, nutmeg and orange juice in a saucepan.
- Bring to boil. Reduce heat and simmer 45 minutes until thickened.
- Stir in Grand Marnier. Cool or serve warm.

May use a combination of natural and golden raisins. May use less sugar and more Grand Marnier.

Yield: 8-10 servings
CATHERINE CAPPS

CRANBERRY FRAPPE

4 cups cranberries
3 cups water
2 cups sugar
1 cup water

2 egg whites
Juice of 1 lemon
    (about 3 tablespoons)
½ cup orange juice

- Boil cranberries in 3 cups water until softened. Drain. Rub cranberries through a strainer.
- Combine sugar and 1 cup water. Bring to boil until reaches 230-234 degrees on candy thermometer or spins a thread.
- Beat egg whites until stiff. Slowly add sugar syrup into egg whites.
- Add cranberry pulp, lemon juice and orange juice. Freeze.

Yield: 8 servings
JANICE SELDOMRIDGE

233

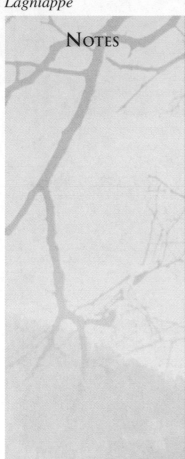

CAROL'S FAJITAS
PORK TENDERLOIN MARINADE

1 large garlic clove, minced
1 teaspoon salt
½ teaspoon pepper
4-5 tablespoons soy sauce

½ (8-ounce) can tomato paste
2 tablespoons vegetable oil
¾ teaspoon dried oregano

- Combine garlic, salt, pepper, soy sauce, tomato paste, oil and oregano. Mix well.
- Pour over meat of choice. Refrigerate overnight. Grill as desired.

This marinade is great on flank steak for beef fajitas, chicken breasts for chicken fajitas or for chicken taco salad. It is delicious for pork tenderloin on the grill.

Yield: ¾ cup
JUDY ERICKSON

HAMBURGER COOKIES

24 vanilla wafers
12 chocolate mint cookies
1 (16-ounce) can vanilla frosting

¼ cup flaked coconut
Red, yellow and green food coloring

- Place 12 vanilla wafers flat side up. Spread small amount of frosting on wafer.
- Top with mint cookie. Color coconut with green food coloring, relish.
- Color ¼ cup frosting with red food coloring, ketchup.
- Color ¼ cup frosting with yellow food coloring, mustard.
- Spread a teaspoon red frosting on mint cookie.
- Sprinkle coconut, relish, over ketchup.
- Spread a teaspoon yellow frosting, mustard, to edge of cookie, on flat side of other 12 wafers.
- Place wafer over coconut, relish.

May toast sesame seeds. Brush top with corn syrup and sprinkle seeds over wafer, bun.

May ask McDonald's for hamburger wrap. Cut to size and wrap wafers. This makes it look authentic.

Yield: 6 servings
SHIRLIE MATTHEWS

FRUIT SANDWICH

Mayonnaise **Banana, sliced**
Sandwich bread

- Spread a thin layer of mayonnaise on two bread slices.
- Place banana slices on bread.

May substitute well drained pineapple slices for banana.

Yield: a few-many
DEBORAH VALENTINE

This was a tradition in Howard's family from Ozark, Alabama. A great summer treat.

GINGERBREAD PEOPLE COOKIES

6 cups all-purpose flour **1 cup molasses**
1 teaspoon baking soda **1½ teaspoons ground cloves**
½ teaspoon baking powder **1 teaspoon pepper**
2 sticks unsalted butter, softened **1½ teaspoons salt**
1 cup packed dark brown sugar **4 teaspoons cinnamon**
2 large eggs **4 teaspoons ground ginger**

- Sift together flour, baking soda and baking powder.
- Cream butter and brown sugar. Beat in eggs and molasses into butter mixture.
- Combine cloves, pepper, salt, cinnamon and ginger.
- Add flour mixture and spice mixture to creamed mixture. Beat on low speed until mixed.
- Divide dough into thirds. Refrigerate 1 hour.
- Roll out dough to ⅛-inch thickness. Cut out with gingerbread cookie cutter.
- Bake 10 minutes until edges are dark but not burned.
- Cool on rack.

Place raisins or candy decorations on cookies before baking.

Yield: 10 servings
LINDA MOORE

This rub recipe is from Mike Mills, Apple City Barbecue team of the 17th Street Bar and Grill in Murphyboro, Illinois. This is the only team to be World Grand Champion three times and only team to earn a perfect score twice in Memphis, TN. He uses this rub on ribs and Boston Butts. It is also the seasoning for his baked beans.

Magic Dust Meat Rub

½ cup paprika
¼ cup finely ground kosher salt
¼ cup sugar
2 tablespoons mustard powder
¼ cup chili powder

¼ cup ground cumin
2 tablespoons ground black pepper
¼ cup garlic powder
2 tablespoons cayenne pepper

- Combine paprika, salt, sugar, mustard powder, chili powder, cumin, pepper, garlic powder and cayenne.
- Store in a tightly sealed container. Rub on meat of choice.

Yield: 2½ cups rub

RAMONA C. MIKEE

Judy's Barbecue Sauce

2 cups apple cider vinegar
2 cups ketchup
½ cup sugar
1 tablespoon chili powder

1½ teaspoons salt
1½ teaspoons pepper
½ teaspoon barbecue spice
5 dashes of Tabasco sauce

- Combine vinegar, ketchup, sugar, chili powder, salt, pepper, barbecue spice and Tabasco in a saucepan.
- Simmer 30 minutes. Store in refrigerator.

Yield: 4 cups

SUSAN PHILLIPS

MASTER GRANOLA RECIPE

2 cups old-fashioned oats
½ cup wheat germ
1 cup dried fruit of choice
1 cup natural almonds
2 tablespoons packed brown sugar

¼ teaspoon salt
¼ cup honey
3 tablespoons vegetable oil
2 tablespoons water
1 teaspoon choice of flavoring

- Preheat oven to 275 degrees.
- Combine oats, wheat germ, fruit and almonds.
- Blend brown sugar, salt, honey, oil, water and flavoring in a saucepan. Heat slightly.
- Pour sauce over dry ingredients. Toss to coat.
- Spread out on a baking sheet. Bake 30 minutes, stirring several times.

Great on yogurt.

Yield: 6 servings
JUDY GARNER

HOMEMADE MAYONNAISE

1 cup cold Wesson vegetable or canola oil
1 egg
1 teaspoon Grey Poupon mustard

½ teaspoon salt
½ teaspoon horseradish
Juice on 1 lemon or more to taste (about 3 tablespoons)

- Combine ¼ cup oil, egg, mustard, salt and horseradish in blender. Process until smooth.
- Drizzle in remaining oil alternating with lemon juice while blending.
- Blend to get desired consistency. Refrigerate immediately.

For a slightly tart mayonnaise, add more lemon juice. If too tart, add more salt.

Yield: 1 cup
MELITE CAMPBELL

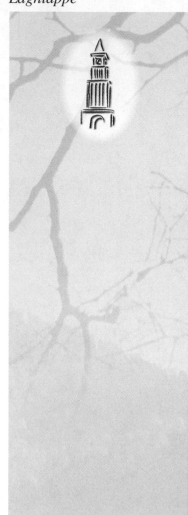

MELISSA'S FAMILY NUT STICKS

DOUGH

1 cup sugar

1 egg

2 egg yolks, reserve whites

½ teaspoon salt

2 tablespoons ground corn flakes

2 tablespoons all-purpose flour

1 pound ground nuts, walnuts or pecans

Dash of vanilla

FROSTING

2 eggs whites, beaten stiff

12 tablespoons powdered sugar

DOUGH

- Combine sugar, egg, egg yolks, salt, corn flakes, flour, ground nuts and vanilla.
- Divide dough into 4 balls. Roll ball into long thin logs.

FROSTING

- Blend stiff egg whites with powdered sugar, 3 tablespoons at a time.
- Frost dough logs and cut into sticks. Place on a greased baking sheet.
- Bake at 325 degrees 15 minutes.

Yield: 36 sticks

CHARLOTTE MCCLOSKEY

PLAY DOUGH

1 cup all-purpose flour

½ cup salt

1 cup water

2 teaspoons cream of tartar

1 tablespoon vegetable oil

Food coloring

- Combine flour, salt, water, cream of tartar, oil and food coloring in an electric skillet.
- Cook on low heat, stirring constantly, until mixture becomes play dough consistency.
- Remove and knead until cool.

Yield: 1½ cups play dough

LINDA S. WOOD

Children love to cook play dough and experiment with different colors. Store in a sealed container or zip-top plastic bag.

MILLER'S MARSHMALLOW PILGRIM HATS

24 chocolate striped shortbread cookies
1 (12-ounce) package semi-sweet chocolate chips

24 large marshmallows
Tube yellow frosting

- Place cookie stripe-side down on wax paper lined tray.
- Melt chocolate chips. Stick toothpick into marshmallow. Dip into chocolate and place on center on cookie.
- Use a second toothpick to hold down marshmallow and pull out first toothpick.
- Refrigerate until chocolate sets. Pipe yellow frosting to make a buckle on front of each hat.

Yield: 24 hats
LAURIE BROGDON ANDERSON

NICK'S TRIED AND TRUE COCKTAIL SAUCE

1 cup ketchup
3-4 dashes of Worcestershire sauce
1 teaspoon brown mustard
4 teaspoons horseradish

2 teaspoons lemon juice
4 shakes garlic salt
2-3 shakes celery salt
Ground pepper
Salt to taste

- Combine ketchup, Worcestershire sauce, brown mustard, horseradish, lemon juice, garlic salt, celery salt, pepper and salt. Mix well.
- Refrigerate at least 4 hours. Bring to room temperature at least 30 minutes before use.

Yield: 4-6 servings
NICK BROWN

Few people realize that most dogs love peanut butter. Add to this the distinctively sweet taste of rolled oats and molasses and you have a cookie that dogs will run a mile to eat.

OATMEAL DOGGIE COOKIES WITH PEANUT BUTTER

3 cups whole wheat flour
½ cup rolled oats
2 teaspoons baking powder
1½ cups milk, room temperature

1 tablespoon molasses
1¼ cups creamy peanut butter
¼ cup chicken broth

- Preheat oven to 375 degrees.
- Combine flour, oats and baking powder.
- In a separate bowl, beat milk, molasses and peanut butter until smooth. Stir in broth.
- Stir into dry mixture until a soft dough forms. If dry, add more broth.
- Turn dough onto a floured surface. Roll out to ¼-inch thickness.
- Cut dough with a 1½-inch round cookie cutter. Rework dough and cut out until dough is used.
- Place cookies side by side on lightly greased or parchment paper lined baking sheets.
- Bake 25 minutes or until very dry and golden browned.
- Cool completely. Turn off oven.
- When cooled, place cookies in a single layer on baking sheets. Return to oven.
- Leave undisturbed, without opening oven door, 8-16 hours.

Some dogs do not tolerate milk.

Yield: 2 pounds (88 cookies per pound)

ANN BURTON

ORANGE CRANBERRY RED WINE RELISH

32 ounces fresh or frozen whole cranberries
¾ cup dry red wine
2 cups sugar
1 cup fresh orange juice
2 tablespoons vanilla

Zest of 2 oranges
Chopped parsley or toasted sliced almonds
Garnish: orange slices without rind

- Combine cranberries, wine, sugar, orange juice, vanilla and zest in a saucepan. Mix lightly.
- Cover and bring to simmer. When simmering, uncover and cook 3-5 minutes.
- Remove from heat. Pour relish into a flat wide container to cool.
- Transfer to serving dish and sprinkle with parsley or almonds. Top with oranges slices without rind.

May refrigerate relish up to 2 weeks in closed container.

Yield: 6-8 cups
ALICE EACHUS

PORK MARINADE

¼ cup soy sauce
¼ cup bourbon

2 tablespoons brown sugar
1½ pounds pork tenderloin

- Blend soy sauce, bourbon and brown sugar. Pour over pork tenderloin.
- Refrigerate at least 8 hours or overnight, turning a few times.
- Grill to desired degree of doneness.

Yield: 4-6 servings
OUIDA AMES

POPPY SEED SALAD DRESSING

1 cup vegetable oil	1 teaspoon dry mustard
1 cup sugar	1 teaspoon salt
⅓ cup apple cider vinegar	1⅓ teaspoons poppy seeds

- Combine oil, sugar, vinegar, mustard, salt and poppy seeds in a blender. Process until smooth.
- Shake well before use as sugar settles to bottom.

Yield: 2 cups

JANE BATTEN

ROQUEFORT DRESSING

4 ounces Roquefort, blue or Gorgonzola cheese	3 tablespoons apple cider vinegar
¼ cup vegetable oil	Pinch of sugar
	Salt and pepper to taste

- Press cheese with a fork in a wooden bowl until it reaches a paste consistency.
- Stir in oil, vinegar, sugar, salt and pepper. Mix well.

Serve with marinated onion slices and romaine lettuce.

Yield: 2 servings

CYNTHIA JUNGER

SWEET FRENCH DRESSING

½ cup vegetable oil	1 teaspoon paprika
¼ cup vinegar	1 teaspoon salt
⅔ cup sugar	½ teaspoon grated onions
⅓ cup ketchup	Juice of ½ lemon (about 1½ tablespoons)

- Combine oil, vinegar, sugar, ketchup, paprika, salt, onions and lemon juice. Beat until smooth.
- Store in a glass jar or cruet in refrigerator.

Yield: 12 servings

JOYCE RALEY

ROSEMARY BUTTER

1 stick butter, softened   1 small garlic clove, minced
2 tablespoons chopped rosemary

- Combine butter, rosemary and garlic. Mix well.
- Cover and refrigerate for several hours for flavors to blend.
- Serve with bread or spread on warm vegetables just before serving.

For health benefits, substitute Benecol for butter.

Yield: ½ cup butter
MICKIE McARDLE

REINDEER FOOD

2 sticks butter
½ teaspoon garlic salt
1 teaspoon onion salt
1 (8-ounce) can peanuts
4½ teaspoons Worcestershire
    sauce

1 (15-ounce) package Cheerios
1 (15-ounce) package corn Chex
1 (15-ounce) package rice Chex
1 (15-ounce) package wheat
    Chex
1 pound pecans

- Preheat oven to 250 degrees.
- Melt butter in a saucepan. Add garlic salt, onion salt and Worcestershire sauce.
- Combine all cereals in a large bowl. Pour butter mixture over cereal and toss to coat.
- Add pecans and peanuts. Pour mixture into a 13 x 9 x 2-inch baking dish.
- Bake 1 hour, 30 minutes, stirring every 15 minutes.

Great snack for kids during holidays.

Yield: 25-30 servings
JUDY GARNER

243

NOTES

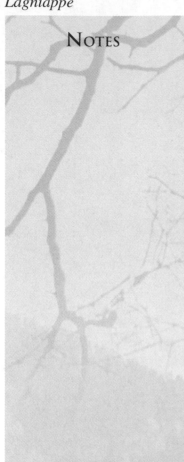

SYDNEY'S SANTA BUTTONS

3 (10-ounce) packages waffle pretzels

1 (17-ounce) package holiday M&M plain chocolate candies, red and green

3 (13-ounce) package Hershey's Hugs chocolates

3 (13-ounce) package Hershey's chocolate kisses

- Preheat oven to 170 degrees.
- Discard all unbroken pretzels. Place pretzels in a single layer on a wax paper-lined baking sheet.
- Place one Hug candy on each pretzel. Use one type of candy per baking sheet.
- Place one chocolate kiss on each pretzel on a separate baking sheet
- Bake 4 minutes for sheet with Hugs and 5-6 minutes with sheet with chocolate kisses.
- Immediately after removing from oven, place one M&M on top of each chocolate pretzel.
- Place baking sheet in freezer 8-10 minutes for chocolate to set.

Yield: 30 servings

LAURIE BROGDON ANDERSON

VERMONT MAPLE SUGAR RUB

2 tablespoons coarsely ground pepper

¼ cup pure maple sugar

⅓ cup packed dark brown sugar

¼ cup Kosher salt

2 tablespoons garlic powder

2 teaspoons dried thyme

- Combine pepper, maple sugar, brown sugar, salt, garlic powder and thyme. Mix well with whisk.
- Store for several weeks in sealed container.

May brush maple syrup or melted butter over salmon fillets if maple sugar is unavailable. Evenly sprinkle fillet with rub. Grill just until done. Do not overcook.

Yield: ¾ cup rub

SHIRLEY MOORE

Restaurants

IN THE WOODS

Deep in the woods, there is silence.
My footsteps fall on decaying leaves
as I wander alone,
lured by peace and beauty.

The air is still,
The sky is clear,
The winter day is mild,
Surrounding me countless pine trees
reach to pierce the sky.

They're much too tall for their girth it seems.
They lay a thick new carpet,
cinnamon colored on the ground
where lacy ferns at my feet,
fan out in clusters, lush and round.

Beside a narrow stream
I stoop to gather stones lying in a sandy bed,
beneath clear, sparkling water.
Round and smooth, they feel
cool and damp in my hands.

An hour passes; I see no one.
This time, this place is given to me.
Alone with nature, I see life and growth —
cycles of continuity, extending to eternity.

Above all, there is a clear command:
Slow down.
Breath deeply.
Bond with earth that is
your origin and your destination.

Joyce Reid Raley

KOBE BEEF MEATLOAF WITH MUSHROOM GRAVY

3 pounds ground beef, Kobe preferred

1 medium yellow onion, finely chopped

2 stalks celery, chopped

2 tablespoons Worcestershire sauce

1 tablespoon garlic powder

3 eggs

1 cup oatmeal

1 tablespoon Kosher salt

1 teaspoon black pepper

- Preheat oven to 350 degrees.
- Combine beef, onions, celery, Worcestershire sauce, garlic powder, eggs, oatmeal, salt and pepper.
- Shape mixture into two logs and place in two 9 x 5-inch loaf pans.
- Bake 55-60 minutes or until meat thermometer reaches 165 degrees.
- Let rest 5 minutes and slice. Place meatloaf slices on platter and serve with mushroom gravy.

Yield: 8 generous servings

JASON FITTS, CHEF/OWNER
APPALACHIA GRILL
BIG CANOE/STEVE TATE HIGHWAY

MUSHROOM GRAVY

2 cups chicken broth

2 cups beef broth

2-3 tablespoons blonde roux

1 cup button mushrooms, chopped

1 cup heavy cream

Salt and pepper to taste

- Bring chicken broth and beef broth to boil in large saucepan.
- Slowly whisk in roux. Cook slowly until mixture thickens.
- Add mushrooms and cream. Reduce heat and simmer 5 minutes.
- Add salt and pepper and mix well.

Blonde roux is equal parts melted unsalted butter and flour. Mix together but do not brown.

Yield: 4½ cups gravy

JASON FITTS, CHEF/OWNER
APPALACHIA GRILL
BIG CANOE/STEVE TATE HIGHWAY

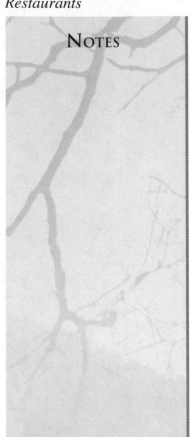

TREVI'S MEATBALLS

¾ cup chopped garlic
1½ cups fresh oregano
¾ cup fresh basil leaves
2 whole tomatoes
3 tablespoons salt
1½ cups grated Parmesan
   cheese

10 pounds ground beef
1 (6-ounce) package Italian
   sausage, ground
1 quart bread crumbs
2 eggs

• Preheat oven to 350 degrees.

• Combine garlic, oregano, basil, tomatoes, salt and Parmesan cheese in food processor and blend.

• Mix together beef, sausage, bread crumbs and eggs in large bowl. Add tomato mixture and mix by hand.

• Shape mixture into meatballs. Arrange meatballs on baking sheet with sides.

• Bake 30 minutes or until meat thermometer reaches 165 degrees.

Yield: 50 meatballs

ANDREW BROWN, CHEF/OWNER
TREVI PIZZERIA
FOOTHILLS SHOPPING CENTER, MARBLE HILL

DRUNKEN PORK WITH SAUCE

½ cup Evan Williams® Bourbon
⅓ cup soy sauce
1 shallot, sliced
½ cup teriyaki glaze
½ cup teriyaki marinade
1-2 sprigs rosemary, stemmed

1 cup packed brown sugar
½ cup water
2 tablespoons vegetable oil
2 pounds pork tenderloin,
   cut into 2 ounce pieces and
   pounded to ¼-inch thick
¼ cup heavy whipping cream

• Combine bourbon, soy sauce, shallot, teriyaki glaze, teriyaki marinade, rosemary, brown sugar and water. Whisk until well blended.

• Heat oil in a skillet. Sear tenderloin on both sides about 2 minutes.

• Add bourbon mixture. Cook until reduced to one-half volume.

• Stir in cream and reduce for 1 minute.

• Serve hot pork with sauce.

Yield: 6 servings

JASON J. MCFARLAND, EXECUTIVE CHEF
ATKINS PARK TAVERN
VICKERY VILLAGE, CUMMING

BRAISED COUNTRY-STYLE PORK RIBS

Peanut oil
3 pounds thick cut country-style
   pork ribs
Salt and pepper to taste
½ cup all-purpose flour
1 medium onion, finely diced
1 medium carrot, finely diced
1 stalk celery, finely diced
2-3 garlic cloves, very finely
   minced
¼ teaspoon red chili flakes
½ cup dry white wine

1 (28-ounce) can Italian-style
   tomatoes
2 cups chicken broth
Zest of ½ lemon
1 bay leaf
4 sprigs thyme or 1 teaspoon
   dried
8 large sage leaves or
   ½ teaspoon dried
Salt and pepper to taste
Hot Saffron risotto
Freshly chopped parsley

- Preheat oven to 325 degrees.
- Heat ½-inch peanut oil in a large skillet. Sprinkle ribs with salt and pepper. Dust lightly with flour.
- Gently place ribs in hot oil. Cook ribs in batches, browning on both sides.
- Transfer ribs to large baking dish able to hold ribs and sauce.
- Reduce heat and add onions, carrots and celery. Sauté 10 minutes, stirring often, until golden browned.
- Scrape any browned bits from pan. Add garlic and chili flakes. Cook 1 minute.
- Pour in wine and bring to boil. Reduce wine by half.
- Add tomatoes, broth, zest, bay leaf, thyme, sage, salt and pepper.
- Bring to boil. Once boiling, pour over ribs to cover halfway up side of meat. Do not cover.
- Cover with foil. Bake 2 hours. Check for tenderness. If not falling from bone, bake 30 minutes more.
- Cool 20 minutes. Carefully skim oil and fat from sauce. If sauce is too thin, remove ribs and keep warm.
- Cook sauce until reduced and thickened.
- To serve, place half cup saffron risotto in six pasta bowls.
- Top with one or two ribs. Ladle on sauce and sprinkle with parsley. Top with lemon zest.

Yield: 6 servings

GUY OWEN, CHEF/OWNER
THE BLUE BICYCLE
671 LUMPKIN CAMP GROUND, DAWSONVILLE

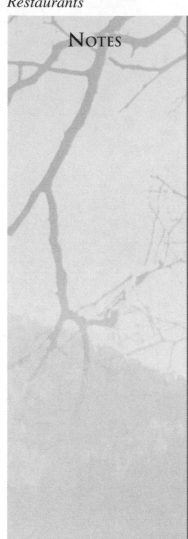

CHICKEN TETRAZZINI

1 cup fresh mushrooms, sliced
1 onion, thinly sliced
Garlic clove, pressed
4 tablespoons butter
½ cup all-purpose flour
1 teaspoon salt
¼ teaspoon pepper

2 cups chicken broth
½ cup heavy cream
1 (8-ounce) package spaghetti, cooked al dente
3½ cups cooked and cubed chicken
½ cup grated Parmesan cheese

- Preheat oven to 350 degrees.
- Sauté mushrooms, onions and garlic in butter until tender.
- Add flour, salt and pepper. Cook 1 minute.
- Pour in chicken broth. Cook until thickened and bubbly. Stir in cream.
- Layer spaghetti in a greased 13 x 9 x 2-inch baking dish.
- Top with chicken and pour on sauce. Sprinkle with Parmesan cheese.
- Bake 30-45 minutes until bubbly.

Yield: 6 servings

BAKERY ON THE SQUARE (CORK 'N' CRUMBLE)

ELLIJAY

TUNA AU POIVRE

2 pounds sushi grade tuna, at least 1-inch thick
2 tablespoons black peppercorns, cracked
1 tablespoon olive oil

¼ cup cognac
1 stick unsalted butter, cut into pieces
Salt and pepper to taste

- Generously rub tuna with peppercorns. Heat skillet on high until very hot.
- Add oil to skillet. Sauté tuna 1-2 minutes per side for medium rare.
- Remove tuna and keep warm. Reduce heat to low. Add cognac to skillet, being careful of flame up.
- Simmer 5 minutes. Slowly add butter. Cook and stir until sauce thickens.
- Add salt and pepper. Slice tuna into strips, place on plate and pour sauce on top.

Yield: 2 servings

ZACH KELL, CHEF/OWNER
DOWNTOWN KITCHEN, CANTON

ROAST DUCKLING À LA ORANGE

ORANGE GLAZE
¾ cup marmalade
2 teaspoons Absolute Mandarin
   vodka

½ teaspoon minced garlic

DUCK
1 whole duck
   (Maple Leaf Farms)

¼ cup poultry seasoning

ORANGE GLAZE
• Blend marmalade, vodka and garlic until smooth. Keep warm.

DUCK
• Preheat oven to 400 degrees.
• Remove neck and gizzards from cavity. Place duck skin side up in a roasting pan.
• Sprinkle each half of duck with poultry seasoning.
• Roast 2 hours or until internal temperature reaches 165 degrees.
• Remove from oven. Set oven to broil. Return duck to oven and broil until skin is crisp, watch carefully.
• Serve one-half duck per person. Top with orange glaze.

Serve with rosemary roasted new potatoes and shaved Brussels sprouts.

Yield: 2 servings

JOE RUEFFERT, CHEF/OWNER
WOODBRIDGE INN
JASPER

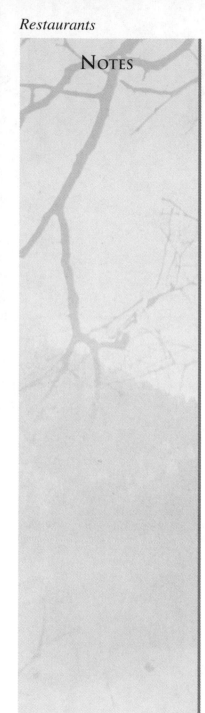

GRILLED HONEY-GINGER GLAZED SALMON

1½ cups honey
¾ cup dry sherry
¾ cup soy sauce
½ cup fresh lime juice

¼ cup finely grated ginger
¼ cup Dijon mustard
6 (8-ounce) salmon fillets

- Blend honey, sherry, soy sauce, lime juice, ginger and mustard. Reserve 1 cup marinade.
- Pour remaining marinade over fillets. Marinate 20 minutes.
- Grill fillets skin side up 3 minutes, basting with marinade.
- Turn fillets skin side down and grill 3 minutes, basting with marinade.
- Remove to plate. Pour reserved marinade over fillets.

Serve with wild rice, green beans, garlic bread and green salad. Garnish with green onions and wedge of lemon.

Yield: 6 servings

RICHARD DICKEY, CHEF/OWNER
FIRESIDE CAFE & PUB
MARBLE HILL

SHRIMP, CORN AND TOMATO SAUTÉ

2 tablespoons olive oil
2 tablespoons butter
4 ears yellow corn, cut from cob
4 vine ripe tomatoes, peeled, seeded and diced
1 (16-ounce) can whole tomatoes in tomato sauce, chopped
2 garlic cloves, chopped

2 pounds shrimp, peeled and deveined
2 sprigs thyme, stemmed
Splash white wine
Kosher salt and white pepper to taste
1 tablespoon unsalted butter

- Heat oil and butter in skillet. Sauté corn, tomatoes, tomatoes with sauce and garlic 5 minutes.
- Add shrimp and cook until shrimp turns pink. Sprinkle with thyme.
- Turn off heat. Add wine and scrape bottom to incorporate browned bits and flavor.
- Stir in salt and pepper. Swirl in butter until butter melts.
- Serve immediately. Great with cooked rice.

Yield: 6-8 servings

LAURI GRIZZLE, CHEF/OWNER
THE MUSTARD SEED CAFE
BALLGROUND

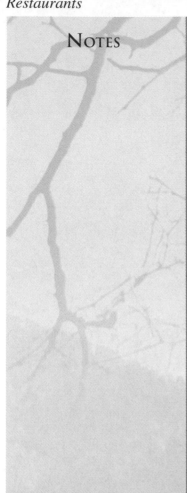

TULIO'S PERUVIAN SHRIMP AND CORN BISQUE

1 cup chopped onions
¼ cup diced celery
¼ cup minced garlic
1 cup roasted red pepper, diced
1 cup diced carrots
¼ cup paprika
¼ cup Old Bay seasoning
¼ cup shrimp base

¼ cup olive oil
1 quart shrimp broth
1 (16-ounce) can whole kernel corn, drained
1 quart heavy cream
Salt to taste
¼ cup port wine or dry sherry

- Combine onions, celery, garlic, peppers, carrots, paprika, Old Bay, shrimp base and oil in a saucepan.
- Cook 5 minutes. Add shrimp broth. Bring to boil. Cook 5 minutes.
- Reduce heat. Add corn and simmer.
- Pour in cream and mix well. Add salt and port wine or sherry.
- Serve hot with bread or crackers.

Yield: 10 servings

TULIO NAVARRO, CHEF
LAKE SCONTI RESTAURANT, BIG CANOE

TOMATO BASIL SOUP

4 teaspoons olive oil
2 yellow onions, finely chopped
2 carrots, shredded
2 celery stalks, finely chopped
5 garlic cloves, finely chopped
1 (6-pound, 9-ounce) can ground tomatoes, preferably organic

2 teaspoons freshly chopped marjoram
4 cups water
2 cups heavy cream
4 tablespoons freshly chopped basil
1 basil leaf

- Heat oil in a large stockpot. Sauté onions, carrots, celery and garlic until tender.
- Add tomatoes, marjoram and water.
- Bring to boil. Cover, reduce heat and simmer 1 hour, stirring occasionally.
- Turn off heat. Stir in cream and basil until blended.
- Garnish with basil leaf in center of bowl.

Yield: 10-12 servings

ANDREW BROWN, CHEF/OWNER
TREVI PIZZERIA
FOOTHILLS SHOPPING CENTER, MARBLE HILL

PECKENPAUGH'S CHICKEN SALAD

5 (6-ounce) boneless skinless
   chicken breasts halves
1 tablespoon McCormick's®
   chicken rotisserie seasoning
½ bunch green onions, finely
   diced
½ sweet red pepper, finely diced
½ bell pepper, finely diced

1 cup chopped pecans
½ cup mayonnaise
½ cup sour cream
¼ cup honey
1 tablespoon salt
1 teaspoon black pepper
1 tablespoon Dijon mustard
Croissants (optional)

- Season chicken breasts with seasoning. Grill chicken until done.
- Allow chicken to cool. Place in refrigerator until cold. Dice cold chicken.
- Combine chicken, green onions, red and bell peppers and pecans.
- In a separate bowl, blend mayonnaise, sour cream, honey, salt, pepper and mustard.
- Add mayonnaise mixture to chicken mixture and blend well.
- Serve on croissants.

Yield: 8-10 servings

GARY SANDERSON, EXECUTIVE CHEF
PENKENPAUGH'S FINE FOODS
VICKERY VILLAGE, CUMMING

MILANO EGGPLANT AND TOMATO PARMESAN

1 medium eggplant, cut into
   ¾-inch slices
2 tablespoons lemon juice
½ cup olive oil
1 large tomato, sliced
¼ cup minced garlic

Chopped rosemary and basil
   to taste
Salt and pepper to taste
¾ cup freshly grated Parmesan
   cheese
Garnish: Rosemary sprigs and
   basil leaves (optional)

- Preheat oven to 350 degrees.
- Brush lemon juice on both sides of eggplant slices. Place on a baking sheet.
- Brush with oil. Bake 5-8 minutes.
- Turn slices over and bake an additional 5-8 minutes.
- Remove from oven. Set oven control to broil.
- Top each eggplant slice with tomato.
- Brush lightly with oil. Sprinkle with garlic, rosemary, basil, salt and pepper.
- Generously cover with Parmesan cheese. Broil until cheese is bubbly.
- Top with rosemary sprig or basil leaf.

Yield: 4-6 servings

JENNIFER MINEO, CHEF/OWNER
BELLA'S CORNER BISTRO
DAWSONVILLE

MACARONI AND CHEESE

CHEESE SAUCE

1 stick butter

1 sweet bell pepper, finely diced

1 jalapeño pepper, seeded and finely diced

½ large yellow onion, finely diced

1 teaspoon garlic powder

¼ teaspoon dried thyme

2 cups half & half

5 dashes of Tabasco sauce

1 teaspoon salt

2 pounds white cheese for melting, half American and half Queseo

MACARONI

1 (18-ounce) package cavatappi

1 large onion, thinly sliced

Olive oil

1 cup fresh spinach leaves

6 ounces Portabella mushrooms, thinly sliced

1 (8-ounce) package goat cheese, crumbled

½ cup Panko bread crumbs

CHEESE SAUCE

- Melt butter in saucepan. Sauté peppers, jalapeño and onions.
- Stir in garlic powder, thyme, half & half, Tabasco and salt.
- Add cheese. Cook and stir until cheese melts and is blended. Keep warm.

MACARONI

- Cook cavatappi according to package directions.
- Caramelize onions in oil until golden browned.
- Cook spinach in small saucepan until wilted.
- Sauté mushrooms. Combine cavatappi, onions, spinach, mushrooms and cheese sauce. Mix well.
- Pour mixture into a greased 13 x 9 x 2-inch baking dish.
- Top with goat cheese and bread crumbs.
- Broil about 2 minutes until bread crumbs are lightly toasted.
- Serve immediately.

Yield: 6 servings

SEAN GALLAGHER, EXECUTIVE CHEF
WINCHESTER WOODFIRE GRILL
CANTON

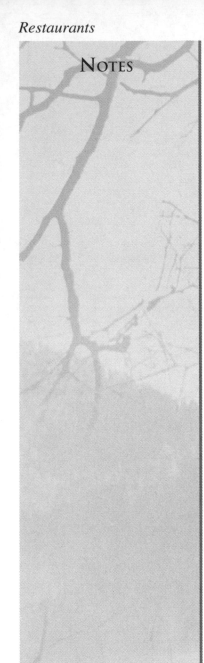

THE FOSTER HOUSE'S BOURBON BREAD PUDDING

PUDDING

10 eggs
1 teaspoon vanilla
4 cups milk

1½ cups sugar
8 cups toasted bread cubes

TOPPING

1 stick butter, melted
2 cups packed brown sugar

1 cup pecans

SAUCE

3 sticks butter, cut into 1-inch cubes
3 eggs

2 cups sugar
1 teaspoon vanilla
¼ cup bourbon

PUDDING

- Beat eggs. Add vanilla, milk and sugar. Beat 2 minutes.
- Place bread cubes in a bowl. Pour on egg mixture to cover. Let soak.
- Pour bread cubes and egg mixture into a large greased pan.

TOPPING

- Preheat oven to 350 degrees.
- Combine butter, brown sugar and pecans.
- Sprinkle topping evenly over bread cubes.
- Bake 18 minutes.

SAUCE

- Combine butter, eggs and sugar in a heavy saucepan. Cook over low heat 5-7 minutes, stirring constantly, until smooth and butter is melted.
- Add vanilla and bourbon.
- When pudding comes out of oven, immediately pour sauce on top.

Yield: 25 servings

THE FOSTER HOUSE
CUMMING

PEPPERMINT-CINNAMON BARK

20 hard peppermint candies
20 hard cinnamon candies
1 (16-ounce) package vanilla flavored candy coating, broken into pieces

½ cup milk chocolate chips
1 teaspoon vegetable shortening

- Crush peppermint and cinnamon candies in a zip top plastic bag with rolling pin.
- Melt vanilla candy in top of double boiler, stirring occasionally.
- Remove from heat and stir until smooth. Add crushed candies, reserving some larger pieces for top.
- Spread coating mixture evenly on a wax or parchment paper-lined baking sheet.
- Sprinkle with reserved candy pieces. Cool 1 hour.
- When candy is hard, melt chocolate chips with shortening in top of a double boiler.
- Drizzle chocolate over bark. Let cool. Break bark into pieces.

Yield: 1 pound candy pieces

LAURI GRIZZLE, CHEF/OWNER
THE MUSTARD SEED CAFE
BALLGROUND

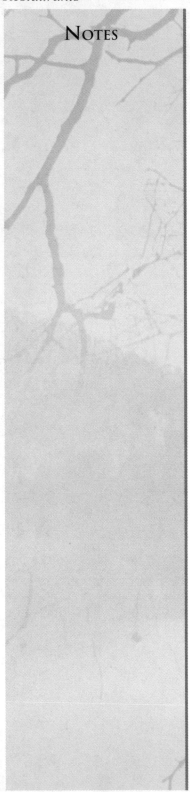

NOTES

A

APPETIZERS (Also See Dips and Spreads)

APPLES

ARTICHOKES

AVOCADOS

B

BANANAS

BEANS AND PEAS

CROCKPOT RECIPES

CRUSTS AND SHELLS

D

DESSERTS

Cakes

Cobblers and Tarts

Cookies and Bars

Frozen Treats

DIPS AND SPREADS

DUCK (See Poultry)

E

EGGPLANT

EGGS

F

FISH

FRUITS (Also see Individual Listings)

G

GRAPES

GRILLING RECIPES

PUMPKIN

Q

QUICHE

R

RAISIN

RICE

S

SALAD DRESSINGS

SALADS